Dealing with Uncertainties in Policing Serious Crime

Dealing with Uncertainties in Policing Serious Crime

edited by Gabriele Bammer

E PRESS

Published by ANU E Press
The Australian National University
Canberra ACT 0200, Australia
Email: anuepress@anu.edu.au
This title is also available online at: http://epress.anu.edu.au/dealing_citation.html

National Library of Australia
Cataloguing-in-Publication entry

Title: Dealing with uncertainties in policing serious crime /
             editor, Gabriele Bammer ... [et al.].

ISBN: 9781921666360 (pbk.) 9781921666377 (pdf)

Subjects: Criminal justice, Administration of--Australia
             Evidence, Criminal--Australia.
             Burden of proof--Australia.
             Criminal investigation--Australia.
             Criminal law--Australia

Other Authors/Contributors: Bammer, Gabriele.

Dewey Number: 364.994

All rights reserved. No part of this publication may be reproduced, stored in a retrieval system or transmitted in any form or by any means, electronic, mechanical, photocopying or otherwise, without the prior permission of the publisher.

Cover design and layout by ANU E Press

Printed by Griffin Press

This edition © 2010 ANU E Press

Contents

Acknowledgements.................................vii
Preface...ix
   Simon Bronitt

Introduction..1
   Gabriele Bammer

Setting the Scene

The Modern Policing Environment......................15
   Sue Wilkinson

Understanding Uncertainty............................27
   Michael Smithson

Enhancing Accepted Approaches

Can Statistics Help?.................................51
   Robyn G Attewell

Quantitative Risk....................................67
   Richard Jarrett and Mark Westcott

Understanding and Managing Bias......................87
   Mark R Kebbell, Damon A Muller, Kirsty Martin

Insights from Adjunct Areas

Criminal Law..101
   Hon. Tim Carmody SC

Politics..115
   Hon. Carmen Lawrence

Business..127
   Neil Fargher

Commentaries from Practice

The Investigating Officer and the Investigation Manager. 141
   Peter Martin

Higher Education in Policing 153
   Tracey Green and Greg Linsdell

Consultancy to Build Capacity in Dealing with Uncertainty
in Law Enforcement. 169
   Steve Longford

Law Enforcement Agencies which Respond to Nationally
Significant Crime. 191
   Alastair M Milroy

List of Contributors 207

Acknowledgements

The production of this book and the associated conference were funded by the Australian Research Council Centre of Excellence in Policing and Security.

Preface
SIMON BRONITT

This collection examines how criminal justice systems deal with and respond to uncertainty in the investigation of serious crime. It draws from a range of disciplines both within and outside policing studies. It traverses public and private sectors, academic and practitioner communities, applied and theoretical perspectives. The editor, Professor Gabriele Bammer, and authors must be commended for bringing a cohesive, integrated and scholarly focus to a topic which has long been a concern for the criminal justice system.

Over centuries the legal system has developed a number of tools for negotiating uncertainties surrounding the guilt of an accused. In the modern trial, courts will assist juries manage evidential uncertainty through judicial instructions and warnings. Most paradigmatically, fact finders are schooled in managing uncertainty through the standard jury directions relating to the presumption of innocence and standard of proof. Juries are told that 'absolute' certainty is impossible, and the 'Golden Thread' running through the web of the criminal law is that the prosecution ordinarily bears the burden of proving its case against the accused *beyond reasonable doubt* (*Woolmington v DPP* [1935] AC 462). While this direction may encourage a feeling of reassurance for participants in the process (jurors having heard this formula repeated endlessly in courtroom dramas), the notion of what constitutes satisfaction beyond 'reasonable doubt' warranting conviction notoriously lacks precision. Indeed, judges often simply revert to distinguishing the criminal standard of proof from the lower civil standard of balance of probabilities, rejecting the use of percentages or other scientific formulae to direct jurors. The presumption of innocence is best understood, juries are told, as a matter of 'common-sense'—a timely judicial reminder that trials place a person's liberty in jeopardy and that utmost prudence is required before returning a guilty verdict! The lesson to be drawn from these examples is that there are few certainties in the imperfect world of our criminal justice system, and that ultimately our legal system has to operate with one eye on the 'best available' evidence, and the other eye on the broader concerns related to fairness and legitimacy.

Policing, like the courts, confronts similar challenges in the face of uncertainty. Intelligence obtained by police or informers may be partial and unreliable. Statements of witnesses may be contradictory or incoherent. Police investigators do not necessarily know *a priori* whether a 'person of interest' is the suspect, witness or indeed victim. Forensic evidence may be open to a variety of (more or less expert) interpretations. Faced by uncertainty at every turn, the role of the professional investigator is to sift through this informational minefield to gather credible material for inclusion in the brief of evidence, which is then placed before the prosecutor for consideration. It is well-known that the 'facts' constituting this police brief come into existence through a complex interaction between the various institutions of the criminal justice system, the relevant procedural and substantive laws, as well as the particular 'theories' about the case held by the police or prosecutors (McConville et al. 1991). This framing of the prosecution case is further overlaid by the wide scope of discretion conferred on both police constable and prosecutor in the way they conduct their investigation and conduct the prosecution.

Due to its adversarial nature, our system of justice will not always generate a comprehensive account of the 'facts' of a case. Leads favourable to the defence may be overlooked or ineptly investigated, with the result that potentially exculpatory material may not be disclosed to the defence at trial, or even suppressed in the public interest for operational reasons. The adoption of prosecution disclosure guidelines by Directors of Public Prosecution in Australia since the 1980s have certainly mitigated some of the dangers outlined above that have historically contributed to miscarriages of justice. However, it would be naïve to think that these risks have been completely removed by simply promulgating guidelines for investigators and prosecutors.

The legal system responds to uncertainty in other ways. Powers relating to arrest, search and seizure of evidence under the common law were initially confined to accused 'caught in the act' of committing an offence. With time, and the emergence of a professional police force in the 19th century, legislatures subsequently recognised that police constables were empowered to arrest, search and seize evidence in cases where the person was merely *suspected* of having engaged in an offence. The concept of reasonable suspicion or belief is a forensic tool for navigating uncertainty—in this context, this relates to the absence of actual knowledge that the person targeted in fact committed the offence. In this way, the concept of 'reasonable belief or suspicion' became a crucial mediating concept for the exercise of investigative powers, and police powers more generally, recognising that absolute certainty would be impractical. The emergence of the reasonable suspicion or belief threshold purports to play a significant role in limiting police powers, applying across a wide range of policing domains from 'move-on' powers in the public order field, through to the deployment of surveillance devices.

The trend during the late 20th century and early 21st century has been towards authorising a wider range of preventive action especially in the counter terrorism field. To demand from law enforcement officials the customary level of satisfaction based on 'belief or suspicion' before exercising powers of search, seizure or arrest might risk a catastrophic attack and mass casualties. As a result, many jurisdictions have opted for pre-emptive or precautionary measures, such as preventive detention or control orders, that can be administratively deployed on a lower civil standard of 'balance of probabilities'. However, responding to uncertainty by the adoption of pre-emptive or precautionary measures is controversial—widening police powers may be ineffective or, worse still, counterproductive by eroding civil liberties that underpin the legitimacy of both policing and liberal democracy. Research in the UK suggests that resentment over broadened police powers among certain communities can lead to the deterioration in police–community relations, adversely impacting on the public's willingness to cooperate with policing and security agencies (Pickering et al. 2008). A recent example of the adoption of precautionary police powers are the UK laws authorising police to stop and search a pedestrian or vehicle in any designated areas on the basis that it was considered 'expedient for the prevention of acts of terrorism'—see s 44 *Terrorism Act 2000 (UK)*. The European Court of Human Rights recently held that the absence of adequate safeguards against the misuse of these powers (requiring that the police believe or suspect, on reasonable grounds, these actions are necessary and proportionate) meant that the exercise of these powers constituted an unjustifiable violation of the right to privacy protected under Article 8 of the European Convention on Human Rights (*Gillan and Quinton v. the United Kingdom* (12 January 2010, unreported) Application no. 4158/05). These powers in the UK were strongly identified with 'racial profiling' by police since data suggested that Blacks and Asians were four times more likely to be stopped and searched without cause than Whites (Pickering et al. 2008). It is vital that pre-emptive measures to combat uncertainty do not come at too high a price, a point underscored by Tim Carmody in his contribution to this book.

This edited collection itself represents an important advance in our thinking about uncertainty and its impact on the policing of serious crime. The project recognises, as does the ARC Centre of Excellence in Policing and Security, the important role that the law enforcement agencies themselves play in promoting a more nuanced and sophisticated understanding of the policies and responses that counter serious crime. As previously noted in the context of counterterrorism policing, this task of preventing crime can be particularly challenging in an environment where both security and policing agencies 'are unable to map the contours of the threat with any certainty' (Pickering et al. 2008, p. 45). This feature of our policing and political environment was explored by the participants at the conference and contributors to this collection. In the post 9/11 environment the central concern of preventing crime has become 'normalised'. The innovative methodology deployed producing this book is a step in promoting a more meaningful dialogue between scholarly and practitioner communities, laying the foundation for new insights, policies and practices for combating serious crime.

References

McConville, M, Saunders, A & Leng, R 1991, *The case for the prosecution*, Routledge, London.

Pickering, S, McCulloch, J & Wright-Neville, D 2008, *Counter-terrorism policing*, Springer, New York.

Introduction
GABRIELE BAMMER

Police have always had to grapple with uncertainties in their investigations of crime, so considerable effort has gone into reducing unknowns by developing technologies, like DNA testing, and procedures, like a record of interview. As crime, especially serious crime, has become more complex and resources have become more stretched it is starting to become evident that reduction cannot be the only approach to uncertainties. But how else can unknowns be tackled?

It turns out that many aspects of understanding and managing unknowns have long been a blind-spot in western intellectual thought (Smithson 1989). However, in recent years, as researchers have increasingly engaged with complex real-world problems, the need to develop richer approaches to uncertainties has become more evident and pressing. Responding to that need is still in early stages. Considerable effort is required to develop a more sophisticated understanding of unknowns, let alone a range of effective options for dealing with them.

One of the central challenges is that—although every complex real-world problem contains many different kinds of unknowns—the way each discipline and practice area handles uncertainty covers only a fraction of the terrain. Further, different kinds of unknowns do not map neatly onto disciplines and practice areas. These limitations were demonstrated in a recent publication, where the insights of 17 disciplines and practice areas (art history, complexity science, economics, emergency management, futures, history, intelligence, law, law enforcement, music, philosophy, physics, policy making, politics, psychology, statistics and theology) were expounded and compared, and where the unknowns involved in responding to communicable disease outbreaks, environmental disturbances and illicit drug use were examined (Bammer & Smithson 2008). That project demonstrated that one way to deal more effectively with the myriad unknowns in social and environmental problems is to bring together different disciplinary experts and practitioners enabling them to learn from each other, as well as to contribute and integrate their insights.

That is the task undertaken by this book, which maps out some of the prime territory for dealing with uncertainties in policing serious crime, as well as reviewing key areas for further development.

This book

The book draws heavily on expertise within the Australian Research Council (ARC) Centre of Excellence in Policing and Security (CEPS), including key practitioners from industry partner organisations, the Executive-in-Residence, Chief Investigators, as well as an Associate Investigator and PhD student. It has also brought in leading contributors from other domains, in a strong partnership between CEPS and other major organisations.

The process used to produce this book involved inviting authors to develop draft chapters, which were circulated to the whole group. Each author was asked to undertake a specific task in line with their expertise, as described in more detail below. The papers were then presented and discussed at a one-day conference which was open to interested participants from the policing and research worlds. After this, the final chapters were written. There were two primary activities designed to integrate the insights. First, four authors were asked to write commentaries reflecting on the other chapters in light of particular aspects of policing practice. The second process is ongoing. Conference participants were asked to document and hand in notes on their own reflections at the end of the meeting. These were collated and circulated and, along with this book, will form the basis for follow-up activities in promising areas.

Sue Wilkinson and Michael Smithson set the scene. Sue Wilkinson describes the major challenges for the profession in responding to serious crime. She shows how crime has changed, especially by exploiting globalisation, as well as by the spread and increasing sophistication of information technologies. She describes modern organised crime as 'international, multilayered, multicultural, highly developed, ambitious, profitable and technologically sophisticated'. Uncertainties are compounded by the unpredictable nature of government priorities and subsequent impacts on resources, lack of inter-operability across jurisdictions and difficulties in cooperating with other countries to fight international crime, as well as differences between countries in legal codes and respect for human rights.

Major developments in research on unknowns are highlighted by Michael Smithson, who also starts to tease out different kinds of uncertainties and their consequences. He specifically describes problems where reduction of uncertainty is not possible or not warranted. He also shows how reducing one uncertainty can increase or generate others. In particular he demonstrates that uncertainties are not always negative, but underpin important forms of social capital like privacy and trust. This has important consequences for reducing uncertainty, which always requires trade-offs, some of which should be avoided.

Introduction

The next set of authors was asked to describe established areas for dealing with uncertainty and to discuss new trends in applying them to policing serious crime. Robyn Attewell, along with Richard Jarrett and Mark Westcott, focus on recent developments in statistics, while Mark Kebbell, Damon Muller and Kirsty Martin concentrate on developments in psychology for dealing with bias.

Robyn Attewell demonstrates how the basic tools of statistics—descriptive statistics, graphs, geospatial mapping, cluster analysis and process control—have continued to evolve, providing effective insights for dealing with serious crime. She also compares and contrasts policing with public health and medicine to discuss how the evidence base for policing could be improved, as well as the limitations to such developments.

A brief introduction to risk analysis is provided by Richard Jarrett and Mark Westcott, showing that many of the qualitative methods currently in use are open to subjective and inconsistent interpretations. They demonstrate an effective method for quantifying consequences and likelihoods of risks, as well as for combining these assessments. They also take this further by examining different kinds of risks—death, injury and illness; economic; social; environmental; symbolic; external; and reputational—and show how these can be rated and combined, allowing for a rich appraisal of a wide range of situations. It therefore becomes possible to construct much more sophisticated and quantified risk matrices to assist police decision-making about allocation of resources and other responses to serious crime, including terrorism.

Mark Kebbell and colleagues describe how short cuts in thinking are essential for effectively responding to the informational complexity of the world. Heuristics are essential aids to thinking, but can have maladaptive outcomes, including leading to bias. They describe a selection of heuristics and biases relevant to policing, namely the representativeness heuristic, the availability heuristic, anchoring and adjustment, confirmation bias and hindsight bias. They also outline advances in debiasing. They demonstrate the particular pertinence of these issues in counterterrorism investigations, which involve both inherent and created uncertainties, and which are both time pressured and high stakes. They argue for the importance of realistic expectations, highlighting the dangers of hindsight bias in particular, especially in politically charged situations.

The third set of authors come from areas which have significant intersections with policing—the law (the Hon. Tim Carmody SC), politics (the Hon. Carmen Lawrence) and business (Neil Fargher). The purpose of providing introductions to these areas is twofold. First, they highlight differences that throw policing procedures into sharper relief. Further exploration may then open the potential to enhance policing effectiveness, for example, in developing cases for prosecution in the courts and in responding to political pressures. Second, advances in these areas in dealing with uncertainties may be able to be adapted to policing purposes. For instance new understandings from the commercial world may be applied to make the 'business' of crime fail.

A review of the foremost uncertainties inherent in the practice of criminal law is provided by Tim Carmody. For any serious crime, important uncertainties arise from the language of the law, liability for punishment, court processes and the use of discretion. Luck also plays a role. In the second half of the paper he lays out some challenges in preventing and penalising crimes such as terrorism. It is vital that legal uncertainties are not allowed to undermine the inherent values on which the legal system is based, that civil liberties and individual freedoms are respected and that society's fundamental tenets of democratic government and the rule of law are upheld.

Carmen Lawrence explores the fundamental issue of fear. While a central role of policing is to reduce fear in the community, there is always a temptation for politicians to exaggerate and exploit fear as a path to maintaining power. Pressures from the media, which thrives on the reporting of crime, exacerbate this temptation. She demonstrates how common psychological processes make communities more vulnerable to manipulation through this fear and how evidence and more nuanced arguments can be blocked out.

Business thrives on uncertainty and Neil Fargher provides an introduction to this world. Profit and risk are directly correlated. For a business to succeed risks have to be taken, but risks and other uncertainties also have to be managed. Policing already uses many strategies from business, so it is helpful to stay on top of mechanisms for reducing uncertainties through managing information, accepting uncertainties through scenario testing and exploiting them through sharing and shifting, using mechanisms such as insurance and derivatives. Policing already understands the value of seeing crime as business and is on the look out for up-to-date understanding of factors that make businesses fail, given that this is the fate of most new businesses and that even profitable established businesses can come to grief. For example, the chapter concludes with a tantalising analysis of drug dealing, demonstrating similarities to professional sports and accounting partnerships, where junior employees put up with low pay and high risk for the chance of being extremely well paid if they reach the top. Legitimate businesses may be able to provide new insights into the criminal world.

The final four authors were given the most challenging task, namely to relate all the other insights back to practical policing issues. They were asked to concentrate on an area of practice in which they have particular expertise. Thus Peter Martin deals with undertaking and managing investigations, Tracey

Green and Greg Linsdell with higher education in policing, Steve Longford with capacity building through consultancy work and Alastair Milroy with the work of specialist agencies established to deal with serious crime.

Peter Martin provides insights into the worlds of the investigating officer and investigation manager. Serious crime investigation is a multidisciplinary effort, where a major challenge is dealing with masses of information. He describes processes, honed through experience, which allow the protracted, complex and controversial nature of serious crimes to be dealt with and he highlights the importance of intuition, the tacit knowledge derived from that experience base. He confirms the importance of dealing with bias, not only among the investigating officers, but also among witnesses. He outlines the importance of the authorising environment, which seeks to provide public value through appropriate allocation of resources to give effect to the law and to achieve efficient outcomes. The authorising environment is essentially the legislative and regulatory support for the investigation, which can also have the downside of diverting effort from the investigation to meet political and media needs, such as pressure to achieve results and demands for information about the investigation to be made public prematurely.

Australia's leading role in the growth and development of higher education to meet the needs of modern policing, as well as how policing is increasingly constituting a discipline in its own right, is described by Tracey Green and Greg Linsdell. Helping police deal with uncertainty is central and becomes more sophisticated as police proceed from recruits to senior managers. They describe the value of a 'club sandwich' approach, which combines underpinning knowledge relevant to policing, ongoing research and evaluation, and application; the same principles which are used in medical education. There are three tenets relevant to all layers of the club sandwich, which are critical thinking, analysis and research. They also demonstrate the importance of higher education in helping police to stay abreast of changing demands and to effectively deal with the authorising environment, as well as describing how today's certainties can be critical uncertainties tomorrow. They highlight the importance of police becoming active partners in research designed to improve policing practice, including initiating investigations and being the lead researchers, which is facilitated by masters and PhD programs. They conclude with a case study of the successful combination of the higher order skills provided by higher education in the solving of a cold missing person's case by a multidisciplinary team.

Higher education alone cannot meet all the demands of policing in dealing with the myriad relevant uncertainties, with consultancy services filling an important niche. Steve Longford describes how his business tackles education and research in the critical area of decision-making. In essence, the business aims to increase understanding of how biases impact upon decision-making and to provide a framework, guidelines and tools that assist with more effective decision-making. He systematically works through decisions and decision processes, including programmable and unprogrammable decisions. He highlights three important biases—cognitive, situational and personal—and describes an inverse correlation between uncertainty and confidence, which he argues must be dealt with by concentrating on uncertainty, not confidence. He describes a range of approaches important for mitigating uncertainty, especially problem-solving; critical thinking; open mindedness; differentiating emotion from reason; arguing from knowledge not ignorance; differentiating between possibility, probability and certainty; as well as between intelligence and evidence; applying Occam's razor; and understanding anchoring. He also examines decision quality, including false positive and negatives.

Alastair Milroy concludes the book with a law enforcement agency perspective. The aim of an organisation like the Australian Crime Commission is to bring together all arms of law enforcement intelligence gathering to unite the fight against serious criminal activities. The challenges that such organisations face include lack of accurate and comprehensive statistics about serious crime; lack of agreement across jurisdictions about priorities; jurisdictional differences in legislation, operating standards, powers and cultures that impede collaboration; and turf wars between agencies and professional groups. An operation against an Asian criminal drug syndicate is used as a case study, where both information gaps in some areas and information overload in others were challenges. Despite the difficulties, the operation had marked successes. But as Alastair Milroy points out a significant uncertainty remains: 'While the task force followed the investigative plan, met key performance indicators, stayed within budget, achieved substantial arrests and charges, the overall impact on serious crime will never be known'.

Each of the authors emphasises the importance of bridging the chasm between research and practice. They identify key areas of intersection between practice concerns and research efforts, as well as areas critical to uncertainty in practice that warrant further research.

Moving forward

There is a long way to go before understanding and managing unknowns takes its rightful place in research and practice effort on complex real-world problems, including the policing of serious crime. There are at least five major challenges which an expanded consideration of unknowns must deal with:

1. appreciating that unknowns are infinite, but research capacity is finite
2. responding to heightened awareness of what we do not know, as what we know increases

3. overcoming the fact that no discipline or other area of intellectual endeavour has the mandate to take an overarching view of unknowns
4. avoiding three problematic responses: a) overconfidence, b) nihilism and despair, and c) providing a hiding place for corruption and incompetence, and
5. agreeing on terminology.

Let us discuss each of these in turn.

Appreciating that unknowns are infinite, but research capacity is finite

There are at least four reasons why unknowns are unlimited:

(i) change is constant, so new unknowns will continue to arise

(ii) research will always uncover new unknowns

(iii) some things are unknowable

(iv) the techniques to research some unknowns are not available.

It is sobering to couple the unlimited nature of unknowns with the fact that the capacity to undertake research is a limited resource. In his book *Inquiry and Change*, Charles Lindblom (1990, p. 162) contended:

> *Professional inquiry is a scarce resource even in a wealthy U.S., never abundant enough to permit study of all important social phenomena and problems, even if the entire adult population became social scientists.*

This holds not just for social scientists, but for researchers in general. Consequently, there can never be enough researchers to study all the important problems existing at any one time.

At present research effort is largely devoted to reducing unknowns, by producing new knowledge. Appreciating that unknowns are infinite helps raise awareness of the need to devote some of the finite research effort to other ways of managing unknowns. Smithson (1989) suggests that these include: acceptance, exploitation, relinquishment, denial and banishment, each of which can be adaptive or maladaptive depending on the circumstances (see also Smithson et al. 2008; Bammer and Smithson 2009). A primary aim of research on unknowns is to better equip decision-makers and other practitioners to deal with uncertainty when responding to complex problems. Knowledge (or evidence) alone is not enough. The remaining unknowns also have to be taken into account.

Responding to heightened awareness of what we do not know, as what we know increases

The argument that we need to put effort into ways of responding to unknowns other than reducing them is strengthened by heightened awareness of unknowns. A useful metaphor here is an island. Let the island represent knowledge in an infinite sea of unknowns. The shoreline is the awareness of what we do not know. As the island grows, the shoreline also expands. Hence we become more aware of unknowns, as well as appreciating the limitations of our capacity to reduce them through research.

Overcoming the fact that no discipline or other area of intellectual endeavour has the mandate to take an overarching view of unknowns

I have already described that each discipline and practice area covers only a fraction of the terrain in terms of the different kinds of unknowns contained in complex problems and that there is no neat correspondence between disciplines or practice areas and different kinds of unknowns, either in terms of what they concern themselves with or in terms of responses. What is more, it is no-one's business to take an overarching view of unknowns and to figure out how to make progress in dealing with them. No discipline or practice area has this mandate. As a consequence there is limited cross-fertilisation between different developments in responding to unknowns, which usually occur ad hoc in the context of research on complex real-world problems. I argue elsewhere (Bammer 2005, 2008) that a new discipline of Integration and Implementation Sciences (I2S) is required to take this overarching role.

Avoiding three problematic responses:
a) overconfidence, b) nihilism and despair, and
c) providing a hiding place for corruption and incompetence

Having a limited understanding of the importance of unknowns can lead to overconfidence. Steve Rayner (2006, p. 5) discusses this in relation to policy making on environmental risk:

> ...policy makers are consistently led to believe that, given time and money, scientific inquiry will reduce relevant uncertainty about environmental

risk. Their scientific advisors hold out the promise that more fine-grained information will clarify the nature and extent of the problem and enable policy makers to craft efficient and effective responses.

Rayner then goes on to point out why this is mistaken, based not only on the new areas research uncovers, but also the often conflicting findings of different investigations. Understanding the unlimited nature of unknowns is also relevant here.

On the other hand, once the extent and inevitability of unknowns is appreciated, tackling unknowns can be overwhelming and it can be tempting to reject research and action completely. Such nihilism is also inappropriate. Good research will provide new insights and, even though actions will always be imperfect, some actions are much better than others.

Third, the unscrupulous can 'game' the ubiquity of uncertainty to cover up incompetence and even corruption. For example, the impossibility of obtaining a full picture of a situation may be offered as an excuse for not taking sensible action. This must not be tolerated.

Agreeing on terminology

An overarching challenge to making progress on unknowns is that there is not yet an agreed terminology. Here I use unknowns and uncertainties interchangeably to designate the whole orbit of what is outside the world of knowledge. Others use the term 'uncertainty' to refer to a specific subset of unknowns, but these subsets are often different. For example, for Smithson (1989) uncertainty refers to partial information and can be subdivided into three categories—vagueness, probability (the domain of statistics) and ambiguity—whereas for Matthews (2009) uncertainty refers to unknowns which cannot be quantified, in contrast to risk which refers to the unknowns which can be quantified. Smithson also points out that other overarching terms, like ignorance, which he tends to prefer, often have pejorative connotations.

There is also no agreed terminology for different kinds of unknowns. For example, Smithson (1989) has developed a typology of unknowns in which he differentiates between error, irrelevance, distortion, incompleteness, untopicality, taboo, undecidability, confusion, inaccuracy, uncertainty, absence, vagueness, probability, ambiguity, fuzziness and non-specificity. The point here is not to discuss or analyse these distinctions (interested readers could see Smithson 1989 or Bammer et al. 2008), but to point out that terminology is complex and not yet agreed.

Conclusion

Responding to these challenges requires painstaking work. One task is to sort out issues of terminology. Another is to gather and categorise different ways of responding to unknowns, along with examples. Further, new ways of understanding and managing unknowns need to be developed. These insights also need to be disseminated and adopted in the research and practice worlds.

One way of moving forward is to focus on specific problems, as this book has done, and to start to expose researchers and practitioners to new ways of thinking about unknowns. It is important to bring in a broad range of perspectives and to present some real intellectual depth, not just a surface view. This requires the creation of an atmosphere where ideas outside individual comfort zones are neither dismissed nor accepted uncritically. Just because an area is hard, does not mean it is worthless. But neither does it mean it is not open to question. Such an exercise can only work when the researchers and practitioners are at the top of their game, as the authors in this book are. It guarantees that the exercise of engaging with difficult ideas is worth the effort.

The book has combined several approaches. One was to invite those familiar with the policing of serious crime to look at their own research or practice with a greater than usual focus on uncertainty. Another was to invite those familiar with unknowns to apply their thinking to the policing of serious crime. The third was to promote exchange between these perspectives, as well as with others interested in the topic (the conference audience).

The challenge now is to build on this initiative. One book and conference can only be a small step forward. We are planning further work to expand thinking about uncertainty, develop new responses to it and enhance the effective uptake of productive insights into the practice of policing. We invite your comments and feedback to Gabriele.Bammer@anu.edu.au.

Acknowledgements

I am grateful to the authors – Robyn Attewell, Tim Carmody, Neil Fargher, Mark Kebbell, Richard Jarrett, Carmen Lawrence, Damon Muller, Kirsty Martin, Michael Smithson, Mark Westcott, and Sue Wilkinson—for participating, especially to Tracey Green, Greg Linsdell, Steve Longford, Peter Martin, and Alastair Milroy for taking on the task of synthesising insights from the other authors. The conference audience were lively participants who contributed additional perspectives, which will be picked up in further work. Damon Muller and Ros Hales provided valuable help in organising the conference. Su Moore provided expert assistance in editing this book. Maree Tait and

Duncan Beard shepherded it through the review and production processes, respectively, and Nausica Pinar designed the cover. Michael Smithson introduced me to the importance of unknowns and provided the grounding needed to progress efforts in understanding and managing them.

References

Bammer, G 2005, 'Integration and implementation sciences: building a new specialization' *Ecology and Society*, vol. 10, no. 2, article 6, <http://www.ecologyandsociety.org/vol10/iss2/art6/> (accessed 26 January 2010).

Bammer, G 2008, 'Adopting orphans: uncertainty and other neglected aspects of complex problems', in G Bammer & M Smithson (eds), *Uncertainty and risk: multidisciplinary perspectives*, Earthscan, London, pp. 27–41.

Bammer, G & Smithson, M (eds) 2008, *Uncertainty and risk: multidisciplinary perspectives*, Earthscan, London.

Bammer, G, Smithson M & the Goolabri Group 2008, 'The nature of uncertainty', in G Bammer & M Smithson (eds), *Uncertainty and risk: multidisciplinary perspectives*, Earthscan, London, pp. 289-303.

Bammer, G & Smithson, M 2009, 'Let's not ignore unknowns', *CEPS Focus on Research, ARC Centre of Excellence in Policing and Security Newsletter*, July, pp. 2–3.

Lindblom, CE 1990, *Inquiry and change. The troubled attempt to understand and shape society*, Yale University Press/Russell Sage, New York.

Matthews, M 2009, Giving preparedness a central role in science and innovation policy, *FASTS (Federation of Australian Scientific and Technological Societies) policy discussion paper*, 6 November, <http://www.fasts.org/index.php?option=com_content&task=view&id=1> (accessed 7 January 2010).

Rayner, S 2006, 'What drives environmental policy?', *Global Environmental Change*, vol.16, no. 1, pp. 4–6.

Smithson, M 1989, *Ignorance and uncertainty. Emerging paradigms*, Springer Verlag, New York.

Smithson, M, Bammer G & the Goolabri Group 2008, 'Coping and managing under uncertainty', in G Bammer & M Smithson (eds), *Uncertainty and risk: multidisciplinary perspectives*, Earthscan, London, pp. 321–333.

Setting the Scene

The Modern Policing Environment
SUE WILKINSON

Introduction

The author Fay Weldon was recently quoted as commenting 'I find the phrase "organised criminals" comforting. When I hear it I thank God somebody, somewhere knows what they're doing and has a plan' (Weldon 2009). She was speaking in jest of course, but if only it were indeed that simple. Organised crime does not necessarily follow a logical process, a plan. If it did, it would be far easier to anticipate, detect, prevent and make effective interventions. As it is, serious and organised crime has changed and adapted with the modern world, exploiting the opportunities it brings. Adaptive, innovative, ahead of the game, organised criminality constantly defies and challenges law enforcement to keep up with it. Investigators find themselves operating within a complex, multilayered, multifaceted environment. It makes for a fascinating area of policing.

In this paper I examine a range of uncertainties that need to be taken into account in the policing of serious and organised crime. I offer descriptions and explanations for the complexity of the challenge, and discuss strategies for managing and addressing the uncertainties—uncertainties that provide not just threats but also opportunities for investigators.

The nature of modern organised crime

Over the past three decades the world has undergone extraordinary change. Globalisation has impacted on every aspect of human life, and has revolutionised the face of organised crime. Communication technologies—telephonic, electronic, digital, satellite—offer both criminals and law enforcement a vast array of options that manifest as opportunities as well as challenges. Such technology has allowed new types of crime to evolve, provided new ways to commit old crime types, facilitated the commission of crime, and challenged traditional methods of detection and apprehension. Further, climate change, as well as economic and political upheavals have resulted in the legal and illegal movement of people across the world, with many countries accommodating a wide range of communities that still retain strong cultural identities and links with their countries of origin. In addition, national and international travel is cheap and easy, allowing organised crime to become an international business. For the sophisticated end of the criminal fraternity, the changing environment within which organised crime can flourish has arguably changed the odds from high risk with high profit, to lower risk with even greater profits.

Evolving crime types include cyber-crime, human trafficking, sophisticated and large-scale fraud, drug trafficking, gun running, counterfeiting and piracy, identity theft and pornography. Emerging crime types include carbon theft and illegal trading, and water theft. These crimes feed further fraud and money laundering, extortion and blackmail. These types of criminality involve layers of organisation, planning, logistics and coordinated activity to manage the large-scale cross-border nature of much of the activity. For example, trafficking people across continents might require cooperation between local crime groups to assist in transit, experts in the provision of identity documentation, and money launderers to deal with the profits. Rivalries can result in homicide, kidnapping and serial extortion between gangs or networks. These crime types cross borders and continents with ease, and facilitated by the benefits of globalisation, a new type of international 'business' has come into being.

Organised crime, though, remains relatively low profile. The cost of organised crime to Australia was conservatively estimated by the Australian Crime Commission (2008) as in excess of $10 billion. Governments across the world make similar assessments, and admit that organised crime probably takes an even higher toll, including fundamentally undermining Gross Domestic Product or GDP. But the nature of organised crime remains hard to quantify in terms that are readily grasped and understood in the public consciousness. Even where, as in Australia, organised crime is acknowledged as a key part of the national security statement and strategy (Department of the Prime Minister and Cabinet 2008), the modern scale and nature of it remains elusive. When organised crime is portrayed in the media or the cinema, it tends to follow more scalable and traditional plot lines—spectaculars involving gangland or bank heists. These crime types still represent aspects of organised crime, but being more established in nature, time-honoured investigation techniques remain effective. The real damage being wreaked upon the world economies is to be found in the cross-border and international dimension.

As well as costs and scale being hard to grasp, another reason organised crime remains relatively low profile is its lack of visibility. Large-scale frauds and deceptions are generally reimbursed to the victims by insurance companies, banks and financial institutions, and not widely publicised for business reasons, and for fear of undermining consumer confidence. The kidnappings, extortions and even murders that result from the activities of organised gangs and criminal networks as they compete for 'turf' or profits tend to remain within the criminal environment without impacting on the wider community. Further, they are not always reported and even law enforcement may remain unaware of them. So the result can be little or no public concern and little coverage in the media.

The products of organised crime are also not very apparent to the average person, despite their presence in local communities. A box of pirated DVDs in a street market often marks the end result of a multimillion dollar international pirating operation. When people purchase these cheap DVDs one or two at a time they are essentially undermining the legitimate operation of the local DVD store and so undermining the local economy. At the same time, national economies are undermined through the wider impact on big business, in turn impacting on GDP and the tax system. Similarly, many see no substantial harm in purchasing cheap cigarettes, liquor or perfume. Dancers in clubs, and prostitutes in local brothels, may be there as a result of international human trafficking or a modern day 'slave trade' as it is often described, and represent the human cost of organised crime. Along with an illegal and underpaid rural or city workforce, they have little visibility in the wider community. Drugs, recreational and pharmaceutical, bought in small but multiple quantities over the internet or on the street, may be the last stage of a pernicious cross-border, international business. A phishing or botnet attack on a home computer may be a small part of a larger crime which has often emanated from half way across the globe. Criminals themselves live in communities, with unexplained and visible signs of wealth and prosperity for all to see, but often with no questions asked. Casinos and gambling venues are vulnerable to exploitation as unwitting money launderers.

To put it crudely, modern day organised crime is rarely manifested as 'blood on the walls' in the same way as homicide or gun crime, so fails to raise the fears and concerns of the wider public or engender a media profile. Even where film and TV dramas and thrillers are developed based on 'real-life', such as *Underbelly* in Australia, they tend to glamorise rather than raise public concern. Without articulated public concern, organised crime is unlikely to become a high profile priority of any government. Here in Australia it (arguably) took a particularly brutal murder committed in broad daylight at the domestic terminal at Sydney airport in March 2009 (when members of a motorcycle gang attacked rivals) to provoke enough fear and concern to stimulate a round of political activity that is starting to address how serious and organised crime is tackled across the states and territories.

The role of the media is worth specific mention. The *'CSI* (Crime Scene Investigation) factor' has gained traction—TV dramas tell a story of neat and swift conclusions to crime investigations, and there are concerns within law enforcement that the expectations of the public, and of juries, are raised to unrealistic levels. The media can play a positive role in raising the profile of organised crime and can play its part in supporting investigations. Conversely, if not properly managed, the media can engender fear and distort the facts and betray confidences. The power and influence of the media should not be underestimated, and a media strategy is an important component of any investigation plan.

Key uncertainties

Uncertainties to be taken into account in policing organised crime are many and various, but can be broadly divided into the following areas: political and economic, international and other jurisdictional, legal, organised criminal networks and communities, and cyberspace. I deal with each in turn.

Political and economic

A major uncertainty for law enforcement to deal with is politics—see also the chapter by Carmen Lawrence (2010). Local and national governments everywhere tend to be more interested in the short term, and their electoral prospects. Local, visible crime and disorder issues tend to take precedence. It is notoriously difficult to achieve longer term investment in any crime strategies because of inconsistency in political priorities. Governments change, as do political priorities, and investment priorities with them. Fighting organised crime is resource intensive, time consuming and expensive. Without the sort of high profile events that have driven, for example, terrorist and security funding over the recent past, the capacity of law enforcement agencies to respond to organised crime has been impacted by a lack of funding. Other funding streams tend to follow local priority setting in the direction of frontline delivery, dealing with local issues. An aspect of organised crime (e.g. human trafficking) can be a high profile issue for a while—with specialist squads set up to tackle it as occurred recently in the UK—only for the squad to be disbanded after a short period of time when funding is withdrawn in favour of other priorities, or cannot be sustained due to economic conditions. Because of their complexity, organised crime investigations can be lengthy and so get caught up in changing circumstances such as these.

International and other jurisdictional

In some parts of the world, the challenge is truly severe—there are places where governments actively sponsor organised crime, or where corrupt governments turn a blind eye to it. There are some countries with a strong tradition of international organised crime where the rule of law is not established. Law enforcement agencies in 'western' countries have to take into account the regimes and priorities of others. Law enforcement agencies can find themselves in a position where international cooperation cannot be safely secured and so investigations are fatally impeded or compromised.

The international nature of organised crime introduces other complexities and uncertainties that need to be taken into account. Foreign language issues have to be managed. Understanding local culture and politics is critical, and these need to be managed by the investigators to maintain progress and integrity in investigations, for example, in countries where corruption is endemic and an accepted way of life. Many jurisdictions now operate a system of international liaison officers who live in countries of interest to assist with bringing local knowledge, networks and contacts to crime investigations.

The exchange of intelligence and information, if not carefully risk assessed and governed by protocols or international MOUs (memoranda of understanding; or in the case of the European Union, international legislation) can bring real risk. For example, the fact that criminality has been identified in some countries can be regarded as bringing shame, or as harmful to national reputations, and enquiries can be blocked by their governments. Where suspects are identified there is a danger that action or retribution can be taken out on their families or acquaintances. The investigation may provoke a related investigation or trial in another country which may not have compatible or appropriate human rights safeguards in place, or may have a system of capital punishment. Human sources or protected witnesses may be placed at risk. Extradition agreements may not be in place. Investigators may need to conduct a thorough risk assessment and adjust the direction and conduct of their investigation accordingly. On occasion, the risks may be assessed as so great that they will outweigh the necessity or benefits of pursuing the investigation further and the investigation may be discontinued.

As the international nature of organised crime grows, the role of diplomats and politicians has increased in assisting law enforcement to address and overcome some of these issues. It is possible to negotiate case-specific agreements to override otherwise incompatible systems, for example, to safeguard the well-being of deportees or foreign prisoners to their countries of origin where otherwise their lives may be at risk, or to facilitate extradition. Similarly, to negotiate safeguards in the exchange of intelligence, politicians and diplomats can have a critical role to play in facilitating the continuation of international investigations.

Within Australia, to some extent the international challenges outlined here are also reflected within the federal system. Essentially, the states and territories are separate jurisdictions, each with its own police force, criminal code and legislation governing investigations and the management of intelligence and information between agencies and across jurisdictions. Interoperability is affected to varying degrees by differences in standards and local priority setting.

Legal

Around the world, across police jurisdictions, and between agencies, there are issues of incompatibility in training, skills and standards, legislation, police powers and procedures, different criminal codes and criminal justice systems. How technology can be used and how evidence and disclosure are handled have to be recognised, respected and negotiated as necessary to allow the continuance of investigations across borders. Communication is a major issue, with interpreters cleared to the appropriate security levels in short supply or unavailable for some languages and dialects.

The conduct of covert investigations can be problematic and has to be managed well to minimise risk. Skills, standards, respect for human rights and the concept and assessment of risk vary across the world. Disclosure issues for use in evidence, and the use of interception product varies, even between very similar allied countries and jurisdictions.

The implications of incompatible privacy legislation and judicial review processes across jurisdictions or countries can result in unintended disclosure that places people at risk and compromises investigations. Agreed protocols and MOUs from the outset of investigations are invaluable to navigate complexity and uncertainty in the pursuit of a crime investigation.

Organised criminal networks and communities

Much attention is being paid to the growth of organised criminal networks. They are, again, often international in nature, with multilayered structures and shifting alliances that serve to protect the 'masterminds' very effectively. However, they are also often identified with particular countries of origin.

With the demography of countries and cities across the world becoming far more multicultural, new and immigrant communities are often isolated. They may not speak the language of their adopted country, may feel culturally estranged and maintain more meaningful contact with communities and family in their countries of origin than they do in their new homes. It can be very challenging for authorities, including the police, to engage and build relationships with these communities who may feel distrustful of authority, and historically and culturally lack faith in police. Communities can become vulnerable to crime and feel unable to seek help. At the same time, criminal elements within communities may evolve but operate in partnership with criminals in their country of origin. There has been a trend in Europe and Asia for organised criminal networks of different nationalities to specialise in particular types of crime, but to work together when it suits them.

Working within new, or existing, culturally and linguistically diverse communities can be hugely challenging for police and wider law enforcement professionals, who need to understand crime and criminality as it affects any one community in order to be able to operate more effectively. Meanwhile, the flow of intelligence and progress of investigations can be stalled while much effort goes into building the trust and longer term relationships needed to support organised crime investigations.

Organised criminal networks are difficult to track, often operating across many borders, with no fixed membership or even crime type. They are therefore challenging for law enforcement agencies to infiltrate or monitor. Their use of technology can be very sophisticated, whether to commit crime, facilitate crime, or to confuse investigators. However, across the world police forces and law enforcement agencies are increasingly working together to disrupt and dismantle identified international criminal networks. It is acknowledged that many networks, whether they are dealing in any combination of fraud, money laundering, drugs, people trafficking, gun running, piracy, cyber-crime or pornography, are effectively opportunistic high profit businesses. Some are organised and sophisticated enough to set themselves up as part of legitimate companies. Others set up apparently legitimate businesses as a cover. Others again are chaotic and unpredictable. All of them tend to be highly profitable, but their international nature makes them challenging to identify and disrupt. It is often said that criminals take advantage of borders and jurisdictional barriers, but police are hampered by them.

Cyberspace

Many see cyber-crime as the biggest crime threat facing the world. It is worth detailing the particular challenge of cyber-crime and its contribution to the uncertainties that investigators must grapple with. There are no borders in cyberspace. Cyber-crime in the new millennium is a mix of 'old crimes' using new technology, such as pornography, paedophilia and identity theft, and emerging crime types such as critical infrastructure attack, cyber-terrorism and online money laundering services.

The use of technology is helping criminals hide their tracks, facilitates their communication, and makes surveillance and monitoring by law enforcement agencies more difficult. Cyberspace affords criminals a relatively safe environment and an opportunity to make a lot of money quickly and then a way to dispose of the money electronically. The growth of phishing and the use of botnets can compromise many thousands of computers at a time across any number of countries and allow criminals access to countless pieces of personal information leading to large-scale fraud, theft, identity theft and denial of service attacks. The nature of the internet makes detection and disruption very challenging but, in turn, makes it possible for law enforcement to become far more effective.

Law enforcement can take advantage of the same technology. Collaborative partnerships with telecommunication companies, the computer industry and internet service providers are critical in assisting police to remain responsive to the challenge. Encryption available 'off the shelf' and as a standard part of new computers has to be taken into account, and the future nature of telephone services will require detection and monitoring methods to be adapted.

Dealing with uncertainty

To sum up, modern organised crime tends to be international, multilayered, multicultural, highly developed, ambitious, profitable and technologically sophisticated. It presents tremendous challenges to investigators who need to be capable of building partnerships across law enforcement agencies, across sectors and across borders. Investigators need to manage languages, cultures, international politics and legislation. The crime they pursue is multifaceted and unpredictable, high profit and often unseen. So how do investigators deal with these challenges and balance the uncertainties in order to make informed decisions about the risks they manage and where they focus their resources and energy?

The safety and security of communities is the top priority of most law enforcement agencies. A clear vision such as this helps when balancing demands and managing risk. The scale of organised crime is such that in any case, law enforcement must make informed decisions as to where the best likelihood of success lies compared to the risk and expense involved in any investigation. A test of reasonableness can be applied. It would not, for example, be reasonable to make a decision not to deploy police to prevent loss of life, but it could be seen as reasonable not to spend money on an enquiry that did not have a reasonable chance of resulting in a successful prosecution. On the other hand, the likelihood of a successful outcome often cannot be accurately assessed before undertaking an investigation. Indeed, the rationale for decisions can run to many pages in a decision log.

Investigators employ a range of tools in making these assessments. The issue of proportionality is always a primary consideration—is the level of resources, money, and time needed to investigate, along with the likelihood of a successful outcome, balanced by the amount of risk and harm posed by the criminal activity in question?

The issue of 'risk' and 'harm' is often hard to assess. An obvious risk to life is simple, as is risk to reputation, but how important are they in the overall scheme of things? Risk to the economy is not so easy to estimate, nor is assessing risk to the community. The harm caused by organised crime is often insidious and hard to quantify. Organised crime can cause underlying fear in a targeted community. It can cause insecurity. For example, a recent survey in the UK found that 13% of people were more afraid of being a victim of cyber-crime than they were of burglary (Dorset Police Authority 2008). Organised crime can undermine quality of life and community confidence, but in a way that is hard to make explicit. Whether or not a crime investigation is in the 'public interest' is often cited as part of a rationale for continuing or discontinuing.

Risk assessments are a useful decision-making tool. Political, economic, sociological, technological, ethical, legal and organisational factors can be taken into account and balanced against each other. Making decisions about whether to investigate complex crime has become a critical exercise for the modern day law enforcement officer. Freedom of information and disclosure provisions have required investigators to record their decisions in order to be able to withstand scrutiny from any number of interested parties, including the media, politicians, the courts, the victim(s), and human rights or civil liberties organisations. In many countries, the right of sworn law enforcement officers to exercise discretion is absolute, although not immune from legal challenge. Standard models and processes are routinely used to support decision-making that is deemed fair, ethical and reasonable.

Given the character, scale and complexity of modern day organised crime, much energy is being invested internationally in prevention. 'Target hardening'— such as ensuring financial institutions are more robust, regulatory practices are in place, industries such as the security sector are less vulnerable, the public more informed—is cost-effective and in the public interest. Agencies around the world are finding ways of working together to tackle crime 'at source'— such as proactively targeting suspected organised criminal networks through intelligence-led policing; working with banks and internet service providers to prevent exploitation of their services; working in partnership with customs and immigration authorities; deploying undercover tactics, including online, to target predators and sex offenders using the internet; engaging in proactive law enforcement activity such as targeting unexplained wealth and tracking suspicious money movements. Perhaps most important, is educating the public to take responsibility—to protect themselves, for example, in avoiding identity theft and protecting their computers.

Joint training and international courses for law enforcement officers are becoming the norm. Strategic assessments are important in predicting how organised crime continues to evolve and to assist with identifying the strategies that will be needed to counter it. Agencies are seeking to recruit from diverse communities, investing in language courses, and setting up formal partnerships and secondments that bring experts, for example in banking or information technology, to work alongside investigators. Flexibility and innovation will be needed on an ongoing basis to meet the challenge.

It is widely accepted that the fight against organised crime is not one for law enforcement alone, but can only be conducted in partnership across all sectors, and at an international level. Organisations such as the United Nations and Interpol have key roles to play at the most strategic level and are increasingly engaged in enhancing international understanding and supporting the cooperation and collaboration needed to tackle organised crime effectively. Building on existing work in coordinating nations, agencies, organisations, businesses and communities to identify and reduce the impact of organised crime remains a major global challenge.

In conclusion, organised crime poses ever evolving and complex challenges to law enforcement, and managing and dealing with uncertainty is a key component of any investigator's role. Constant review and evaluation of likely risk and harm is needed to inform the key tests of reasonableness and proportionality. The application of transparent logical risk assessment to such an unpredictable and challenging environment brings reassurance and confidence to the public and practitioner alike.

This paper is not intended as an academic study of organised crime. It represents my personal views and is based upon my own experience in policing serious and organised crime. It does not represent the views or official policy position of any agency or organisation in Australia or overseas.

References

Australian Crime Commission 2008, *Organised crime in Australia*, Australian Crime Commission, Australia.

Department of the Prime Minister and Cabinet 2008, *The first National Security Statement to parliament*, address by the Prime Minister of Australia The Hon. Kevin Rudd MP, 4 December, Canberra.

Dorset Police Authority 2008, *Dorset police community safety survey 2008*, main report of study findings, November 2008, <http://www.dpa.police.uk/pdf/cecc_22.01.09%20-%2006%20-%20the%20community%20safety%20survey%202008.pdf> (accessed 21 January 2010).

Lawrence, C 2010, 'Politics', in G Bammer (ed.), *Dealing with uncertainties in policing serious crime*, ANU E Press, Canberra.

Weldon, F 2009, *The Observer*, interview by L Seigle, 30 August, <http://www.guardian.co.uk/lifeandstyle/2009/aug/30/fay-weldon> (accessed 14 January 2010).

Understanding Uncertainty

MICHAEL SMITHSON

An overview of uncertainty in this practice-oriented setting may seem too academic by half. Why indulge in an exercise around *understanding* uncertainty? Surely we should be focusing on the business of *removing* uncertainties, by improving our predictions of when and where criminal activity or threats to security will arise, the effectiveness of our methods of investigation, intelligence and case-solving, and our understanding of the root causes of crime and security threats.

Those are laudable goals. Nevertheless, they entail implicit assumptions about the nature of the uncertainties involved in policing and security, and how stakeholders understand these uncertainties and the risks associated with them. They also are formed by a perspective that views uncertainty as entirely negative, something to be rid of. This overview examines these assumptions and makes some rather bold claims, such as the following:

- Many important uncertainties may be incomparable with one another. People think and behave as if there are different kinds of uncertainty.
- Many important uncertainties are irreducible.
- Even when uncertainties are reducible, they may not be worth reducing.
- Even when they are worth reducing, conventional uncertainty reduction methods may not be useful to decision-makers.
- Reducing one uncertainty may increase or generate other uncertainties.
- People have uses for uncertainty, and some of those uses underpin important forms of social capital. Reducing those uncertainties destroys social capital.
- We always trade away something when we try to reduce uncertainties. Sometimes we should be reluctant to make the trade.

Another justification for an overview is the disjointed nature of the available perspectives on uncertainty, risk, and related topics. Many disciplines, professions and practice domains have perspectives on uncertainty, and some of them are sophisticated, but these are usually not well understood by others outside those disciplines or domains. They are not self-integrating either, and an overview can be helpful in this regard.

Frameworks for understanding unknowns

It is difficult to communicate clearly about uncertainty, and to do so without employing terms that have negative connotations. In many disciplines the most popular general term seems to be 'uncertainty'. This is the case, for example, in psychology, economics, and engineering. Still another alternative is 'ignorance' itself, which I will use as the overarching term in this chapter even though the primary focus will be on uncertainty. For interesting discussions of nomenclature in this domain, see Gross (2007) and Smithson (2008a).

Ignorance also is a slippery concept. A major problem in attaching a definition to it is that we cannot avoid making claims to know something about who is ignorant of what. Any claim about ignorance entails a knowledge-claim regarding the nature of said ignorance. Instead of a 'frontal-assault' definition which would trap us into making unwarranted claims to know everything, we need a definition that takes the claimant's viewpoint into account. A definition (Smithson 1989) that seems to handle these problems reasonably well is as follows: A is ignorant from B's viewpoint if A fails to agree with or show awareness of ideas which B defines as actually or potentially valid. This definition allows B to define what she or he means by ignorance. It also permits self-attributed ignorance, since A and B may be the same person. Most importantly, it incorporates anything B thinks A could or should know (but does not) and anything that B thinks A must not know (and does not). B's notions about ignorance may be as context-dependent and subjective as required.

The intuition that there might be different kinds of ignorance has motivated a number of scholars to propose various distinctions and taxonomies. Even such a seemingly well-known concept as probability has undergone splits into distinct schools of thought. Many reviews of probability theories divide schools of probability into three camps: Logical or a priori probability, frequentist probability and Bayesian probability. All three schools agree on the probability calculus; where they differ is on the basis and scope of probability. Many Bayesians, for instance, are willing to attach probabilities to unique unrepeatable events, whereas frequentists will not permit that.

Outside of probability theory, one of the most popular distinctions between different kinds of ignorance is absence or neglect versus distortion. Another common distinction is reducible versus irreducible ignorance. The term 'negative knowledge' has been proposed by Knorr Cetina (1999) to encompass knowledge of the limits of knowing, mistakes in attempts to know, things that interfere with knowing, and what people do not want to know. A fourth distinction in some languages (Smithson 1989) is between the active voice (ignoring) and the passive voice (being ignorant). The active voice shall be referred to here as 'irrelevance' and the passive voice as 'error'.

Lower-level distinctions among kinds of error that have proven useful are as follows. Error may arise either from incomplete or distorted views, or both. Distortion may consist of a systematic bias or inaccuracy (e.g. under- or overestimation), or confusion (mistaking one thing for another). Incompleteness in kind is outright absence of information, whereas incompleteness in degree constitutes what we shall term 'uncertainty'. Uncertainty, in turn, includes probability, vagueness, ambiguity, and conflict (see Smithson 1989; Smithson 1999; Smithson 2008b). Figure 1 displays Smithson's (1989) taxonomy.

Figure 1: Taxonomy of ignorance

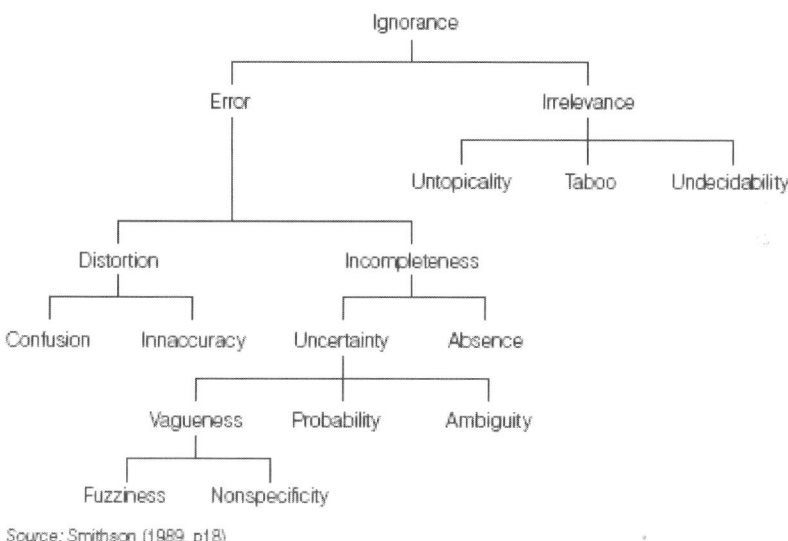

Source: Smithson (1989, p18)

In mathematics and related areas, the past four decades have seen a rapid proliferation of formal frameworks for dealing with uncertainty (as used in this chapter) in ways that depart from standard probability theory. Fuzzy set theory, roughs sets, and fuzzy logic are frameworks for dealing with vagueness and related kinds of nonprobabilistic uncertainty (for an overview, see Klir & Yuan 1995). The primary claim for fuzzy set theory is that it handles categories (sets) in which items can have partial membership (e.g. a 'reddish' colour or a 'tall' person). Likewise, fuzzy logic permits degrees of truth to be attached to propositions.

Probability theory itself has been generalised mainly by extensions to theories of 'imprecise' probabilities such as possibility theory, Dempster-Shafer belief theory, and several others that incorporate these two as special cases (key references here are Shafer 1976; Walley 1991). The past two decades have seen the establishment of these frameworks on firm axiomatic foundations and an increasing number of applications.

What is the practical significance of all this? How can general frameworks of the kind exemplified in this section help commanders, detectives, attorneys, or even jury members make decisions about real cases? I will argue for the utility of general frameworks through five topics:

1. how the number of alternatives or outcomes affects the decisions we make
2. understanding that uncertainty reduction is not always worthwhile
3. when more information actually increases uncertainty
4. on choosing the right analytical tool for the job
5. trade-offs and dilemmas in dealing with ignorance and uncertainty.

These topics have been chosen because each has practical effects on decisions in complex real-world settings, those effects are somewhat counterintuitive, and they pertain directly to aspects of one or more general frameworks.

Framing a decision: how many outcomes?

The number of alternatives to choose from affects what we choose and how we make choices. Commonsense intuition has it that the more alternatives the better; a greater number of alternatives gives us 'room to move.' However, there is plenty of evidence that too many alternatives make us indecisive (Anderson 2003). This effect is partly due to the sheer amount of thought required by a large number of alternatives, but also to the likelihood that some of these alternatives will seem so similar to one another as to make choosing among them difficult.

There is another kind of influence that the number of alternatives has on our decision-making, and its effects are greatest when that number is small. This effect originates from an apparently reasonable facet of probability theory. Standard probability assessments applied to settings in which there is a finite set of possible events are *partition-dependent*. The 'partition' refers to how events are categorised, and 'partition dependency' here simply means that the number of event categories influences how probabilities are assigned. On grounds of insufficient reason, a probability of $1/K$ is assigned to K mutually exclusive possible events when nothing is known about the likelihood of those events. For example, in a race involving three greyhounds, a decision-maker who knows nothing about any of the dogs would assign a value of $1/3$ to the probability of each greyhound winning. But if there are five dogs in the race, then the same decision-maker would assign a probability of $1/5$ to each dog's chances.

All well and good, but so what? It is not difficult to find real decision-making situations in which the choice of K is problematic. First, people can be fooled into adopting incorrect partitions. In a pioneering experiment, Fox and Rottenstreich (2003) demonstrated that when asked 'How likely is it that Sunday will be the hottest day of the week,' many people answered '1/2' whereas when asked 'Out of the seven days of the week, how likely is it ...' most gave the more defensible estimate '1/7'. The first version of the question primed people to think that either Sunday will or will not be the hottest day and therefore a twofold partition. The second version primed them to think about Sunday being one day out of the seven in a week, a sevenfold partition.

Second, there are many practical situations in which no 'correct' partition exists. Nevertheless, the choice of partition crucially affects how a decision is framed. An example is how to categorise test results. For example, a test for measuring iron deficiency (serum ferretin) can be categorised into two options: greater or less than 45 mmol per litre or into three options, less than 35mmol/l, more than 35 and less than 75mmol/l, and more than 75mmol/l. The website of the Centre for Evidence-Based Medicine at the University of Toronto (2007) presents an example of a female patient who has been administered a serum ferritin test for diagnosing iron deficiency anaemia. Her test yields 40 mmol/l. Their hypothetical evidence for the diagnostic application of this test is shown in the upper part of Table 1, suggesting that a result of 45 mmol/l or less has a likelihood ratio of 8.24 and a post-test probability of 70/85 = .82 of having the disorder. The obvious recommendation for this patient is treatment.

Table 1: Hypothetical anaemia test scenario

Serum ferritin test result	Iron deficiency anaemia		Likelihood ratio
	Present	Absent	
positive (< 45 mmol/l)	70	15	8.24
negative (> 45 mmol/l)	15	135	0.20
	85	150	

Serum ferritin test result	Iron deficiency anaemia		Likelihood Ratio
	Present	Absent	
< 35 mmol/l	60	3	35.29
> 35 < 75 mmol/l	15	35	0.76
> 75mmol/l	10	112	0.16
	85	150	

However, what if the partition used for the serum ferritin test was the one shown in the lower part of Table 1? The evidence base is the same, but now the patient lands in a category where the likelihood ratio is only 0.76, hardly sufficient to compel us to recommend treatment. Perhaps further investigation or tests would be warranted instead.

Now, the question of whether to divide the mmol/l scale into two, three, four, etc. options is unanswerable. There is no reason that compels us to prefer two categories over three or vice versa. In medicine, the partition usually is determined simply by the number of decisional alternatives available to the practitioner (e.g. {treat, do not treat} versus {treat, more tests, do not treat}). The point is that neither partition is normatively preferable to the other, but each yields a different decision. It is not hard to find similar examples in policing. Consider evaluating the likelihood that a suspect in a homicide case is guilty if the partition is {murder, accident} versus {murder 1, murder 2, manslaughter, negligence, accident}.

A general consequence of partitioning is that, not only can the modification of a partition alter decisions, it can also alter the relationship between the decision-maker's preferences and her/his standards of evidence. It has implications for the work of police, for example in the collection of evidence and proof of guilt in courtroom trials. In the context of legal standards of proof, Connolly (1987) points out that for many people the threshold probability of guilt associated with the phrase 'beyond reasonable doubt' is in the [.9, 1] range. That is, most people would return a conviction only if they were persuaded that the suspect had at least a 90% chance of having committed the crime. For a logically consistent juror, a threshold probability of .9 implies the difference between the subjective value of acquitting versus convicting the innocent, is 9 times the difference in the subjective value of convicting versus acquitting the guilty.

Connolly demonstrates that the relative valuations of the four possible outcomes (convicting the guilty, acquitting the innocent, convicting the innocent, and acquitting the guilty) that are compatible with such a high threshold probability are counterintuitive. Specifically, '... if one does [want to have a threshold of .9], one must be prepared to hold the acquittal of the guilty as highly desirable, at least in comparison to the other available outcomes' (Connolly 1987, p. 111). He also shows that more intuitively reasonable valuations lead to unacceptably low threshold probabilities according to most people's interpretations of 'beyond reasonable doubt'.

So, the higher the standard of proof, the more likely guilty suspects will be acquitted. Smithson (2006) shows that the incorporation of a third middle option (such as the Scottish Not Proven verdict) with a suitable threshold can resolve this quandary, permitting a rational agent (i.e. one whose valuations of outcomes are compatible with their standards of proof) to retain a high conviction threshold and still regard false acquittals as negatively as false convictions.

However, the price paid for this solution is a more stringent standard of proof for outright acquittal, in other words, it is harder for someone to be acquitted outright. In a series of empirical studies of mock-juror decision-making in which a Not Proven alternative was made available, Smithson, Deady and Gracik (2007) found that those who returned a Guilty verdict believed the suspect was very likely to have committed the crime, those returning an Acquittal believed the suspect was very unlikely to have done so, and those returning a Not Proven verdict gave probabilities of guilt in the middle of the scale. In fact, the Not Proven probabilities were within the range where a rational agent utilising a high threshold for conviction would return a Not Proven verdict.

So, as in the medical example, the choice of partition (i.e. having 3 options rather than 2) alters the decisional outcomes. Contrary to a widely held view that the Not Proven alternative would result in a decrease in *convictions*, Smithson and colleagues found that it resulted in a decrease in outright *acquittals*. Note that this effect is not due to irrationality on the part of the participants in their study; indeed, a rational decision-maker would do the same.

An even worse problem in some respects arises from the fact that our probability judgments are partition-dependent (Fox & Rottenstreich 2003). To begin with, the $1/K$ rule does not distinguish between a judge who has strong reasons for believing that the K outcomes are equally likely and a judge who does not have a clue. An experienced bookie might assign probabilities of $1/3$ to each of the dogs in our three-dog race because he has reviewed each of the dog's previous form in great detail and knows they are evenly matched. But his probabilities are indistinguishable from the punter who has no knowledge about any of the dogs and assigns $1/3$ through the aforementioned principle of insufficient reason (a probability of $1/K$ is assigned to K mutually exclusive possible events when nothing is known about the likelihood of those events). The bookie knows quite well what probabilities to assign. The punter has no idea what probabilities to assign.

This problem has practical consequences when not all the outcomes are known about in advance. A seminal study by Fischhoff, Slovic, and Lichtenstein (1978) concerning people's assignments of probabilities to possible causes of a given outcome (e.g. an automobile that will not start) revealed that possible causes that were explicitly listed received higher probabilities than when the same causes were implicitly incorporated into a 'Catch-All' category of additional causes (see Table 2 for an example; List 2 uses the Catch-All category 'Other'). One explanation proposed for this effect amounts to the old proverb 'Out of sight, out of mind', and the effect has since been referred to as the 'Catch-All Underestimation Bias' and also sometimes the 'pruning bias' (Russo & Kolzow 1994).

Table 2: Fault lists for automobile

List 1	List 2
Out of petrol	Out of petrol
Dirty spark plugs	Dirty spark plugs
Flat battery	Other
Fuel leak	
Out of oil	
Motor seized	
...	

Why is this problematic for decision-makers or planners? In many real-world situations we do not know what all of the possible outcomes are. If we are estimating the probability of these outcomes, we therefore have to employ a Catch-All category for the ones we do not yet know about. The Catch-All Underestimation Bias implies that we will not allocate enough probability to the Catch-All, and thus will underestimate the probability of novel, unexpected events. Therefore, we are likely to be unprepared for these surprises when they occur.

In a more general vein, Support Theory (Rottenstreich & Tversky 1997) is a framework that begins with the claim that people do not follow the logic of conventional probability theory. Instead, unpacking a compound event (e.g. cancer) into disjoint components (e.g. breast cancer, lung cancer, bone cancer etc.) tends to increase the perceived likelihood of that event. An immediate implication is that unpacking an hypothesis and/or repacking its complement will increase the judged likelihood of that hypothesis. Human judges are not behaving according to probability theory here, but what are they doing instead? One explanation is that they intuitively evaluate the likelihood of a compound event by the number of ways they think that it can happen. The more distinct paths to an outcome they are aware of (i.e. the finer-grained the partition), the more likely that outcome seems.

Are there solutions to the partition-dependence problem? The most plausible answer lies in what seems the most arcane among the topics raised in the preceding section: generalised probability theories. Focusing on probability judgments, suppose we allow judges to use a lower and an upper probability estimate (i.e. a type of imprecise probability). A judge who has no idea about the probabilities of any of the outcomes (e.g. the ignorant punter at the dog races) can assign a lower probability of 0 and an upper probability of 1 to every one of them. That is, a set of probability assignments that does not depend on the number of outcomes. Moreover, this judge's assignments will be distinguishable from a knowledgeable (or confident) judge who makes more precise probability assignments (e.g. the experienced bookie who knows the dogs are equally matched and therefore assigns each a 1/3 chance of winning).

When is uncertainty reduction worthwhile?

The commonplace assumption that reducing unknowns will always aid decision-making ignores the fact that reducing unknowns is not cost-free, nor does it always pay off. Perhaps the most obvious argument against this assumption begins with the observation that usually reducing ignorance or uncertainty requires acquiring and processing information. Information seeking and processing both cost time, effort and other resources. We should therefore ascertain, if possible, whether such expenditure is going to be worthwhile. I shall describe an example where uncertainty reduction arguably fails on this point due to the difficulty of obtaining accurate information on which to base a decision.

Smithson and Muller (2009) examined how knowledge about the characteristics of missing persons who are found to be homicide victims can be used to provide guidance for decisions regarding the investigation of missing persons cases. They ask whether improved predictors of high risk missing persons cases will enable commanders to have a reasonably high probability of correctly deciding to allocate resources to these cases. The question posed by them is directly relevant to the concerns raised here. If the effort required to find or develop effective predictors for these cases is to pay off, it should result in commanders making correct decisions most of the time. If, on the other hand, too much effort is required for too little gain then seeking more effective predictors is not a viable course of action.

Although the majority of missing persons are located quickly—in Victoria in 2005–06, for example, 90% were located within seven days—some are found dead and may be homicide victims (James, Anderson, & Putt 2008). When a person has been reported missing, police consider issues such as whether the circumstances are suspicious, or there is evidence of the commission of a crime. A high risk case is assigned a high priority, and if the person is not found within a few hours, a more intensive follow-up investigation is commenced (James et al. 2008). So the decision in question here is whether to allocate the resources required for the more intensive investigation. That decision hinges on how the risks are assessed.

In a large-scale UK study Newiss (2006) examined 32,705 cases of missing persons in the UK between 2000 and 2002, and determined that 0.6% were found dead, although not necessarily victims of homicide. An obvious recommendation is ascertaining the factors that may predict the likelihood of a missing person ending up dead and, conditional on death, being a homicide victim. These investigations could be combined with survival analysis of the kind employed by Newiss, to determine whether there is a relationship between the length of time a person has gone missing and the likelihood that the person is a homicide victim. Newiss (2006), however, argues that the best available factors are unreliable predictors, at least for the purpose of decision-making.

What is the basis of Newiss' pessimism? Smithson and Muller (2009) show that the accuracy of any predictive model is strongly compromised by the sheer rarity of deaths among missing person cases. In particular, they demonstrate that even if the risk factors tell us that when there is a homicide, the probability that the factors are present is .99 and when there is no homicide the probability that the factors are absent is .99 (far better than can be obtained from the predictors identified by Newiss), the probability of a correct 'diagnosis' would be poor: the probability of a homicide given that the factors are present is only .376. Thus, if police decided to allocate more resources to cases where these risk factors were present they could expect to be wrong about 62% of the time.

To get to the point where correct diagnosis was an even money bet (probability of a homicide given that the factors are present = .5) would require the probability of factors absent given no homicide to be .994. To move the probability of a correct diagnosis to .9 would require that latter probability to be .9993. Needless to say, these standards are unachievable: it is effectively impossible to get a criterion that is accurate enough to reliably inform a decision as to whether to investigate a missing person case as a homicide. Therefore, even when highly accurate diagnostic criteria are available for such decision-making, the most likely outcome is an 'erroneous' decision. The pursuit of more accurate diagnostic criteria in the name of guaranteeing correct decisions becomes pointless.

When does more information increase uncertainty?

Coupled with the commonplace assumption that uncertainty reduction is an unalloyed good is another assumption that more information always will reduce uncertainty. More information does not always have this effect; it can do the opposite. I will describe four ways in which more information can *increase* uncertainty. The first two are fairly obvious, but the latter two are more counterintuitive and point to deeper philosophical issues with considerable practical impacts.

Perhaps the most self-evident is when additional information results in conflicting assessments. Not only does more information raise uncertainty by introducing conflict, but people perceive the uncertainty arising from conflicting information as different from (and worse than) uncertainty arising from probability or ambiguity (Smithson 1999). Moreover, if the conflict is due to disagreement among alternative sources then people tend to distrust all of those sources, not just the sources they regard as inferior to the best source. Even in mathematical decision theory frameworks, how best to combine information from disagreeing sources and base decisions on them remains an open question.

Another more subtle way that more information can increase uncertainty is when the information is irrelevant. This issue crops up in areas where evidence is at a premium such as forensic science, but for the moment we will consider a simple stripped-down example. Suppose we have 80 cases where a go/no-go decision has been made on the basis of case characteristic A, and in 50 of those cases the decision turned out to be correct. Is characteristic A useful (i.e. does it perform better than flipping a coin)? The proportion of correct decisions is 50/80 = .625 and a 95% confidence interval around this proportion is [.516, .723], so we should conclude that characteristic A probably is better than flipping a coin.

But a critic points out that we also should take into account whether characteristic B is present or absent. To take B into account is to take on more information, therefore making a more informed decision. There is a downside, however. Characteristic B is present in 40 cases and absent in the other 40, and it turns out that B also splits the correct decisions equally, into two groups of 25 each. The proportion of correct decisions is still the same, regardless of whether B is present or absent. But if we consider the B-present cases separately from the B-absent ones, our 95% confidence interval widens because we are using smaller samples. The interval now is [.470, .758] and therefore includes a probability of .5, so we are unable to say whether the proportion of correct decisions taking characteristics A and B into account is any better than flipping a coin.

Our uncertainty is greater because B is irrelevant. Suppose instead that when B is present there are 30 correct decisions out of 40 and when it is absent there are 20 correct out of 40. Now B is relevant, and it also makes us more certain about when A is useful. When B is present the proportion of correct decisions is 30/40 = .75 and the 95% confidence interval around that proportion is [.598, .858], whereas when B is absent the proportion is 20/40 = .5 and the 95% confidence interval is [.352, .648]. We conclude that A is useful when B is present but not when B is absent. Moreover, a 95% confidence interval around the difference between these proportions is [.038, .433], so we may conclude that they probably do differ.

In the first example, if we knew in advance that B was irrelevant then we would not bother taking it into account. However, often we do not know beforehand whether information is going to be relevant. Moreover, people tend to take as an article of faith that *any* information is worth taking into account and, if more information becomes available, people generally become more confident about their judgments or predictions regardless of whether the information is relevant or not.

Lurking behind this example is a fundamental issue known by probabilists as the *reference class problem*. If we are to estimate the probability of an event or the risk associated with a case, what class of events or cases should we use? In current debates about the uses of DNA evidence, this problem has cropped up regarding the estimation of laboratory error-rates in DNA testing. Should we lump all laboratories together and estimate a common error-rate? If not, what characteristics of the laboratories should be taken into account? How far down into specifics should we go? If we ignore important distinctions among laboratories then we may be comparing apples with oranges, but if we make too many distinctions then we end up with vacuously imprecise estimates because we have too little data for each particular kind of laboratory. The trade-off between the diagnosticity of the characteristics and sample size is clear, but the basis for deciding on a reference class is not.

A third way that more information can increase uncertainty is when the amount or complexity of the information overloads processing capacity. This is a common bugbear in intelligence work. Should the decision-maker consider *ignoring* information? If so, on what basis? Several studies suggest that experts actually use fewer cues than novices in making decisions when there is a lot of information or time pressure (e.g. Omodei et al. 2005). It would seem that part of their expertise resides in judgments about which information is irrelevant and can be ignored. In a rare investigation of how people deliberately ignore information, Kutsch and Hall (in press) utilised Smithson's (1989) taxonomy in their study of IT project managers, and found that in addition to Smithson's subcategories untopicality, undecidability, and taboo, a fourth kind of irrelevance reported by IT managers involved a perception of information as useless because it did not have an immediate effect on the project.

Finally, reducing one uncertainty may increase another when they are closely coupled. Smithson and Muller (2009) present an example of this issue in their exploration of a decision concerning whether to put resources into improving police or court accuracy in homicide arrests and trials. They show that improving police accuracy in bringing truly guilty suspects before the courts has a trade-off, namely that increasing police accuracy decreases the proportion of convictions when the defendant is innocent but increases the proportion of acquittals where the defendant is guilty.

Choosing the right tool

Normative decision frameworks such as expected utility theory simultaneously require well-structured decisional tasks for them to be applicable and leave some of the most important aspects of those decisions to the decision-maker. If the task is ill-structured or even if there is more than one applicable analytical approach, the general framework outlined in this chapter can guide us in selecting the most appropriate approach. In this section we explore two instances of choosing the 'right tool'. The first is a relatively well-structured task, whereas in the second the problems are so ill-structured that none of the usual normative approaches can be applied.

Smithson and Muller (2009) argue that the conventional statistical models for determining the characteristics that distinguish solved from unsolved homicides are of little use to decision-makers planning a homicide investigation, but another equally valid statistical method suits planning purposes reasonably well.

Research into unsolved homicides typically focuses on whether there are any distinguishing characteristics shared by unsolved cases. The most powerful statistical technique for this purpose is logistic regression and its variants. The dependent variable is whether the case was solved or not, and the logistic regression model then predicts the likelihood that a case with particular characteristics ends up being cleared or not.

The justification for this approach rests on the argument that if low-solvability cases are identified at the outset, the allocation of additional investigative resources and/or changes in the relevant characteristics that are malleable early in the investigation might increase the chance of solving those cases. However, from a commander's viewpoint this justification sounds rather weak. First, what if there are no distinguishing case characteristics that can be changed? Second, the model does not actually tell us that throwing more resources into the investigation will increase the probability that the case is solved unless lack of resources is one of the factors predicting unsolvability. Third, by dichotomising solvability, logistic regression treats a 'self-solver' that was closed in one day no differently from a 'whodunnit' that took 5 years to close.

An approach that distinguishes between a one-day and five-year-long investigation is survival analysis (also known as 'event history analysis'). Instead of predicting whether a case is solved or not, survival analysis predicts the proportion of cases remaining unsolved after a specific duration of investigation. 'Survival' is therefore the time it takes to close the case. Cases that are unsolved are treated as 'censored' in the sense that their survival times are unknown. Statistical models predicting the likelihood that a case is solved treat a solved case that took one day and another that took three years as identical, whereas survival analysis distinguishes between them. Survival analysis draws strength from databases that have high clearance rates, unlike statistical models that predict solved versus unsolved cases. Indeed, the lower the percentage of censored (uncleared) cases, the better the resultant model.

Roberts (2007) and Lee (2005) use survival analysis to identify factors influencing the rate of homicide case clearance, but do not comment on its potential as an investigative planning and support tool. They do note, however, that survival analysis identifies a different set of predictors of solvability from those found via logistic regression. Survival analysis could be used to predict the length of time expected to solve a case, which clearly would help commanders in planning resource allocation. Indeed, survival analysis could be applied to resources other than time (e.g. accumulating expenditures).

Although survival analysis has promise as a decision support tool for planning, its current usefulness is limited by a lack of appropriate data. Survival analysis requires a start and end date (or date of arrest or closure) for each case. At the time of writing, most major homicide datasets (the Australian National Homicide Monitoring Program database, the UK Home Office Homicide Index, the FBI's Supplemental Homicide Report from the Uniform Crime Reports, and the Chicago Homicide Dataset) do not include the end date for cases. In any event, the main point of this example is that even in a relatively well-structured setting the choice of a technique can differ depending on whether our purpose is prediction or planning.

Now let us turn to an example where the issue of what tools to use is more fundamental. 'Near-miss' incident reporting systems are widely used in the airline industry, and these reports are accumulated in large databases. Flight safety investigators are responsible for analysing incident reports and identifying any underlying risks. These personnel usually have engineering training and, given their brief, could be expected to rely on probabilistic risk assessment methods. However, as Macrae (2009) observes, flight safety investigators find that they cannot use probabilistic risk assessment, or even estimate probabilities in evaluating risks.

Ironically, the main barrier to using probability is an insufficient number of actual crashes or serious incidents. Although the risks being managed include catastrophic risks such as an airliner crash, the vast majority of incidents report events that result in minor consequences. Literally half the requisite data are missing. As Macrae points out, the meaning for safety is often ambiguous in the sense that something went wrong but was corrected or contained. Moreover, while incidents may apparently belong to a common category, the relevant informational details often are unique and/or of poor quality. Small teams of these investigators pore over several thousand reports of this kind per year. Thus, they work with what Macrae terms weak signals, ambiguous signs, and possible warnings of unknown risks.

If the safety investigators are not doing probabilistic risk assessment, what are they doing instead? Macrae found that investigators utilise four interpretive strategies oriented toward revealing potential risks via signs of inadequacies or gaps in current knowledge:

1. identifying underlying patterns or common features of failure
2. drawing connections from incidents to safety issues, or to past major accidents
3. identifying discrepancies or inconsistencies in operational processes, or knowledge about those processes
4. perceiving novel events, particularly events that current knowledge and models could not fully account for.

These strategies are backed by conservatively sceptical views that the state of knowledge is incomplete and fallible, that the information in the reports is incomplete and sometimes inaccurate, and that the investigator's own perceptions and analyses are likely to be flawed. Thus, the investigators substitute probabilistic risk assessment with a preoccupation with the inevitability of ignorance, combined with a strong intolerance of it and a deeply risk-averse orientation. All three of these characteristics are adaptive responses, given the paucity of relevant data and the magnitude of the potential risks.

Trade-offs and dilemmas

Ignorance and uncertainty underpin certain forms of social capital (Smithson 2008a). Three examples are specialised knowledge, privacy, and trust. The first two exemplify multilaterally negotiated ignorance arrangements as opposed to unilateral ones such as secrecy or deceit. Trust is an example of social relations and modes of social conduct that mandate or even require toleration of partial ignorance.

Specialisation is a social ignorance arrangement. Aside from its obvious basis in cognitive limitations and expanding knowledge bases, specialisation is an example of risk-spreading in three respects. First, no participant has to take on all of the risks of direct learning (versus vicarious learning which is less risky). Second, the risk of being ignorant about crucial matters is spread by diversifying ignorance. Third, the risks associated with the consequences of bearing knowledge (e.g. responsibility or culpability) also are diversified.

Likewise, privacy also is a socially mandated arrangement involving voluntarily imposed uncertainty and ignorance. Privacy often has been construed as control over access by others to information, mainly about the self. The most common motives for privacy are quite obvious, amounting to freedom from surveillance and exploitation.

There is widespread agreement among scholars that trust carries with it some form of risk or vulnerability. An important component of that risk is a requirement that the truster remain partially ignorant about the trustee. Trust relationships (e.g. friendships) entail a specific kind of privacy. If a person believes another is monitoring them or insisting that they self-disclose or account for their actions, that person will infer that the other does not trust them. Trust relationships therefore require toleration of ignorance.

Because ignorance and uncertainty underpin some kinds of social capital, it follows that dealing with ignorance or uncertainty may involve trading away social capital. This trade-off merits careful thought but often simply is overlooked in the rush to regulate uncertainty out of existence.

For example, the classical frameworks for management science during the 1950s and 1960s advised managers to eliminate or absorb uncertainty. The most popular remedies included buffering, smoothing, forecasting, and various forms of strategic planning. These remedies primarily amounted to formulating plans and regulatory policies to reduce or banish uncertainty. Most of these organisational approaches for dealing with uncertainty could be summed up in the phrase 'uncertainty avoidance'. In addition to protecting the organisation, motives for avoiding uncertainty included maintaining control and avoiding discreditation, adverse publicity, or controversy.

The 1970s and 1980s saw a somewhat more tolerant view of uncertainty arise in this literature. Evidence began to emerge that not all managers are risk-averse, with some strategically selecting uncertain environments in which they can gain a competitive edge or scope for entrepreneurship. Likewise, critics of conventional command-control and regulation practices pointed out that tolerance of ignorance and uncertainty has potential benefits for organisations, in the form of a local culture of innovation and entrepreneurship, as well as realising the kinds of social capital mentioned earlier.

So, dealing with ignorance and uncertainty is a mixed-motive enterprise, involving trade-offs. Humans both want and do not want unknowns. Consider risk orientation. The same person can be risk-averse in one setting and risk-seeking in another. Prospect Theory (Kahneman & Tversky 1979) posits that people are risk-averse when they stand to gain something and risk-seeking if they stand to lose something. Regulatory Focus Theory (Higgins 1998), on the other hand, states that people focused on preventing an event will be risk-averse and those focused on making something happen (promotion of an event) will be risk-seeking. Both theories have considerable empirical support. Thus, in real-world settings where decision-makers must contemplate a mixture of possible gains and losses and prospects of both prevention and promotion, risk orientation will be pushed and pulled by trade-offs between these two pairs of opponent concerns.

For gaining an appreciation of the mixed-motive nature of engagement with ignorance and uncertainty, there is no substitute for examining some examples of real-world trade-offs and dilemmas that arise from dealing with ignorance in real environments (Smithson 1989):

- 'Collingridge's Dilemma' actually is a trade-off. The less well-entrenched a system is and the shorter the time it has been operating, the more easily and inexpensively it can be changed; but the greater is our ignorance of its likely effects or problems. By the time ignorance of those effects has been reduced, it is too expensive and difficult to change the system. In this trade-off, time is both knowledge and money.
- The 'info-glut' dilemma is a genuine dilemma of the common-pool resource kind. Any stakeholder with an educational or persuasive interest will wish to broadcast its message in a public forum. Too many messages in an unregulated forum, however, may result in the public tuning out messages altogether. The scarce resource in this case is not information or knowledge, but attention.
- 'Mattera's Dilemma' is an example of a conundrum in social regulation that has both trade-off and dilemmatic components. The trade-off arises from the fact that a regulatory climate favouring creativity and entrepreneurship requires the toleration of ignorance in the service of freedom. Insistence on full knowledge and control eliminates the latitude needed for creativity and entrepreneurship. The dilemmatic component arises from the fact that the greater the attempts to regulate behaviour, the more reactive people become and the more they attempt to generate ignorance in the would-be controllers by withholding information or giving false information. If both parties pursue their self-interests then the end result is a system of constraints and controls built on disinformation.
- The 'indemnity' dilemma is a mixture of a collective trade-off and a public goods dilemma. Play, games, fun, volunteering, and various other public goods require at least some risk-taking. However, a risk-averse public, aided by opportunistic lawyers and profit-oriented insurers, can create a litigious market in which public goods like fun and voluntarism are unaffordable or simply outlawed.

Choosing frameworks

Can one framework suit everyone? In concluding their extensive review of prescriptive theories of decision-making, Kleindorfer, Kunreuther and Schoemaker (1993, p. 209) found themselves wanting to construct a 'meta-theory of prescriptive choice'. Their hope was that by describing the nature of the decisional problem and the resources available, the decision-maker could select an appropriate decisional method. In Smithson (in press), I argue along similar lines that certain methods of studying ignorance suit particular topics and questions better than others, and that it may be possible to choose such methods in an informed manner.

The meta-theory of Kleindorfer and colleagues has two dimensions: informational complexity and values complexity. They view these as being traded off against one another by prescriptive decision-making frameworks, in some ways resembling the trade-offs and dilemmas discussed in the preceding section. At one extreme, expected utility theory and many other forms of mathematical modelling leave values questions aside entirely and deal exclusively with information processing. At the other, religious and ideological fundamentalisms focus exclusively on non-negotiable beliefs, values, duties and entitlements as moral guides to decisions.

The meta-theory of Kleindorfer and colleagues may be simplistic, but it homes in on perhaps the crucial issue regarding the uses of frameworks for dealing with ignorance and uncertainty: What do we want the framework to do for us? Do we want it for predicting, or understanding and explaining, or justifying, or planning, or what? Tetlock (2002) compares four 'templates' of the decision-maker on these terms. He dissects the differences in priorities, goals, and methods across the decision-maker as an intuitive scientist, intuitive politician, intuitive prosecutor, and intuitive theologian. His take-home message is that there are incompatibilities between these templates and, therefore, no single approach is going to work for all of them. The 'scientist' is most concerned with truth-tracking, the 'politician' with accountability to constituents, the 'prosecutor' with the ground rules for accountability, and the 'theologian' with protecting fundamental values or ideals.

Tetlock's analysis could be applied to any of the topics and examples discussed in this chapter. Consider, for instance, the quandary of the commander faced with the missing person as potential homicide victim. The conclusion reached was that the pursuit of more accurate predictors of missing persons at risk of being homicide victims *in the name of guaranteeing correct decisions* is pointless (note the points of emphasis). This does not mean, of course, that the pursuit of more accurate predictors of at-risk missing persons is pointless for other purposes. From a scientific or perhaps a certain ideological viewpoint, this pursuit might be intrinsically valuable. Likewise, for the commander-cum-politician wishing to be seen to be doing their utmost to identify at-risk cases, endorsing the search for better predictors could be useful for legitimacy. Nonetheless, that search will not suit a commander who wants it to deliver a better-than-50% chance of making the right decision.

How, then, might practitioners set about deciding what to do about ignorance and uncertainty? In the absence of a comprehensive meta-theory (an exercise well beyond the scope of this chapter), I can at best offer some guiding points based on what we have covered here:

- What kinds of unknowns are involved? Do stakeholders disagree about their nature? Are any of the unknowns due to taboos or other kinds of proscription?
- Which unknowns can be compared with one another, quantified and/or measured? Which, if any, translate into risks? Which constitute options or 'room to move?'
- What are the decision-maker's primary goals and concerns? Do they fit one or more of Tetlock's templates?
- Which unknowns are irreducible? Which cannot be banished?
- If unknowns are reducible, are they worth reducing and if so, by what means?
- Will reducing an unknown increase or generate others?
- What uses can the unknowns be put to, and by whom? Will reducing them destroy social capital or close off potentially valuable opportunities?

The overall guiding idea, then, is before undertaking a 'risk assessment', a decision-maker may need to embark on an 'ignorance assessment'. While there is no sure recipe for decision-making under ignorance or profound uncertainty, the framework presented here enables a decision-maker to build a reasonably coherent and structured understanding of the unknowns at hand and what needs to be considered in dealing with them.

References

Anderson, CJ 2003, 'The psychology of doing nothing: forms of decision avoidance result from reason and emotion', *Psychological Bulletin*, 129, pp.139–167.

Centre for Evidence Based Medicine 2007, University of Toronto, http://ktclearinghouse.ca/cebm/practise/ca/diagnosis/important.htm> (accessed 1 March 2010).

Connolly, T 1987, 'Decision theory, reasonable doubt, and the utility of erroneous acquittals' *Law and Human Behavior*, vol. 11, pp. 101–112.

Fischhoff, B, Slovic P & Lichtenstein S 1978, 'Fault trees: sensitivity of estimated failure probabilities to problem representation', *Journal of Experimental Psychology: Human Perception Performance*, vol. 4, pp. 330–344.

Fox, CR & Rottenstreich, Y 2003, 'Partition priming in judgment under uncertainty', *Psychological Science*, vol. 14, pp. 195–200.

Gross, M 2007, 'The unknown in process: dynamic connections of ignorance, non-knowledge and related concepts', *Current Sociology*, vol. 55, pp. 742–759.

Higgins, ET 1998, 'Promotion and prevention: regulatory focus as a motivational principle', in MP Zanna (ed.), *Advances in Experimental Social Psychology*, vol. 30, pp. 1–46, Academic Press, San Diego, CA.

James, M, Anderson, J & Putt, J 2008, 'Missing persons in Australia', *Research and Public Policy* series no. 86, Australian Institute of Criminology, Canberra.

Kahneman, D & Tversky, A 1979, 'Prospect theory: an analysis of decision under risk', *Econometrica*, vol. 47, pp. 263–291.

Kleindorfer, PR, Kunreuther, HC & Schoemaker, PJH 1993, *Decision sciences: an integrated perspective*, Cambridge University Press, Cambridge.

Klir, GA & Yuan, B 1995, *Fuzzy sets and fuzzy logic*, Prentice-Hall, Englewood Cliffs, NJ.

Knorr Cetina, K 1999, *Epistemic cultures: how the sciences make knowledge*, Harvard University Press, Cambridge, MA.

Kutsch, E & Hall, M (2009), 'Deliberate ignorance in project risk management', *International Journal of Project Management*, vol. 28, pp. 245–255.

Lee, C 2005, 'The value of life in death: multiple regression and event history analyses of homicide clearance in Los Angeles County', *Journal of Criminal Justice*, vol. 33, pp. 527–534.

Macrae, C 2009, 'Making risks visible: identifying and interpreting threats to airline flight safety', *Journal of Occupational and Organizational Psychology*, vol. 82, pp. 273–293.

Newiss, G 2006, 'Understanding the risk of going missing: estimating the risk of fatal outcomes in cancelled cases', *Policing: An International Journal of Police Strategies and Management*, vol. 29, no. 2, pp. 246–260.

Omodei, M, McLennan, J, Elliott, GC, Wearing, AJ & Clancy, JM 2005, '"More is better?" A bias toward overuse of resources in naturalistic decision-making settings', in H Montgomery, R Lipshitz & B Brehmer (eds), *How professionals make decisions*, Lawrence Erlbaum, Mawah, NJ, pp. 29–42.

Roberts, A 2007, 'Predictors of homicide clearance by arrest: an event history analysis of NIBRS incidents', *Homicide Studies*, vol. 11, no. 2, pp. 82–93.

Rottenstreich, Y & Tversky, A 1997, 'Unpacking, repacking, and anchoring: advances in support theory', *Psychological Review*, vol. 104, no. 2, pp. 406–415.

Russo, JE & Kolzow, KJ 1994, 'Where is the fault in fault trees?', *Journal of Experimental Psychology: Human Perception Performance*, vol. 20, pp. 17–32.

Shafer, G 1976, *A mathematical theory of evidence*, Princeton University Press, Princeton.

Smithson, M 1989, *Ignorance and uncertainty: emerging paradigms*, Springer Verlag, New York.

Smithson, M 1999, 'Conflict aversion: preference for ambiguity vs. conflict in sources and evidence', *Organizational Behavior and Human Decision Processes*, vol. 79, pp. 179–198.

Smithson, M 2006, 'Scale construction from a decisional viewpoint', *Minds and Machines*, vol. 16, pp. 339–364.

Smithson, M 2008a, 'Social theories of ignorance', in R Proctor & L Schiebinger (eds), *Agnotology: the cultural production of ignorance*, Stanford University Press, Stanford, CA, pp. 209–229.

Smithson M 2008b, 'The many faces and masks of uncertainty', in G Bammer & M Smithson (eds), *Uncertainty and risk: multidisciplinary perspectives*, Earthscan, London, pp. 13–25.

Smithson, M (in press), 'Ignorance and uncertainty' in VA Brown, J Russell & J Harris (eds), *Tackling wicked problems: using the transdisciplinary imagination*, Earthscan, London.

Smithson, M, Deady, S & Gracik, L 2007, 'Guilty, not guilty, or … ? Multiple verdict options in jury verdict choices', *Journal of Behavioral Decision Making*, vol. 20, pp. 481–498.

Smithson, M & Muller, D 2009, 'Decisions in homicide investigations and trials: uncertainty reduction is not always the answer', unpublished manuscript.

Tetlock, PE 2002, 'Social functionalist frameworks for judgment and choice: intuitive politicians, theologians and prosecutors', *Psychological Review*, vol. 109, pp. 451–471.

Walley, P 1991, *Statistical reasoning with imprecise probabilities*, Chapman Hall, London.

Enhancing Accepted Approaches

Can Statistics Help?
ROBYN G ATTEWELL

Introduction

There is plenty of uncertainty associated with crime. From a layperson's point of view, it is part of the allure. From Agatha Christie to Kathy Reichs, from *Homicide* to *Underbelly*; from *Hawaii Five-O* to *Law and Order*, and all the myriad, forensics-based TV dramas, crime has long been a popular and dependable entertainment theme. I expect it is not just the 'who?' out of the 'whodunnit?' that draws people in, but also the 'how?' and the 'why?', and the possibility that the perpetrator just might get away with it. From the comfort of one's own home, we try to get into the headspace of the 'villain' and fathom what drives them to cross the line and risk the consequences of breaking the law. Equally absorbing is to get into the headspace of the detectives. They are faced with similar uncertainties, but from a different viewpoint. What actual offence has been committed? Were there witnesses? What evidence is at the crime scene? Is there a suspect? Is there sufficient evidence for an apprehension, a charge, a guilty verdict? Even if the suspect is found guilty and sent to prison, can they be rehabilitated or is it just a matter of time before they re-offend?

For the sort of crime most commonly depicted on television or as the subject of crime fiction, I think the public's fascination with the uncertainties of crime is built on the premise that they are unlikely to become a victim of serious crime or cross paths with the mafia. In addition, few would expect ever to find themselves in such dire or extreme circumstances that they would be compelled to break the law. Terrorism, on the other hand, is different. With terrorism, as the name itself suggests, uncertainty and fear are brought into the realm of everyday life. Cyber-crime is slightly different again. We are not so absorbed by it, since we tend to be unaware that crimes such as identity theft, online scams, and even online sexual exploitation might be only a mouse-click away from us, or our children. Crimes such as these are increasingly prevalent and, in fact, thrive on the fact that the public are unaware of how susceptible they are.

My task is to provide an understanding of uncertainty in policing serious crime from my background in statistics. My perspective is not quite that of the general public, nor the police practitioner, but of someone relatively new to policing (I joined the Australian Federal Police at the end of 2007) and from the outside. As a statistician I am pretty comfortable with numerical uncertainty. In earlier work (Attewell 2008), I postulated that statisticians have much to offer in terms of dealing with uncertainty. We like to count things, draw samples, test hypotheses, and fit probability models, but can statistics really help in a patrol car or at a crime scene, an operations control centre or an executive management meeting at headquarters? Policing serious crime is a key function of the Australian Federal Police. The Australian Federal Police is responsible for protecting Australia's security, as well as preventing and investigating crimes against Commonwealth law such as importation of border controlled drugs, people smuggling, human trafficking, fraud and other economic crime, cyber-crime, environmental crime, terrorism and serious organised crime.

In this chapter I start by exploring what policing may learn from public health and medicine about the use of statistics. I then review some significant challenges to the effective use of statistics, followed by areas where statistics is making major contributions to dealing with uncertainties in policing serious crime.

Disease and crime: peas in a pod?

Most of my statistical perspective is grounded in biostatistics which is the application of statistics in the study of disease and, more generally, the human condition. This is an area in which statistical principles have been well accepted and applied. I do not mean that all doctors know what a chi-square test is or could interpret a logistic regression. However, advances in knowledge in epidemiology and the treatment of disease have occurred through research which has been undertaken with the application of sound statistical methodology. The evidence base for prevention and treatment of disease has moved from personal experience and chronicles of case histories to global randomised controlled trials, longitudinal cohort studies and meta-analyses. The movement within the fields of public health and medicine towards a quantitative evidence base is so strong that the pharmaceutical industry, for example, is very highly regulated. New drug treatments are not able to be registered or receive government subsidy unless supported by a structured compilation of efficacy and safety data. It has to be proven beyond reasonable doubt that new medications work and their positive impact on the target disease outweighs any negatives through adverse side effects.

Similarly, policing could benefit from being further along the continuum in the adoption of statistical principles and incorporation of scientific methodology into research and practice. This is not a new notion. See, for example, Laycock (2001), who calls for a greater link between research and practice in policing. In fact, Porter (1986) points to the origins of statistical thinking, not only in the health discipline, but also in the social science sphere in France in the early 1800s. He writes, 'Statistics could provide an understanding not only of the prevailing causes of death and disease, but also of crime and revolution, respectively, the chronic and epidemic disorders of the human spirit'. He further reminds us of the work of Quetelet (lived 1796–1874)—variously described as an astronomer, mathematician, statistician and sociologist—who was one of the first criminologists in that he was interested in how crime rates varied with factors such as age, sex, profession and location. Much has been achieved since then, including comprehensive reviews of what works in preventing and reducing crime (Sherman 1992, 1998, Sherman et al. 2002) and, indeed, a whole movement towards an evidence-based approach with data analysis playing a key role along with intelligence analysis in intelligence-led policing (Ratcliffe 2008).

There are many interesting similarities between disease and crime, although there are also important differences (see Box 1). Sherman (1992) also draws the analogy between doctors and police officers. But how does this help? From a purely mathematical point of view, the dichotomous nature of the outcomes (healthy/unhealthy, crime committed/not committed), as well as the requirement to look at trends and comparisons of incidence and prevalence mean that the statistical approaches that work well in medicine do translate to crime. Differences occur, however, in the inability to control the environment in which crime takes place and the difficulty in collecting relevant information on criminals and criminal activity, which means that traditional epidemiological approaches such as randomised controlled trials will be less widely applicable in the evaluation of various policing strategies. It should be noted, though, that Sherman and colleagues (2002) do cite examples of both controlled and quasi experiments in policing.

In the remainder of this paper, I provide examples of where basic statistical principles and techniques, many of which have been applied successfully in medicine, are being used to address uncertainty in policing crime, as well as where we are falling short of the mark, with regard to serious crime. In particular, I will focus on data collection, measurement, surveys, mapping, descriptive statistics and graphics. Let me begin with some of the challenges, which mainly relate to the collection of data.

> **Box 1: Disorders and disorderly conduct: the correspondence between disease and crime**
>
> Disease and crime are characterised by dichotomous states: sick/well, guilty/not guilty and two main stakeholders: patients/doctors, criminals/police. Both doctors and police are professionals with high ethical standards in whom the public place much faith. Disease and crime both have negative associations. Hospitals and prisons are places to avoid, but are nevertheless essential and costly institutions in our society. Even the terminology overlaps. The words, 'cases' and 'investigations' are commonly used in both fields. There is a continuum of minor ailments to life threatening disease, so too for crime from petty theft to murder. Disease treatment and crime punishment options also range in scale from diet/exercise regimes to surgery, and from fines or restorative justice to more punitive measures. Some patients have more than one condition. Some persons commit more than one type of crime. Some diseases are genetic. Some criminals are psychopaths. Patients relapse. Criminals re-offend. Some diseases, pandemics, have global impact; so do global terror acts. In fact, sometimes the threat of the disease, or the threat of the crime, can have just as much or more impact than the disease or crime itself. Diagnosis and treatment are becoming more sophisticated. This is also the case for crime detection and investigation, with technical advances in surveillance and forensics. New diseases emerge, such as HIV/AIDS, or evolve historically, such as influenza. The same can be said for crime. For example, consider the changing preferences in illicit drugs and the evolution of the manufacture of synthetic drugs, or the emergence of online scams and the evolution of face-to-face confidence tricks. There are also policy and management parallels. Pandemics and terrorism have much in common in that they require both global and local approaches. Prevention of disease and prevention of crime are also both widely acknowledged as being key, since just focusing on better detection and treatment of disease or better crime detection and conviction rates will only lead to further overburdening hospital and prison systems. Further, neither disease nor crime will ever be able to be completely eradicated, so the prioritisation of resources requires careful evaluation and justification.
>
> There is plenty of disparity as well. Sickness usually is not planned, but crimes often are. Disease often has a biological basis that is well understood, which allows for specific cures to be developed for specific diseases. Crime on the other hand, may be a result of many factors related to human behaviour. The 'cure' may never be clear cut. Patients want to get better, and therefore, usually provide information, undergo tests, agree to various treatment options. Criminals do not want to be caught, and are rarely willing to provide substantial information, leading to it being gathered through other means such as coercive powers requiring witness protection. Doctors often have established protocols to follow, but police may have more discretion in pursuing an investigation, depending on resources and priorities.

Challenges

Scepticism abounds

Unfortunately, just the mere mention of the word 'statistics' is enough to raise some suspicion, but there is particular scepticism related to 'crime statistics'. This is from both outside and within the policing profession. The community tend to lose confidence on hearing reports of police focusing on low end crimes to meet performance targets. Police lose confidence in management if they feel that their efforts are not accurately reflected in official figures.

The public also lose faith in the police service when official crime figures and trends do not match their perceptions regarding the incidence of crime. Official figures show that crime is trending downwards, but the public are influenced by repeated media reports of crime in their cities, on their doorsteps. As Carmen Lawrence (2010) also describes in her chapter, fear of crime becomes out of proportion with actual risk. Innes (2004) has examined the relationship between media reporting of crime and public perceptions of risk and postulates that certain incidents or 'signal crimes' have particular impact. So it is not surprising that there is a discrepancy between recorded crime and public perception.

We see it in Australia on a regular basis; most recently in the state of Victoria, resulting in an inquiry by the State Ombudsman, (Brouwer 2009), described in more detail below, but also previously in New South Wales (Dixon 2005). Similarly in Britain, where official crime statistics indicated a reduction in overall crime and violent crime in 2007–08 in England and Wales (Kershaw et al. 2008), the public were increasingly concerned about personal safety in the light of many reportedly random and apparently unprovoked knife attacks. Interestingly, the 2008–09 figures published recently (Walker et al. 2009) still do not show any upward turn in overall or violent crime statistics.

Apples and oranges

The State Ombudsman's report on an investigation into the validity of crime statistics in Victoria (Brouwer 2009), which was tabled in the Victorian Parliament, was a response to concern that the crime figures and police numbers were being distorted. The Ombudsman found that there was underreporting of crime due to both poor recording practices and inadequate data systems. He concluded, however, that there was no systematic, deliberate manipulation of the data. Nevertheless, much public debate ensued, reflecting not only that this is a particularly sensitive topic for the public, government and police alike, but also that there are complexities that need to be understood. One of the complicating factors is recurrent in Australia where the various states and territories do not all do things in the same way. This is especially so in policing, with eight separate police forces plus the Australian Federal Police. Until 2008 the Victorian police used different criteria from the other jurisdictions to record crime in their databases. Most states use a *prima facie* system in that essentially, all crime reported is recorded, but Victoria previously used an 'evidentiary' system where only the crime with evidence was recorded. Inconsistencies and administrative changes such as these invalidate comparisons between jurisdictions and across time.

The Australian Bureau of Statistics (ABS) plays an important role in compiling and promoting nationally consistent data. They produce data on offenders, victims, courts, prisoners and corrective services under the National Criminal Justice Statistical Framework which was first released in 2001 (ABS 2007). One of the coding systems of particular relevance to the topic of serious crime is the National Offence Index (ABS 2009). It is an ordinal ranking of offences by perceived seriousness; from traffic offences to murder (with approximately 150 other crime types in between these). It is used to determine a principal sentence if multiple offences occur and ensures nationally comparable offence information from across jurisdictions.

Underestimation adds to uncertainty

Underreporting of crime is a major source of uncertainty and a root cause of much of the concern regarding crime statistics. This is widely acknowledged and referred to universally as the 'dark figure' of crime (Biderman & Reiss 1967). Underestimation occurs through lack of detection, underreporting by the public and underrecording by the police. It impacts on official crime statistics. This has led to the augmentation of police-recorded crime statistics with surveys of the general public (generally referred to as crime victim surveys) or surveys of offenders. The gaps between the police-recorded statistics and the self-reported statistics of victims or offenders are marked, but depend on the type of crime. For example, Clare and Morgan (2009) noted that only 31% of assaults were reported to the police in Australia in 2005, but they also highlight that this may depend on the victim's perception of the act as a criminal event. There are many other methodological issues with these types of surveys. For example, the survey sample needs to be large enough to provide reasonably accurate estimates for relatively rare crimes. The sampling frame needs to be sophisticated enough to address the problem that the people who are most likely to be victims are probably the least likely to be in a position to participate in a survey.

Key examples of these kinds of surveys are the British Crime Survey in the United Kingdom and the National Crime and Safety Survey conducted by the Australian Bureau of Statistics. There is also the International Crime Victims

Survey coordinated by several European countries and by the United Nations Interregional Crime and Justice Research Institute (Van Dijk et al. 2007). The United Nations Office on Drugs and Crime also promotes the cross-national collection of statistics on a different group of crimes such as bribery/corruption, fraud and extortion in both the private sector (Crime and corruption business surveys) and the public sector (Corruption/integrity surveys). For an example, see Alvazzi del Frate (2007). In Australia, the first national Personal Fraud Survey was conducted in 2007 (ABS 2008). It was estimated that 5% of the adult population had been a victim of a personal fraud—3% through identity fraud and 2% by responding to a scam such as lotteries, pyramid schemes or phishing.

These surveys, however, still have limitations in terms of scope. They do not include children, and yet children are often the targets of very specific, serious crimes, such as sexual exploitation and underage labour. The surveys also do not cover the problem of estimating the magnitude of so-called 'victimless' or 'consensual' crimes where there is unlikely to be a complainant. These include not only activity in contravention of the law in which the main impact is on the perpetrator (e.g. illicit drug use and prostitution), but also other crimes against the state or government when there is generally no single, direct victim. Examples include the trafficking and importation of illegal drugs, sale of pornography, illegal gambling, immigration crime, intellectual property crime, piracy, terrorism and all aspects of organised crime such as money laundering and corruption.

Indeed, the dark figure of crime just gets 'murkier' once we move into the realm of trying to estimate the incidence and impact of serious and organised crime. The lack of victims or complainants in this area of crime is highlighted in the Witness Protection Report by the Parliamentary Joint Committee on the National Crime Authority (1988).

In summary, there are difficulties in demonstrating the effectiveness in policing through difficulties in obtaining accurate and valid estimates of crime incidence. Despite the wide availability of administrative police databases and survey information, both nationally and internationally, these are limited by problems of scope and coverage, as well as inconsistent definitions across jurisdictions.

Advances

Mapping

One broad area of successful application of statistical techniques in policing (as well as public health) is in geospatial analysis. This involves plotting crime incidents by location and formally comparing the incidence of events by their spatial distribution to identify hotspots of criminal activity. This is either done for individual incidents (point based) or for aggregate data in pre-defined geographical units (area based), for example, precincts or local government areas. Crime mapping—and using it to target police responses—was one aspect of an entire police management strategy referred to as CompStat that was developed by the New York City Police Department. That strategy was associated with marked decreases in community crime statistics at the time (late 1990s). Since then, it has been applied in many locations, including the Australian Capital Territory, New South Wales and Queensland (Ratcliffe 2008, Mazerolle & Rombouts 2007). To date, the main application appears to have been used in localised community policing.

An interesting new spatial application that could ultimately have an impact on policing is the analysis of waste water in order to map the patterns of illicit drug use. This is achieved through the detection of drugs and their metabolites in sewerage (Frost & Griffith 2008) and is already being trialled in Europe.

The Australian Federal Police is currently employing geospatial techniques to characterise the movement in and out of Australia of funds associated with criminal activity. Understanding money flows is a key strategy in addressing organised crime groups. The aim of this work is to identify financial hotspots in Australia and offshore, profile different routes for different crime types and establish a benchmark that can be monitored over time.

Cluster analysis

Clustering is a multivariate data analysis technique that has many applications in the policing arena apart from the geospatial analysis described above. Cluster analysis classifies individual data items into groups which have similar characteristics. The Australian Federal Police are currently funding research applying this technique to fraud data (Higginson 2009), with the aim of characterising fraud against Australian Commonwealth agencies comparing it to fraud in relation to individuals or businesses. The data analysed includes the size and context of the offences and information about the offenders. This is part of a larger research project that also looks at how to best monitor activity related to fraud investigations, identifying factors which predict successful prosecution.

Process control

Statistical process control has traditionally been applied in industry to ensure that consistent quality is maintained in a production process. Statistical models are used to estimate variation in time series and thereby differentiate unusual occurrences from normal behaviour. The Australian Federal Police has invested in research applying these techniques to monitor its own activity and performance (Haynes et al. 2007). The benefit of this application is that variation in monthly series of case counts, drug seizures or other performance indices can be assessed graphically to either dismiss or investigate unusual data points and also address longer term trends. The control charts typically consist of a time series plot of monthly data, which displays considerable variability around an average level of activity. A control area within which 95% of the data is expected to occur is also provided on the plot (Figure 1). The control limits are based on a comparison period or reference period (generally a period of up to five years' historical data, for example within the vertical dashed lines in Figure 1). Any points outside the control limits are identified as outliers. Any variation within the control limits can be effectively discounted as within expected limits of statistical random variation. From a statistical point of view some difficult problems were addressed in this work. The usual application of this technique is based on the standard normal distribution, however certain series, such as drug seizures and proceeds of crime, were skewed. Different probability distributions, such as the negative binominal and gamma distributions, provided a much better fit to the data.

Descriptive statistics

Not all statistical applications in policing need to incorporate high-powered statistical models. In 2008, a descriptive summary was compiled to establish a statistical profile of online child sex offenders. This was based on a survey of offenders completed by the investigating officers and was aimed at characterising the socio-demographics of the offenders, the content of the child exploitation material and the means by which the offences occurred. This consisted primarily of tabulations, straightforward graphical presentations and chi-squared tests on two-way tables (testing independence between two factors/characteristics). The outcome of this research is to assist investigators in this area, particularly in terms of detection, to inform prevention strategies and policy initiatives. The research is ongoing in the sense that the profiling will be more accurate when expanded to a larger and more representative sample using the same questionnaire. Indeed, the results have been shared in international fora and there is collaboration with other researchers to contribute to a meta-analysis relating to criminal history and risk of offender recidivism. These data summaries will be used to contribute to further research to understand the likelihood of, and the triggers for, progression from online offending to actual sexual assaults of children.

Figure 1: Control chart showing reference period (within the dashed vertical lines) and 95% control limits (upper and lower horizontal lines). This is a generic plot where the y-axis could be cases, drug seizures or any other variable of interest.

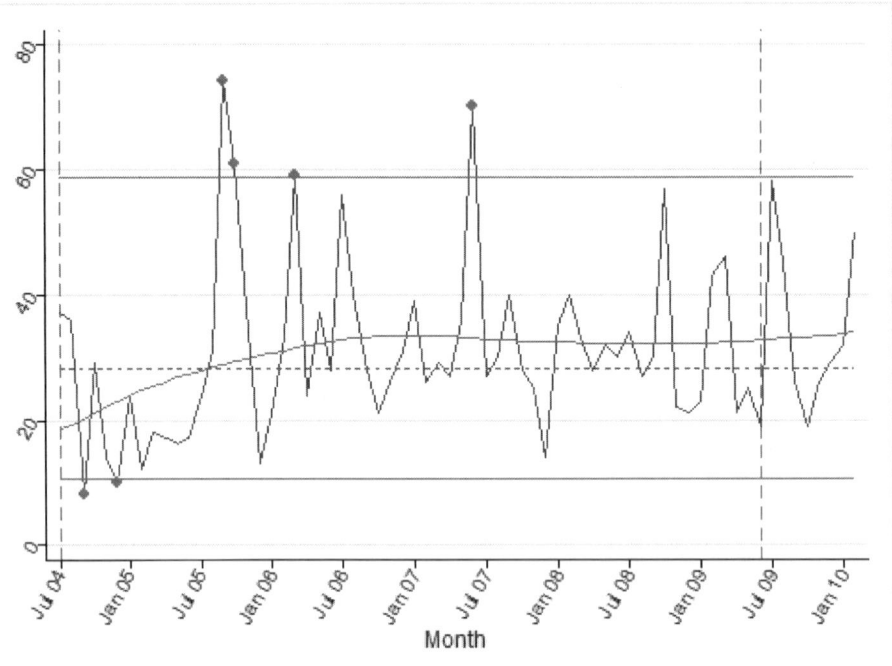

Graphs

Graphs are another basic tool that should not be underestimated in terms of how to convey a clear message from a mass of information. They are one of the key components of the Australian Federal Police's current approach to building an operational planning tool for prioritisation of serious organised crime targets, referred to as the target enforcement prioritisation index (TEPI). Figure 2 is a simplified depiction of a typical plot.

Each target is rated on two different types of factors: first, the elements that indicate the potential effectiveness of the organised crime target, such as resources, skills and relationships. This is the target dimension (the vertical axis). Second, the law enforcement dimension is made up of the elements that influence law enforcement decision-making, such as investigational complexity, cost, risk, likelihood of success, value to agency and external direction (the horizontal axis). These two dimensions form the x-y coordinate space for comparing different potential targets. The total of the individual target ratings is plotted against the average enforcement rating (the large square symbols in Figure 2). The five component enforcement ratings are also depicted along the total target level (asterisks in Figure 2). The targets most likely to be prioritised will score highly along both dimensions and lie in the upper right hand or 'glory' quadrant. On the other hand, low priority targets will have low scores on both scales (the lower left or 'barge pole' quadrant). The most interesting quadrant is the upper left and is referred to as the 'Call for volunteers' quadrant. Targets within this quadrant may need to be investigated due to their high target value, but they present organisational challenges that require consideration and treatment. A single graph can be used to compare multiple targets (as in Figure 2), trace the progress of a target as new information is incorporated, conduct sensitivity analysis on the source data making up the scales or identify intelligence gaps between the estimated position (on the graph) and other positions predicted by other sources or agencies.

Figure 2: Simplified graphical presentation of priority index information for two separate potential targets using a TEPI model being developed by the Australian Federal Police

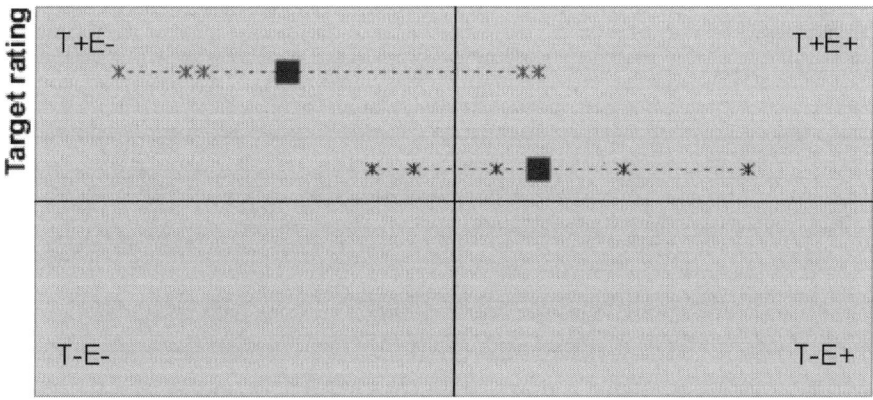

Discussion

The role of statistics in addressing uncertainty associated with policing crime is achieved through the systematic collection, analysis and presentation of data associated with crime.

There are major parallels between the application of statistics in public health and medicine and the application of statistics in policing. Unfortunately, this does not extend—to any great extent—to convenient study designs such as randomised controlled trials of different policing strategies. However, policing could benefit from having a stronger evidence base, closer links between research and practice, developing standardised classification systems, collaboration across jurisdictions, both nationally and internationally, and looking at cost-benefit analysis of prevention strategies. This would assist with informing policy, ensuring effective interventions.

But what about serious crime? The wins from a statistical perspective are harder to show. Statistics generally come into their own when there is too much data to deal with manually, which is often not the case for serious crime. Graphs provide a relatively simple way of understanding data which is otherwise inaccessible through sheer size or complexity. Exploratory data analysis, mapping, and simple descriptive statistics all help to elucidate patterns that are hidden in large data sets. However, in many cases, we just do not have the data to work with, either in the sense that the events are sparse (terror attacks), difficult to classify consistently (disruption of organised crime activity), difficult to detect (people smuggling), there are no complainants (drug trafficking, organised crime), or the data are generally only accessible through liaison with other agencies (cyber-crime, drug importation). By highlighting the difficulties in accurately estimating the incidence of criminal activity, I have shown that statistics can also add to uncertainty. Measuring police performance in terms of changes in criminal activity is therefore fraught with difficulty.

Nonetheless, there are several examples of the successful application of standard statistical techniques in the context of serious crime, such as following money trails through mapping, characterising clusters of fraud or child sex offenders and providing graphical images to steer management decisions on prioritisation and performance monitoring. Further application is merely a matter of persistence and imagination.

Disclaimer: These are the views of the author and do not necessarily represent the official position of the Australian Federal Police.

References

Alvazzi del Frate, A (ed.) 2007, *Study on crime and corruption in Cape Verde*, UNODC, <http://www.unodc.org> (accessed 29 November 2009).

Attewell, RG 2008, 'Statistics: an essential tool for model citizens', in G Bammer & M Smithson (eds), *Uncertainty and risk: multidisciplinary perspectives*, Earthscan, London, pp. 81–90.

Australian Bureau of Statistics 2007, *Information paper: national criminal justice statistical framework*, cat. no. 4525.0, Australian Bureau of Statistics, <http://www.abs.gov.au> (accessed 7 September 2009).

Australian Bureau of Statistics 2008, *Personal fraud, 2007*, cat. no. 4528.0, Australian Bureau of Statistics, <http://www.abs.gov.au> (accessed 17 August 2009).

Australian Bureau of Statistics 2009, *National offence index, 2009*, cat. no. 1234.0.55.001, Australian Bureau of Statistics, <http://www.abs.gov.au/AUSSTATS> (accessed 7 September 2009).

Biderman, AD & Reiss, JR 1967, 'On exploring the "dark figure" of crime', *The Annals of the American Academy of Political and Social Science*, vol. 374, no. 1, pp. 1–15.

Brouwer, G 2009, *Crime statistics and police numbers*, Ombudsman Victoria, Victorian Government Printer, Session 2006-09 P.P. no. 173, March, <http://www.ombudsman.vic.gov.au/resources/documents/Crime_statistics_and_police_numbers_report.pdf> (accessed August 2009).

Clare, J & Morgan, F 2009, 'Factors affecting perceived criminality: evidence from victims of assault', *Trends & Issues in Criminal Justice*, no. 376, Australian Institute of Criminology, Canberra, <http://www.aic.gov.au> (accessed 15 January 2010).

Dixon, D 2005, 'Why don't the police stop crime?', *Australian and New Zealand Journal of Criminology*, vol. 38, no. 1, pp. 4–24.

Frost, N and Griffith, P 2008, *Assessing illicit drugs in wastewater: potential and limitations of a new monitoring approach*, European Monitoring Centre for Drugs and Drug Addiction, Portugal.

Haynes, M, Sheedy, G & Wockner, L 2007, *Time series and control charts for illicit drug seizures and proceeds of crime*, internal report for the Australian Federal Police, University of Queensland Social Research Centre, Reference J7019, Queensland.

Higginson, A 2009, *Faces of fraud: a typology of* serious and complex *economic fraud against Australian commonwealth agencies*, presented at the British Society of Criminology (BSC) conference, 29 June–1 July 2009, Cardiff, UK.

Innes, M 2004, 'Crime as a signal. Crime as a memory', *Journal for Crime Conflict and the Media*, vol. 1, no. 2, pp. 15–22.

Kershaw, C, Nicholas, S & Walker, A (eds) 2008, *Crime in England and Wales 2007/08*, findings from the British Crime Survey and police recorded crime, <http://www.homeoffice.gov.uk/rds> (accessed 17 August 2009).

Lawrence, C 2010, 'Politics', in G Bammer (ed.), *Dealing with uncertainties in policing serious crime*, ANU E Press, Canberra.

Laycock, G 2001, 'Research for police: who needs it?', *Trends & Issues in Crime and Criminal Justice*, no. 211, Australian Institute of Criminology, Canberra, <http://www.aic.gov.au> (accessed 15 January 2010).

Mazerolle, L & Rombouts, S 2007, 'The impact of COMPSTAT on reported crime in Queensland', *Policing: An International Journal of Police Strategies & Management*, vol. 30, no. 2, pp. 237–256.

Parliamentary Joint Committee on the National Crime Authority 1988, *Witness protection*, Commonwealth of Australia, Australian Government Publishing Service, Canberra.

Porter, T 1986, *The rise of statistical thinking, 1820–1900*, Princeton University Press, Princeton.

Ratcliffe, J 2008, *Intelligence-led policing*, Willan Publishing, Devon.

Sherman, LW 1992, 'Attacking crime: police and crime control', in MH Tonry & N Morris (eds), *Crime and justice volume 15: modern policing*, University of Chicago Press, Chicago and London.

Sherman, LW 1998, *Evidence-based policing. Ideas in American policing*, Police Foundation. Washington DC.

Sherman, LW, Farrington, DP, Welsh, BC & MacKenzie DL (eds) 2002, *Evidence-based crime prevention*, Routledge Taylor and Francis Group, London and New York.

Van Dijk, J, Van Kesteren, J & Smit, P 2007, *Criminal victimisation in international perspective: key findings from the 2004-05 ICVS and EU ICS*, Ministry of Justice WODC, The Hague.

Walker, A, Flatley, J, Kershaw, C & Moon, D (eds) 2009, *Crime in England and Wales 2008/09,* Findings from the British Crime Survey and police recorded crime, vol.1, Home Office, UK, <http://www.homeoffice.gov.auk/rds/pdfs09/hosb1109summ.pdf > (accessed 17 August 2009).

Quantitative Risk
RICHARD JARRETT AND MARK WESTCOTT

Introduction

A key question in policing serious crime is the allocation of resources, by which we mean not just the quantity but also the type or quality of the resource. This implies a need to generate options and to develop decision-making processes that lead to action. In the book arising from a recent symposium on Uncertainty and Risk, it was noted that there was 'an interesting tension between researchers and consultants—researchers focus on the gaps in what is known ... and consultants are oriented to synthesis in order to develop ... an approach to the issue at hand' (Bammer et al. 2008, p.290). By this definition, we are in the consultants' camp, since we are concerned to provide the means by which to make the best decisions possible, albeit in the face of uncertainty.

We have been involved in a number of risk assessment and risk management processes which ultimately lead to the allocation of resources. Much of the risk assessment is undertaken, as it should be, by groups that include staff, outside experts and stakeholders. We provide the mathematical framework that draws the material together, leading to decision-making processes that are valued and trusted by those involved. Many issues raised in that recent symposium occur in practice—disagreements over standards, definitions, the relative importance of different types of hazard—but the need to get a resolution that works is a powerful force in driving this process to a conclusion. The early sections of this chapter look at some of the important and interesting issues related to risk.

Much has been written about potential flaws in the risk assessment process (e.g. Cox 2008a). One of these is the qualitative nature of some methodologies, where terms like 'critical', 'possible' and 'occasional' are used without clear definitions appropriate to the context. This can lead to ambiguity and undesirable subjectivity. It inhibits fruitful discussion and decisive action. A quantitative approach to risk assessment reduces such problems, and brings the remaining problems into sharper focus. We illustrate this proposition by looking in more detail at a particular risk assessment tool, the Risk Matrix, which ranks and compares risks but is often used qualitatively. Our proposal, presented in more detail in Jarrett and Lin (submitted), is to determine meaningful quantitative values for consequence and likelihood, the two components of risk in our interpretation. Specifically, we propose that consequence and likelihood scores be determined respectively as logarithms of objective measures of consequence (in terms of cost or surrogates of cost) and rate of occurrence. These numerical scores can be added to provide a risk score, which can be mapped to an expected cost. This is described in more detail in the second half of the chapter.

Such a formalism provides a broad overarching structure for risk assessment which aims to be practically useful, as objective as possible and to avoid logical inconsistencies. It does not pretend that hazards have consequences and likelihoods that can be accurately determined. Rather, it provides a risk ranking method which is unambiguously defined, and accepts that individual hazards placed within it will have levels of uncertainty associated with their exact position, due either to lack of data or to varied opinions among experts.

What is risk?

Over 2,000 years ago, the Roman statesman and philosopher Cicero wrote that the safety of the people is the supreme law (Rudd 1998, p.152). But 'complete freedom from risk is an unattainable goal, and safety [is] related to the level of risk that society regards as reasonable ... in the context of, and in comparison with, other risks in everyday life' (Department of Health 1998, Section 2.6). For this reason, Kempton (1998) says 'decision makers, be they government or members of the public, need to be better educated in interpreting estimates of risk'.

The Royal Society (1992, Section 1.3.2) defines risk as 'the chance, in quantitative terms, of a defined hazard occurring. It therefore combines a probabilistic measure of ... occurrence ... with a measure of the consequences'. Hazard is 'a situation ... that has the potential for human injury, damage to property, damage to the environment, or economic loss'. Note the distinction made between risk and hazard, terms sometimes used interchangeably in discussion.

Risk, then, has two components: a probability of occurrence and a consequence. How these are combined depends on the context, but in many cases a product of them is appropriate. This multiplication implies that the values of the components must be like physical measurements; they cannot be ranks, for example. Hence 'quantitative' occurs in the definition of risk above, and in the title of our paper.

Social scientists, among others, often need a different definition of risk. Their views are succinctly summarised in Section 1.3.4 of Royal Society (1992). Issues include subjective and socially conditioned perceptions of risk. These are particularly relevant when considering risk management.

The term likelihood is often used instead of probability, though strictly they are not synonymous. In this paper we shall use rate of occurrence, rather than probability, as the surrogate for likelihood. This leads to a specific quantitative interpretation of our risk values.

In the following sections we expand on some of these ideas.

Components of a risk analysis

When considering or analysing risk some of the matters that need to be considered are:

- the hazardous event whose occurrence would cause the risk
- the consequence (harm) associated with that event
- the population at risk
- the risk per unit of exposure
- the level of exposure of members of the population.

Exposure is a factor that can be easily overlooked. Members of a population can have very different levels of exposure to a hazard. For example, distance from a chemical facility will affect significantly a person's risk from a toxic release from the facility (the prevailing wind direction might also be relevant).

Changing any of the components changes the risk. Not considering them all can lead to erroneous conclusions. For example, raw accident statistics are not a direct measure of safety (Kempton 1998); exposure must also be considered. Hilton (1993) notes that the reduction in cycling casualties in Australia of about 25% following the introduction of compulsory wearing of helmets can be explained almost totally by a commensurate reduction in distance cycled.

A more detailed description of how to carry out a Risk Analysis can be found in *The Australian and New Zealand Standard on Risk Management* (Standards Australia 2004a), first developed in 1995, and the accompanying Handbook (Standards Australia 2004b). The need and background for such a standard are described by Cross (1995), together with a summary of the risk management process.

Scales of measurement

The nature of the measurements available for a risk analysis has important consequences. The theory originated with Stevens (1946); a good summary, including the mathematical basis, can be found in Ford (1993). There are essentially five scales of measurement, exemplified informally below by possible 'measurements' on fruit.

- *nominal* (is the fruit an apple or an orange?)
- *ordinal* (grade apples by size)
- *interval* (what weight class does an apple belong to?)
- *ratio* (what weight is an apple?)
- *absolute* (how many apples?)

To do arithmetic on data, the measurements must be on an interval scale, at least. Ranks, the best-known example of ordinal data, cannot be sensibly added, for instance. The standard Risk Matrix, to be introduced shortly, uses ordinal scales for both consequence and likelihood and this creates problems with combining them to form a measure of risk.

Quantitative risk analysis typically uses data on one of the last three scales. However, a lot of policy and social discussion involves data on a nominal or ordinal scale. This can cause difficulties when interpretation or comparison is required.

Hodge and Walpole (1999), using systems in defence as their example, discuss types of data by considering levels of complexity as shown in Figure 1, taken from their paper. The connection with our discussion is that detailed quantitative analysis usually occurs towards the left-hand end of the curve, where agreement and certainty are high. However, the results of such an analysis are then often used and discussed at the right-hand, or 'social' end of the graph, where agreement and certainty can be much less clear.

Perception of risk

Even if there is a reliable calculation of risk, based on sound data or an agreed model, this can legitimately be perceived in very different ways. Perception is a subjective and personal matter. Here are some examples.

1. If a medical procedure has a relatively high risk and an individual perceives it as non-essential, they are unlikely to undergo the procedure. If, however, the alternative is death within a very short time, the risk might be considered acceptable.
2. The risk associated with climbing high mountains would be considered unacceptably great by most individuals, including the authors. However, Andrew Lock, the first Australian to climb all 14 mountains over 8000m

(see http://www.andrew-lock.com), presumably regards this risk as quite acceptable.

3. There is a tendency to regard a hazard as more serious if it kills a large number of people should it occur, even if the overall death rate from the hazard is no greater than that from another hazard which occurs more frequently but kills far fewer people per occurrence. In Australia, the 2008 national road toll from road accidents was 1,464 (Department of Infrastructure, Transport, Regional Development and Local Government 2009). As far as we know, there is no evidence that Australians have decreased their road travel because of this figure, so presumably the risk is considered acceptable by most. If, however, this number of people died in 2 or 3 major air incidents in one year, it is almost certain there would be major public outcry, the use of air transport would (at least temporarily) decrease, and major changes to air transport policy and operations would occur.

4. This is discussed in the literature as 'societal risk' (Vrijling & van Gelder 1997) and typically gives greater weight to more severe consequences in the consequence-probability combination used to calculate risk. There is a specific example in the section 'Discussion of Quantified Risk Matrices' below. A recent paper, with further references, is Horn et al. (2008).

Figure 1: General hierarchy of systems (from Hodge & Walpole 1999)

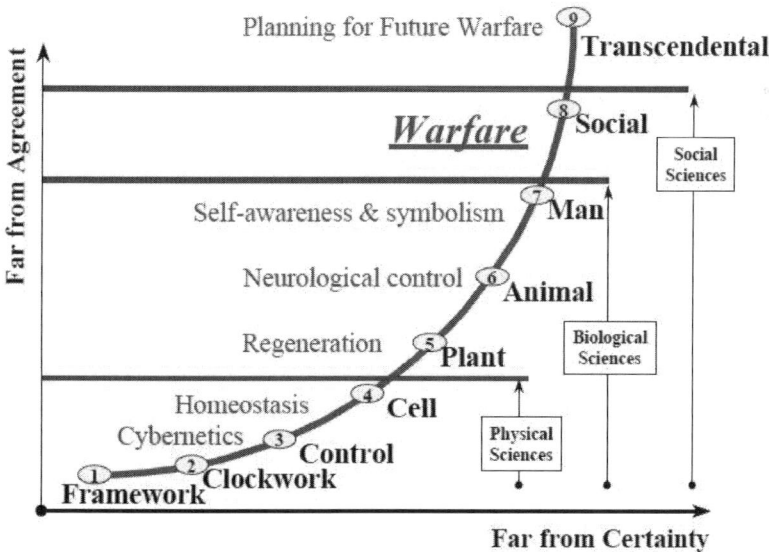

Quantification of risk

Our view is that risk assessment should aim to provide quantitative estimates, even if there is uncertainty in those estimates. The primary motivation for this is an issue of 'measuring instruments' that, in this case, need to provide a clear and unambiguous yardstick against which consequence and likelihood can be assessed. Van Duijne et al. (2008) note that 'scale values such as "unlikely" and "improbable" can be interpreted as almost similar, yet risk assessors are forced to choose one of these options if both values appear on the same scale'. Without precise definitions for consequence and likelihood, the uncertainty contains two components of variation—one related to people's different interpretations of the measuring instrument and a second related to their uncertainty in where to place a particular hazard on the scale. The aim is to remove the first of these, by using clear and unambiguous definitions.

A typical Risk Matrix, shown in Table 1, has rows as levels of consequence and columns giving levels of likelihood. Identified hazards are placed within the Risk Matrix by choosing the appropriate row and column. Standards Australia (2004a, 2004b) provide a broad methodology and specific examples. Anderson (2006) claims to have identified more than 800 versions of Risk Matrices through a search on Google. The levels in the two margins are clearly ordered, or ranked. Without further explanation they are no more than that; in particular, there is no notion of relative magnitude, so their measurement scale is ordinal. Their combination into a measure of risk is qualitative and subjective; for example, should the combinations {critical, improbable} and {negligible, occasional} be regarded as comparable risks, as they are in Table 1?

Table 1: A general Risk Matrix

Consequences	Likelihood				
	IMPROBABLE (E)	REMOTE (D)	OCCASIONAL (C)	PROBABLE (B)	FREQUENT (A)
CATASTROPHIC (4)					VERY HIGH
CRITICAL (3)				HIGH	
MARGINAL (2)			MEDIUM		
NEGLIGIBLE (1)		LOW			

Recent criticisms of Risk Matrices (Cox 2008a) question their suitability and reliability for adequately ranking the risk of a variety of hazards. Many of these criticisms relate to the degree of arbitrariness in the definition of the scales for consequence and likelihood. Table I in Cox (2008a) gives a specific example, and further discussion can be found in Edwards et al. (2009).

The gradations of risk, or iso-risk contours, in Table 1 are roughly diagonal. This suggests their developers have a more quantitative framework in mind. If so, it should be spelled out explicitly. The Risk Matrix shown in Jarrett and Lin (submitted) has levels for both consequence and likelihood scaled in logarithmic steps, as proposed previously by Swallom (2005), van Eijenhoven and van Ravenzwaaij (1989) and Anderson (2006), *inter alia*. Table 2 provides an example with logarithmic scales (based on powers of 10), and levels based on integer steps. For example, if cost is measured in dollars, then a consequence score of 8 corresponds to a consequence of $\$10^8 = \$100M$, and covers consequences that are thought most likely to fall in the range $[10^{7.5}, 10^{8.5}) = [\$30M, \$300M)$. Similarly, a likelihood score of -2 corresponds to a rate of occurrence of $10^{-2} = 0.01$ per annum (if that is the period over which likelihood is assessed) and covers rates in the range $[10^{-2.5}, 10^{-1.5}) = [0.003, 0.03)$.

Table 2: The Risk Matrix with logarithmic scores and risk levels

Overall Consequence Score	Likelihood Score				
	Rare -4	Unlikely -3	Possible -2	Likely -1	Very Likely 0
Catastrophic 10	Medium	High	Very High	Extreme	Extreme
Major 9	Low	Medium	High	Very High	Extreme
Moderate 8	Very Low	Low	Medium	High	Very High
Minor 7	Negligible	Very Low	Low	Medium	High
Insignificant 6	Negligible	Negligible	Very Low	Low	Medium

This does not imply greater accuracy in the assessments, but aims to provide a well-defined measuring instrument against which individual hazards can be judged. This reduces the uncertainty that can arise from use of more subjective scales.

The risk score is the sum of the consequence score and the likelihood score. It has a natural interpretation as the logarithm of the Risk or Expected Cost per year associated with a particular hazard. Here,

$$Risk = Expected\ Cost = Consequence \times Likelihood$$

and the scores sum because multiplication becomes addition on a logarithmic scale. For example, if the likelihood were a rate of 0.1 events per year and the consequence were $\$10^8$, then, on average, for nine years out of 10 the cost would be $\$0$, while one year in ten the cost would be $\$10^8$. Averaged over the 10 years, the cost would be $\$10^7$ per year, which is referred to as the Expected Cost. In this case, the consequence score would be 8, the likelihood score would be -1 and the risk score would be the sum of these, namely 7.

In contrast with Table 1, which is entirely qualitative, cells in Table 2 with the same risk description have the same risk score with a well-defined interpretation. The descriptions can be changed but whichever words are used their meaning in this context is quite clear. This is the objective basis foreshadowed above.

The cutoff values used to define risk levels, as shown in Table 2, will depend on (i) the actions to be taken for each risk level, and (ii) agreement that this is the action one would take for a hazard at that risk level. Table 3 provides a typical description of action (GAO 1998) to be taken for certain risk levels, so agreement is needed on the appropriate cutoff point for each action envisaged. A preferable model, however, would be to consider mitigation strategies and their costs, and determine action on the basis of some combination of reducing the highest risks and making the biggest overall reduction in risk given the finite resources available for mitigation.

Table 3: Examples of actions associated with risk levels (from GAO 1998)

Risk Level	Action required
1	Unacceptable (reduce risk through countermeasures)
2	Undesirable (management decision required)
3	Acceptable with review by management
4	Acceptable without review

The Consequence Matrix

Consequences for particular hazards, where strictly monetary, can be assessed and estimated. However, consequences often are not expressible in purely monetary terms. In a particular government-based risk assessment in which we were involved, there were seven consequence categories, as shown in Table 4, including 'death, injury or illness' and 'environmental', along with 'economic'. The aim is to broaden the definition of consequence and to assist in defining the potential consequences of a particular hazard. Table 4 gives descriptions for the 'moderate' consequence score for each of these seven consequence categories. Similar descriptions are given for each of the other consequence scores, and these can be incorporated into a matrix, in which columns represent consequence categories and rows are the consequence scores (see also Standards Australia, 2004b, Table 6.2). There are three important features of this proposed Consequence Matrix:

- An increase of 1 unit in consequence score corresponds to a tenfold increase in the 'economic' consequence category.
- Where impacts cannot be measured in dollars, judgment and agreement between stakeholders are needed to ensure that, as far as possible, the

descriptions corresponding to a particular consequence score are seen as representing hazards of similar 'impact'. Hence each of the descriptions for moderate consequences in Table 4 is of comparable impact.

- The score allocated for each of the consequence categories is the highest score for which one or more of the dot points would be realised, should such a hazard occur.

Under this proposal, a score of, say, 8 in any column of the Matrix can be regarded as being of similar importance.

The consequence scores for a given hazard need to be combined across categories without diminishing the effects of any high consequence scores. A score of 8 corresponds to an economic impact of the order of \$100M (=$\$10^8$). Since a score of 8 in another consequence category represents an event of similar impact, this might be regarded as having a similar 'cost'. So adding the category scores after taking a power of 10 corresponds to adding the implied costs, and taking the logarithm (log) of the sum turns it into a consequence score again. In formal terms, this can be expressed as:

- take 10 raised to the power of each category score
- add these numbers together to give an overall total
- take the logarithm to base 10 of this total to get the combined consequence score.

The overall consequence score will be higher than the maximum score across a row, by an amount related to how many times that maximum score occurs. For example, if the consequence scores are 4, 8, 6, 8, 7, 5, 4 in the seven categories, the overall consequence score is

$$\log_{10}(10^4+10^8+10^6+10^8+10^7+10^5+10^4) = \log_{10}(211{,}120{,}000) = 8.325$$

This is preferable to the average score of $(4+8+6+8+7+5+4)/7 = 6.00$, which reduces the impact of the scores of 8 to such an extent that the hazard would be regarded as having quite minor consequences. It is also preferable to the maximum (8), since it recognises that high severity in more than one category is 'worse' than having it in just one category. The maximum score achievable when the highest individual score is 8 is $\log_{10}(7\times10^8) = 8.85$, if all seven categories are scored at 8.

Table 4: Examples of descriptions for consequence categories

Category	Description for Moderate Consequence (Consequence Score = 8)
Death, injury or illness	Multiple fatalities
	Mass very seriously ill or seriously ill casualties
	State and/or territory health system fully committed with local health system overwhelmed and/or
	Australian Government assistance considered, state and/or territory response required.
Economic	Impact of $30–300 million.
	Impacts on business include:
	Travel to and within Australia disrupted
	Substantial disruption to industry and/or commerce
	Disruption of one or more national industry sectors with recovery likely to last one to three months.
Social	Significant and/or short-term challenge to Rule of Law, lasting up to 1 month
	Civil liberties, freedom of speech, association, movement, or religion denied or restricted for up to 1 month locally, and threatened at state level for up to 7 days
	Widespread disruption to, or destruction of, the state physical and communications infrastructure, and other essential services (including critical social infrastructure) for up to 7 days
	Isolated disruption to, or degradation of, the local education system up to 1 month, or specifically isolated disruption to state system up to 7 days.
	Extreme disruption to local participation in community, arts, cultural, sporting, and leisure activities for up to 1 month, or significant disruption at state level for up to 7 days.
Environmental	Damage to a conservation value of a marine bioregion, including species, communities or areas identified as of particular conservation significance where recovery extends from three to ten years
	Introduction of exotic marine/terrestrial pest species resulting in a localised incursion with substantial long-term environmental impacts or a widespread incursion with environmental follow on effects where recovery extends from three to ten years
	Industrial scale harvesting of, or trade in, any native species
	Exacerbation/causation of probable long-term decline in an important population of, or habitat for, a listed species
	Commercial harvesting of, trade in, or removal from the biomass of any listed species and/or
	Killing or removal from the biomass of individual representatives of a species listed as critically endangered.
Symbolic	Significant reparable damage to a nationally important symbol that is internationally recognised
	Significant irreparable damage to a nationally important symbol and/or
	Destruction of a locally important symbol.
External	Setback and damage to bilateral relations
	Frequent deliberate challenges to Australia's sovereignty by a foreign state.
Reputational	Major criticism and temporary damage to the government's parliamentary reputation
	Inquiry with detrimental findings and significant criticism leading to temporary damage to the government's reputation
	Moderate damage to Australia's national business reputation.

The likelihood

Likelihood can also be expressed as a likelihood score that moves by 1 unit for each tenfold change. Jarrett and Lin (submitted) propose that probability be replaced by rate of occurrence, in which case the likelihood score can be extended arbitrarily in either direction. The likelihood score is related to the rate of occurrence by

$$\text{Rate of occurrence (/time period)} = 10^{\text{Likelihood Score}}$$

If likelihood is on an annual basis, then a likelihood score of 0 represents hazards that occur on average $10^0 = 1$ time per year. Since the rate may not be constant over time (or space), a time scale (or spatial scale) appropriate to the situation should be chosen.

Likelihood can often be assessed using past data, either internal to the organisation or external. It is harder to evaluate when the rate is low, especially in situations where such hazards have never happened before. Security risks, such as criminal or terrorist activity, often fall into this category and make it particularly difficult to estimate the likelihood (Cox 2008b). Dealing with likelihood in situations of intentional harm, where there are forces or individuals trying to find ways to breach systems of controls, is considered later.

Combining different hazards in different regions

Risk scores are typically determined for a range of hazards, often of different types and geographically dispersed. We might want to combine risk scores in various ways; for example, across threats within a region, for a given threat across regions, or across both threats and regions.

Suppose there are p hazards, with consequence scores C_i and likelihood scores L_i ($i=1,...,p$). The risk scores are then $R_i = C_i + L_i$. Combining across the hazards is done in the same way that consequence scores are combined:

- take 10 raised to the power of each risk score
- add these numbers together to give an overall total
- take the logarithm to base 10 of this total to get the combined consequence score.

This is based on the premise that adding the expected costs across hazards is sensible, giving a combined Risk Score of

$$R = \log\{ \text{Sum}(10^{Ri}) \} = \log\{ \text{Sum}(10^{Ci+Li}) \},$$

and the Expected Cost is just the antilog of this risk score.

It is also possible to associate a consequence score and a likelihood score with the combined set of hazards. The rate of occurrence for a set of hazards is the sum of the rates of occurrence. Since the likelihood score is the log of these rates, the combined likelihood score is given by

$$L = log\{ Sum(10^{Li}) \}.$$

The combined consequence score C for the set of hazards should satisfy the rule that $R = L + C$, from which it follows that

$$C = log\{ Sum(10^{Ci+Li}) \} - log\{ Sum(10^{Li}) \}$$
$$= log[\{ Sum(10^{Ci+Li}) \} / \{ Sum(10^{Li}) \}].$$

Thus the combined consequence is a weighted average of the consequences of the individual hazards, weighted by the rates at which they occur. The combined likelihood score provides a rate of occurrence for a series of hazards which may have very different consequences. The combined consequence score does not now represent a single hazard, but is a summary statistic for a distribution of consequence scores represented by the set of hazards.

Discussion of quantified risk matrices

We previously gave our general views on why quantitative estimates of risk are important. Here we expand on them in the context of Risk Matrices:

- The proposed method ties consequence and likelihood scores to real, measurable quantities, thus promoting objectivity. Furthermore, data, either available or collected into the future, can provide estimates, validate previously determined values or, in cases of sparse data, augment expert elicitation data (i.e. data based on best estimates made by relevant experts).
- The proposed method is readily adapted to specific situations. For example, instead of number of events per annum, likelihood could equally be the number of events per 10 years (thus adding 1 to the likelihood scores proposed), or monthly (essentially subtracting one). Similarly, consequence scores could be considered as logarithms (base 10) of the cost in millions of dollars (thus subtracting 6).
- Expected Cost provides a direct calculation of risk and hence defines how the two factors in risk are combined and how the contours of equal risk should be drawn.

- Expected Cost is related to an insurance premium, without the margin to cover costs/profits.
- Where Expected Cost is calculated for both the presence and absence of proposed (and costed) mitigation activities, a true cost-benefit analysis of the value of mitigation can be undertaken.
- There are cases where Expected Cost might not be acceptable as the measure of risk. Other measures of risk can be used; for example, Value at Risk (VaR) in financial applications (see McNeil et al. 2005). In the context of societal risk (see earlier under Perception of Risk), van Eijenhoven and van Ravenzwaaij (1989) say 'to allow for the relative unwantedness of accidents with large consequences, it has been decided that a consequence n times greater must correspond to a chance n^2 smaller'. In this case, the Risk Score becomes

$$Risk\ Score = 2 \times (Consequence\ Score) + (Likelihood\ Score),$$

giving the consequence score a greater weight and effectively making the diagonals in Table 2 steeper. This increased weight to the consequence score is also suggested in Standards Australia (2004b, p. 49).

Policing serious criminal, including terrorist, activity

How would these methods be applied to policing serious crime or terrorist activity? Willis (2006) gave five recommendations to the Department of Homeland Security (DHS) in respect to terrorism risk modelling and assessment:

The US Government should consistently define terrorism risk in terms of metrics like expected annual consequences

DHS should seek robust risk estimators that account for uncertainty about terrorism risk and variance in citizen values

DHS should use event-based models to assess terrorism risk

Relying on event-based models does not mean relying entirely on a top-down process

The US Government should invest resources to bridge the gap between terrorism risk assessment and resource allocation policies that are cost effective.

These sentiments resonate well with our views on the matter and the comments could equally be applied to other serious criminal activity. The Handbook on Security Risk Management (Standards Australia 2006) advocates an approach that considers such risks to be composed of three aspects, namely:

- threat, which is taken to be the likelihood of attack
- vulnerability, which is taken to be the likelihood of success given that an attack is launched
- consequence, which is the damage achieved if an attack is launched and is successful.

As with the earlier definitions, Risk or Expected Cost can be expressed as the product of these three quantities. Each of these can be converted to a score, as described earlier, and these scores added to provide a risk score. Consequence and vulnerability can be assessed by the same methods described earlier in this chapter. Indeed, the additional consequence categories defined earlier have special significance in this context, since the aim of a terrorist attack is often not merely to cause economic damage or loss of life, but to seriously embarrass governments and increase international tensions.

The assessment of threat as a likelihood is more contentious. There is a strong view (e.g. Cox 2008b) that likelihood is inappropriate here since (i) terrorist attacks are purposeful and intentional, not probabilistic or random, and (ii) even if probabilistic, the uncertainties are far too great for any likelihood assessment. However, security forces do undertake assessments and report their results. In Australia, the National Counter-Terrorism Plan (National Counter-Terrorism Committee 2005) provides a list of four Alert Levels and a description of each level in terms of a terrorist attack, as shown in the first two columns of Table 5. These relate to the likely occurrence of an attack and are essentially qualitative. The last two columns of Table 5 show our suggested likelihood scores and timescales; the basis for which is discussed below. A geographic or context dimension can be added, locating the terrorist activity around a particular person or place.

Table 5: Proposed mapping of Australian counterterrorism alert levels to likelihood scores

Alert Level	Description	Proposed Likelihood Score	Indicative rate (Australia wide)
1=Extreme	Terrorist attack is imminent or has occurred	1	One per month
2=High	Terrorist attack is likely	0.5	One every 4 months
3=Medium	Terrorist attack could occur	0	One per year
4=Low	Terrorist attack is not expected	−0.5	One in three years

Our view is that these Alert Levels can be converted to likelihoods with sufficient accuracy to be useful. For example, the 'Extreme' alert level says an 'attack is imminent or has occurred'. In other documents the wording used is 'expected within the next two weeks'. This defines a time scale and hence can be converted to a rate of occurrence. Suppose we interpret this as 'there is a probability of 50% of an attack in the next two weeks'. Generally, this would apply only over a relatively short period, but if it were maintained for a whole year, then this probability of 50% every two weeks leads to an expected number of 13 events per year, corresponding to a likelihood score of 1.1. Given the uncertainties associated with this, we propose a likelihood score of 1 for Threat Level = 1.

If a one-step change in Alert Level represented a tenfold change in likelihood of attack, the likelihoods decrease too quickly, so Alert Level = 3 (Medium: an attack 'could occur') would give a likelihood score of -1 (once in 10 years) which seems too low. Instead, Table 5 shows a mapping of Alert Level to likelihood score where a one unit step in Alert Level corresponds to a 0.5 unit step in the score for likelihood of attack. This gives a more sensible match.

Risk is now considered as the product of two likelihoods (the second of which is conditional on the first occurring) and one consequence. In terms of our scores, we simply add the two likelihood scores and the consequence score, and the resulting risk score has the usual interpretation (the score for vulnerability is 0 when the probability of success is 1, -1 when the probability of success is 0.1, and so on). From a policing point of view, the accumulation of hazards by region could be used to determine resourcing across regions, through a reduction in any of the three terms involved in the risk calculation. Similarly, the accumulation of a hazard type across regions gives a more global view of the relative risks associated with each hazard type.

There may be complex interrelationships between different hazards in different regions. While this does not have a direct impact on the overall risk, it can have a major impact on the potential variability around that estimated risk. This highlights the need for modelling, something which is rather easier to do for crime, where there are more data available, than for terrorist activity. As an example, consider the issue of protecting critical infrastructure against terrorism using risk analysis. Haimes and Longstaff (2002) note that there is increasing interdependence between interconnected infrastructures and that a terrorist attack on one can have adverse impacts on others. In Australia, an analysis of such interdependency has been done through the CIPMA project (CSIRO 2007), which involved Geoscience Australia and CSIRO, together with significant funding and input from government and the major operators of infrastructure assets. The modelling concentrated on vulnerability and consequence, in relation to a series of defined scenarios. While extremely valuable, it was not a full risk assessment exercise, since (following our definitions) it did not include the threat; that is, the likelihood of attack.

The threat aspect is likely to be very dynamic and responsive. That is to say, if resources are committed to reducing vulnerability or consequence in a particular region, then it is likely that the activity (in our terms, the threat) will move elsewhere. It may not be reduced overall, but the target for that activity may shift, either to another region, or indeed to another type of activity. The notion of the 'attractiveness' of targets is a topic on which we are undertaking further work at present.

Conclusions

Any risk assessment that defines a risk level based on consequence and likelihood has an implied mathematical relationship. By providing a risk matrix with explicit categories, that relationship becomes evident and objective. The uncertainty that remains is confined to the placement of hazards into a well-defined structure and reflects variously the lack of data, the variety of views among participants, and uncertainty about the future.

Consequences cannot always be assessed purely in terms of monetary value. This paper allows other categories of consequences to be put onto the same scale and then shows how to combine consequence scores across these categories into an overall consequence score.

The assessment of consequence and likelihood here is rooted in values which, in principle, can be supported or validated by data. This has major benefits. It helps to create more objectivity, even when expert elicitation is used, by tying the assessments to real numerical values. Data, whether available now or collected in the future, can be used to provide estimates, validation for previously determined values or, in cases of sparse data, to augment expert elicitation data. Further, the risk levels obtained are interpretable; for example, in insurance terms.

The methodology, since it is described in terms of consequences and likelihoods, might be thought to apply strictly to those situations where hazards arise through accidents or natural causes. However, the methodology is extended here to situations where hazards arise through intentional acts, such as criminality, including terrorism. Concerns have been expressed about the appropriateness of the methodology for these situations, particularly in relation to the assessment of likelihood. However, the contention is that risk and risk mitigation must increasingly be prepared to consider hazards across both purposeful and non-purposeful acts, in order to make appropriate use of finite risk mitigation resources.

References

Anderson, K 2006, 'A synthesis of risk matrices', *Newsletter of the Australian Safety Critical Systems Association*, December, pp. 8–11.

Bammer, G, Smithson, M & the Goolabri Group 2008, 'The nature of uncertainty', in G Bammer & M Smithson (eds), *Uncertainty and risk: multidisciplinary perspectives*, Earthscan, London.

Cox Jr, LA 2008a, 'What's wrong with the risk matrices?', *Risk Analysis*, vol. 28, no. 2, pp. 497–512.

Cox Jr, LA 2008b, 'Some limitations of "risk = threat × vulnerability × consequence" for risk analysis of terrorist attacks', *Risk Analysis*, vol. 28, no. 6, pp. 1749–1761.

Cross, J 1995, 'The risk management standard', *The Australian Journal of Emergency Management*, vol. 10, no. 4, pp. 4–7.

CSIRO 2007, 'Protecting Australia's critical infrastructure with CIPMA', <http://www.csiro.au/partnerships/CIPMA.html> (accessed 18 January 2010).

Department of Health 1998, *The Food Standards Agency: a force for change*, Government white paper presented to Parliament by the Minister of Agriculture, Fisheries and Food, Cm 3830, The Stationery Office, London, <http://www.dh.gov.uk/en/Publicationsandstatistics/Publications/PublicationsPolicyAndGuidance/DH_4007106> (accessed 18 January 2010).

Department of Infrastructure, Transport, Regional Development and Local Government 2009, *Road deaths Australia, 2008 statistical summary*, <http://www.infrastructure.gov.au/roads/safety/publications/2009/rsr_04.aspx> (accessed 18 January 2010).

Edwards, CBH, Westcott, M & Fulton, NL 2009, 'The application of hazard risk assessment in defence safety standards', *Proceedings of Improving Systems and Software Engineering Conference* (ISSEC), 10–12 August 2009, Canberra, pp. 135–146, <http://www.issec.com.au/weblease/tpcommon/src/tp1FullPage.cfm?idPageCopy=14899&idClient=969> (accessed 12 March 2010).

Ford, G 1993, 'Measurement theory for software engineers', in Lecture notes on engineering measurement for software engineers, CMU/SEI-93-EM-9, Software Engineering Institute, Carnegie-Mellon University, <www.http://handle.dtic.mil/100.2/ADA266959> (accessed 15 March 2010).

GAO (United States General Accounting Office) 1998, *Combating terrorism: threat and risk assessments can help prioritize and target program investments*, National Security and International Affairs Division, Report Number GAO/NSIAD-98-74, Washington DC.

Haimes, YY & Longstaff, T 2002, 'The role of risk analysis in the protection of critical infrastructures against terrorism', *Risk Analysis*, vol. 22, no. 3, pp. 439–444.

Hilton, M 1993, *Cycle helmets: the case for and against*, Policy Studies Institute, London.

Hodge, R & Walpole, G 1999, 'A systems approach to defence capability planning – a work in progress', *Proceedings of SETE99 Conference on Systems Engineering, Test and Evaluation*, Adelaide, 20–22 October 1999, pp. 21–32, <http://www.dasi.unisa.edu.au/materials/99papers/T04-Hodge.pdf> (accessed 18 January 2010).

Horn, M, Fulton, N & Westcott, M 2008, 'Measures of societal risk and their potential use in civil aviation', *Risk Analysis*, vol. 28, no. 6, pp. 1711–1726.

Jarrett, RG & Lin, X 2009, 'A practical approach to quantitative risk assessment', submitted.

Kempton, RA 1998, 'How safe is safe? Communicating risk to decision makers', from an article in RKM Hay (ed.), *Science and the Scottish Parliament – Proceedings of a Symposium of the Edinburgh International Science Festival*, quote from <http://www.bioss.ac.uk/topics/howsafe.html> (accessed 18 January 2010).

McNeil, AJ, Frey, R & Embrechts, P 2005, *Quantitative risk management*, Princeton University Press, Princeton.

National Counter-Terrorism Committee 2005, *National Counter Terrorism Plan*, 2nd edn, September, <http://www.nationalsecurity.gov.au/agd/www/nationalsecurity.nsf/AllDocs/85A16ADB86A23AD1CA256FC600072E6B?OpenDocument> (accessed 18 January 2010).

Royal Society 1992, *Risk: analysis, perception and management. Report of a Royal Society study group*, The Royal Society, London.

Rudd, N 1998, *The republic and the laws*, translation of Marcus Tullius Cicero's *De re publica* and *De legibus*, Oxford University Press, Oxford.

Standards Australia 2004a, *Risk management. AS/NZS 4360:2004*, Standards Australia, Sydney.

Standards Australia 2004b, *Handbook 436, Risk Management Guidelines - Companion to AS/NZS 4360:2004*, Standards Australia, Sydney.

Standards Australia 2006, *Handbook 167, Security Risk Management - Companion to AS/NZS 4360:2004*, Standards Australia, Sydney.

Stevens, SS 1946, 'On the theory of scales of measurement', *Science*, vol. 103, no. 2684, pp. 677–680.

Swallom, DW 2005, 'A common mishap risk assessment matrix for United States Department of Defense aircraft systems, *Proceedings of the 23rd International System Safety Conference*, San Diego, California.

van Duijne, FH, van Aken, D & Schouten, EG 2008, 'Considerations in developing complete and quantified methods for risk assessment', *Safety Science*, vol. 46, no. 2, pp. 245–254.

van Eijndhoven, JCM & van Ravenzwaaij, A 1989, 'Optimizing risk analysis relating to external safety in the Netherlands', *Risk Analysis*, vol. 9, no. 4, pp. 495–504.

Vrijling, JK & van Gelder, PHAJM 1997, 'Societal risk and the concept of risk aversion', in C Guedes Soares (ed.), *Advances in safety and reliability*, Pergamon, Oxford.

Willis, HH 2006, *Analysing terrorism risk*, written testimony submitted to the House Financial Services Committee, Subcommittee on Oversight and Investigations, and the House Homeland Security Committee, Subcommittee on Intelligence, Information Sharing, and Terrorism Risk Assessment, July 25, RAND Corporation, <http://www.rand.org/pubs/testimonies/CT265/> (accessed 18 January 2010).

Understanding and Managing Bias
MARK R KEBBELL, DAMON A MULLER,
KIRSTY MARTIN

A large amount of evidence, mostly from research in psychology, suggests that decision-making and information processing abilities are often not optimal because the informational complexity of the world overwhelms human cognitive abilities and creates bias. This is exacerbated by contextual pressures, such as time constraints, dynamism and changing goals. Our aim in this chapter is to identify some of the key cognitive biases that contribute to uncertainty, as well as emerging mechanisms to manage them. We also discuss the importance of promoting realistic expectations of the police and security services in their responses to such uncertainty.

While these issues are relevant to all types of serious crime investigations they are exacerbated in counterterrorism investigations, which involve both inherent and created uncertainties, as well as significant time pressure and high stakes. While the inherent uncertainty in terrorists' motivations and actions cannot be easily influenced, the management of counterterrorism operations can have a direct influence on the amount of uncertainty that is introduced to the situation through strategies for decision-making and information interpretation.

To keep within the confines of this chapter, we have been selective in the issues we address, predominantly focusing on counterterrorism operations, but also drawing on knowledge about understanding and managing bias in other types of serious crime. It is important to note that this is not a comprehensive review of the role of bias in creating uncertainty but rather an insight into an area that requires attention.

In a counterterrorism operation decisions regarding intelligence collection, interpretation of available information and courses of action are made in a context characterised not only by time pressure and high stakes, but also severe data limitations, data overload, ill-structured tasks, risk, shifting and competing goals, dynamism, action feedback loops, group work and external and public oversight, all of which create uncertainty (Zsambok & Klein 1997). In such circumstances, the applicability and feasibility of time-intensive, analytical decision-making methods is reduced and counterterrorism operation members may be forced to rely more on faster intuitive and heuristic based methods (Hammond 2007). Heuristics are cognitive short cuts to reduce complex problems into simple rules that work effectively. While heuristics can be adaptive, they can also lead to biases and inaccuracies (Almond et al. 2008; Slovic et al. 1977). As we describe, heuristic use in counterterrorism operations can be both adaptive and maladaptive.

There are a number of cases on the public record where the police and security services have been successful in identifying terrorists. For example, in Australia 17 terrorists have been successfully convicted without a terrorist attack occurring on Australian soil (Porter & Kebbell 2009). However, let us consider two examples where bias has been critical in counterterrorism operations, each illustrating different challenges: errors in the use of information resulting in a false negative where individuals of high risk were rated as low risk and errors that facilitated over-responding to intelligence whereby individuals of low risk were rated as high risk. Operation Crevice provides an example of the first of these challenges. It was an investigation into a terrorist plot to bomb a shopping centre in England that generated a body of information that required virtually the entire operational resources of MI5 to process. This included the analysis of the results of searching 30 addresses, 45,000 hours of monitoring and transcription, 34,000 hours of surveillance, and 4,020 telephone calls (Intelligence and Security Committee 2009). Such an enormous volume of information potentially overwhelms the cognitive abilities of individuals, increasing the likelihood that heuristics are used and thus increasing the potential for bias. One such maladaptive bias involved overlooking important information which led to a failure to investigate two terrorists. The two men, Mohammed Siddique Khan and Shazad Tanweer, were associated with the terrorist cell under surveillance and subsequently attacked London on 7 July 2005 (Intelligence and Security Committee 2009).

The mistaken shootings of Mohammed Abdulkahar in Forest Gate, London, UK (Independent Police Complaints Commission 2007a) and Jean Charles de Menezes in Stockwell, London, UK (Independent Police Complaints Commission 2007b), as well as the detention and subsequent release of Mohammed Haneef in Brisbane, Australia (Clarke 2008) indicate the problem of identifying people as terrorists when there is not sufficient evidence to prove a case. Cognitive biases can contribute to such mistakes, hence the importance of recognising and managing these biases in counterterrorism operations.

Here we first examine a selection of heuristics and cognitive biases, and provide examples of how they are relevant to counterterrorism operations. We then present a number of strategies for debiasing, or reducing the effects of these biases. Many of these debiasing techniques do not seem to have been empirically examined in the context of counterterrorism policing, however they have the potential to help mitigate against biases in this field.

Key heuristics and biases

The literature on heuristics and biases is voluminous and only a selection is discussed here (for a more detailed review see Almond et al. 2008). As previously mentioned, heuristics can help to navigate the complexity of decision-making in counterterrorism operations and it is important to note that their use can have positive or negative impacts, including the production of biases, depending on the circumstances. In this section we discuss the representativeness heuristic, the availability heuristic, anchoring and adjustment, confirmation bias and hindsight bias, providing examples of their positive and negative influences on counterterrorism operations and other serious crime.

The *representativeness heuristic* is a mental short cut which allows judgments to be made about a person or event based on perceived similarity to a particular known group or event (Tversky & Kahneman 1974). This heuristic can be adaptive, allowing intelligence operations to move forward in the face of ambiguous and potentially deceptive information, by allowing analysts to rely on knowledge about similar situations or offenders. This heuristic can also be maladaptive when reliance on this mental short cut leads to subsequent decisions being made largely on the basis of false assumptions. Mears and Bacon (2009) discuss this as a form of 'attribution error' that is common in medical decision-making. An example can be seen in Operation Crevice where Mohammed Siddique Khan and Shazad Tanweer appear to have been thought of as criminals rather than terrorists because of their conversational references to criminal activities (Intelligence and Security Committee 2009).

The *availability heuristic* leads to information that can quickly be brought to mind gaining more prominence than other equally valid evidence (Tversky & Kahneman 1974). This heuristic can be advantageous when the most relevant information for a task is more available than peripheral information, leading to accurate decision-making. On the other hand, information overload is a recognised problem in complex counterterrorism operations and the availability heuristic may lead to more recent evidence being given more weight than is justified. If equally important older evidence cannot easily be recalled by investigators this may lead to error. In light of the increased attention and concern surrounding terrorism and its perpetrators, greater amounts of information are collected, and the likelihood that the availability heuristic will be unconsciously utilised to handle data overload also increases. The sheer volume of information that springs from national security hotlines, terrorist propaganda, covert intelligence collection and informants already creates a significant challenge for analysis, and the availability heuristic may lead analysts to incorrectly privilege information simply because it is recent and easily recalled, rather than because of its inherent importance.

A plausible negative influence of the availability heuristic can be seen in the shooting of Jean Charles de Menezes (Independent Police Complaints Commission 2007b). The four London suicide bombings 15 days previously that killed 56 people and injured over 300, the unsuccessful attempted detonation of four suicide bombs the previous day, and the fact that the bombers were at large, may have made the threat of suicide bombings particularly available in the minds of officers.

Anchoring and adjustment is a heuristic which involves an individual selecting a starting point (anchor) and then gradually adjusting that point as new information requires it (Tversky & Kahneman 1974). Some examples of anchors in counterterrorism operations may include a potential risk that a suspect poses or the level of risk that an attack will occur.

These anchors may evolve from an individual's previous experience or from a partial assessment of the facts. Adjustment occurs as more information is assessed or becomes available, however research suggests that these adjustments are often not enough (Tversky & Kahneman 1974). For example, with regard to the shooting of Jean Charles de Menezes the starting point concerning his likelihood of being a suicide bomber appeared to be assessed as high. Research suggests that police often adopt a 'guilt bias', where they act as if a suspect is guilty, rather than being innocent until proven guilty (e.g. Leo 2008), which is an example of anchoring. If the default anchor is guilt, adjustments from evidence that supports the suspect's innocence may be insufficient. Thus whilst anchoring may allow an operation to move forward without a constant need to be re-assessed, adjustments may not adequately allow for exonerating evidence or incriminating evidence on other potential suspects to be revealed.

Confirmation bias leads to information that is consistent with expectations being sought and information that is contradictory being ignored or devalued (Cook & Smallman 2008; Klayman & Ha 1987; Wason 1960). In an experimental study with detectives, Ask and Granhag (2005) found evidence of confirmation bias in the form of misinterpretation of evidence to support the initial hypothesis. In their study detectives were provided with scenarios in which a murder suspect looked either more or less guilty. They were then given ambiguous witness evidence, and the evidence was generally interpreted in a manner indicative of guilt in the high guilt condition and less so in the low guilt condition.

In counterterrorism operations, intelligence analysts may make assumptions about factors such as terrorist cell construction or typical perpetrator features and may seek confirmation of these leads without considering alternative possibilities—particularly if they have made a commitment to a course of action based on these assumptions. Confirmation bias potentially affected the Haneef case (Clarke 2008), in that ambiguous information, such as Dr Haneef booking a one-way ticket to India, was interpreted as indicating his involvement in a terrorist plot.

Hindsight is the retrospective view of events and how they unfolded; *hindsight bias* describes overestimation of how easy it should have been to be successful and oversimplification of what should have been done (Fischoff 1975; Hawkins & Hastie 1990). This has been a particularly prominent issue in counterterrorism operations which often result in post-operational reviews, frequently with some degree of political motivation. Such reviews are likely to be affected by hindsight bias, in which it is difficult, and arguably impossible, to ignore the effect of later information on a decision made in the absence of that information. Hindsight bias has been a significant public issue in cases such as the London bombings and the Haneef case, where—with the benefit of hindsight—commentators have been extremely critical of the police response. This has impacted on the procedures, policies and practices of future operations and thus is of critical importance. We return to this bias in our conclusions.

Thus far it has been shown that while the use of heuristics can help to reduce the amount of uncertainty and complexity in counterterrorism operations, it may also result in biases that cause errors. As these processes are inherent in human cognition they are difficult to avoid. However, some methods may minimise problems associated with heuristics and biases. We now turn to ways of debiasing.

Mechanisms for debiasing

Given that cognitive biases are such a persistent challenge it is important that, in a counterterrorism operations environment, attention is focused on removing or minimising these effects. Wilson and Brekke (1994) divide biases into two groups, one of which is characterised by uncontrollable mental processes (such as cognitive biases) and the other being failure of rule knowledge or application (applying the wrong rule leading to the wrong conclusion). Thus one way of debiasing is for individuals to be aware of the magnitude and direction of the bias, and motivated to correct for it. However this will only work where the bias is actually controllable (Wilson & Brekke 1994). In the case of counterterrorism operations, this method involves increasing awareness of bias and reducing bias by ensuring team members at all levels are consciously aware of heuristics they may use, and the biases that may result from these, and how this relates to their work. Creating awareness of biases is an important component of training and must be supported through organisational culture. Improving the metacognition, or extent to which members are aware of their thinking, is a vital strategy for providing opportunities to reduce damaging biases during operations.

There is some question as to whether simple awareness of the potential for bias alone is likely to be successful at reducing biases, which generally operate at an unconscious level (Wilson & Brekke 1994). For this reason explicit debiasing strategies may be adopted. Some examples utilised in law enforcement and national security include visualisation, the analysis of competing hypotheses, key assumptions check, structured decision-making, red-teaming, devil's advocate, Team A/Team B, and scenario development. We provide a brief overview of the first four.

Visualisation can be used to keep uncertainty explicit, which is important for reducing bias at both analyst and decision-maker levels of counterterrorism operations. At the analyst level, relying on recent or easily retrieved information and seeking only confirming evidence can be avoided by using visualisation programs to keep all important information visible. At the decision-maker level, products used to assist decision-making should have explicit recognition of where levels of uncertainty regarding information are high or data is lacking. Without this clarity, courses of action may rely on false assumptions drawn from unclear intelligence. Visualisation tools are a good example of how uncertainty can be made explicit for both levels. Analysts may use visualisation programs to keep disconfirming evidence, probabilities of deception, and amounts of supporting information in front of them to help reduce the likelihood of this information being lost in data volume. At the decision-maker level, intelligence products that visually present the information, uncertainty and missing information may also reduce the likelihood that the individual will work from false assumptions.

Although it is not often presented as a debiasing strategy, visualisation software is increasingly being used as an aid to the analysis of criminal intelligence and investigative case management (Dean & Gottschalk 2007). Research has demonstrated that, in some situations, visualisation techniques can be an effective strategy for reducing confirmation bias in the assessment of intelligence (Cook & Smallman 2008). Due to the intuitive appeal of visual representations of complex data, it is likely that many other such approaches exist in law enforcement. The debiasing potential of such systems, many of which are already in place, is an obvious area for further research into mitigating the effects of cognitive biases.

Several methods of keeping uncertainties explicit exist as 'tradecraft' for intelligence analysts (Central Intelligence Agency 2009). These include methods such as the Analysis of Competing Hypotheses and Key Assumptions Check. The Analysis of Competing Hypotheses (Heuer, 1999) has been advocated for the understanding of intelligence, particularly when the consequences of error are likely to be high. It has also been found to reduce the likelihood of confirmation bias (Cheikes et al. 2004; Billman et al. 2006). This procedure consists of eight systematic steps that can be applied to an analytical problem to encourage good decision-making:

1. identifying different hypotheses about what is happening in the domain of interest. Heuer suggests that the more uncertain a situation is, and the greater the impact of a decision, the more alternative scenarios should be hypothesised
2. making a list of the significant evidence and arguments for each hypothesis
3. refining the hypotheses into a matrix with evidence that is assessed for the degree to which it supports the arguments
4. deleting the evidence that has no diagnostic value
5. developing tentative conclusions about the relative likelihood of each hypothesis and trying to find evidence to *disprove* hypotheses rather than proving them
6. assessing the sensitivity of the conclusions to a few sources of evidence, with the implication being that if those sources of evidence are incorrect or subject to a different interpretation then the conclusions may be wrong
7. reporting conclusions that will include not only the most likely conclusion but also alternatives
8. articulating what evidence should be collected in the future to ensure that their assessments are not being deviated from.

A related technique to the Analysis of Competing Hypotheses is the Key Assumptions Check. This involves reviewing the current intelligence line on an issue and articulating all the premises that are accepted as true for this analytic line to be valid. Then the analyst is encouraged to challenge each assumption and its validity. Finally, the analyst must consider under what conditions these assumptions might not hold. Empirical evaluation of this technique in this domain is, to our knowledge, yet to be conducted.

Other methods concern providing counterterrorism operations with structured methods of decision-making that prompt individuals, at all levels, to consider uncertainties in the situation. As previously discussed, the contextual features of counterterrorism operations, particularly uncertainty, induce heuristic-based decision-making. By providing counterterrorism operations with structured methods of decision-making, heuristic use is complemented with some level of analysis and consideration of alternatives. To date, however, most research in a forensic context has looked at structured decision-making from a correctional, rather that counterterrorism perspective.

For example, the Static-99 is a tool used for assessing the risk of future sex offending in convicted sex offenders and is calculated using historical, fixed (or static) factors: personal demographic information, official criminal history, and the gender of and relationship to victims. This procedure is reasonably accurate, though far from perfect, and typically outperforms clinical judgment (Beauregard & Mieczkowski 2009; Grubin 1998; Sjöstedt & Långström 2001) because it removes many of the factors associated with bias, including those involved in making judgments that do not relate to risk, such as how likeable or attractive the individual is, how friendly they are to the assessor, and whether they fulfill the assessor's stereotypes of an offender. As mentioned previously, availability, representativeness, anchoring and adjustment as well as a variety of other heuristics also have the potential to add to bias. Structured decision-making is a more objective way of looking at data that can encourage a more systematic and critical exploration of information in counterterrorism situations, and overlaps with other ways of encouraging critical assessment.

To date however, structured decision-making does not seem to have been empirically evaluated to any significant extent in this domain. Some important advantages of the structured decision-making approach are that it provides an evidence base and audit trail for the decision-making process and it can be designed to ensure consistency of judgments. This allows different people to assess information in the same coherent way and allows for an audit trail to be formed of decisions that are made. This is an important issue in counterterrorism operations where decisions and actions are often scrutinised in hindsight, should events be controversial.

Promoting realistic expectations

Whilst good decision-making in counterterrorism operations is clearly important, it must be borne in mind that analysts and decision-makers have many competing demands. For example, while the best strategy from an analytical perspective might be to collect, collate and analyse more information, the public may require rapid demonstrable action to be taken and, from a leadership perspective, police and security officers may need to be kept active and motivated. Furthermore, in many situations, perhaps most obviously illustrated in the case of imminent terrorist attack, time-pressures mean that the option to delay decision-making is not available. Thus, it is essential that the public are able to understand the complexity of the demands in counterterrorism operations and are also aware of hindsight bias. The Intelligence and Security Committee (2009, p.5), writing about the London bombings, put it well in their comments about what it was reasonable to have known beforehand:

> *We have concentrated on what information was available at the time of CREVICE and before the 7/7 attacks. Although it is always easy, with the benefit of hindsight, to criticise decisions made in the past, we have looked at what was known and what should have been known prior to the attacks.*

Unfortunately the press and public do not always adopt a similar level of realistic expectations.

Conclusions

Complex criminal investigations such as counterterrorism operations have considerable risk of maladaptive cognitive biases and as such there is a need for an awareness of these biases and strategies to manage them. A great deal of uncertainty exists in gathering, collating, analysing and acting on intelligence in counterterrorism operations and, as a result, bias may exist in the interpretation of this information. The consequences of mistakes in such operations range from merely being ineffective in the use of taxpayers' money, to loss of life by failing to identify and prevent terrorist actions. More structured ways of thinking have significant potential to enhance effective management of uncertainty resulting from cognitive bias. Nevertheless, with the always limited resources of investigating agencies, there is a trade-off between continuing to collect information that might lead to identifying more suspects and reveal more crimes, or focusing attention on those that are known. Here the police and security services tread a fine, difficult, and uncertain line.

References

Almond, L, Alison, L, Eyre, M, Crego, J & Goodwill, A 2008, 'Heuristics and biases in decision-making', in L Alison & J Crego (eds), *Policing critical incidents. Leadership and critical incident management*, Willan Publishing, Devon, pp. 151–180.

Ask, K & Granhag, PA 2005, 'Motivational sources of confirmation bias in criminal investigations: the need for cognitive closure', *Journal of Investigative Psychology and Offender Profiling*, vol. 2, no. 1, pp. 43–63.

Beauregard, E & Mieczkowski, T 2009, 'Testing the predictive utility of the STATIC-99: a Bayes analysis', *Legal and Criminological Psychology*, vol. 14, no. 2, pp. 187–200.

Billman, D, Convertino, G, Shrager, J, Massar, JP & Pirolli, P 2006, *Collaborative intelligence analysis with CACHE and its effects on information gathering and cognitive bias,* Human Computer Interaction Consortium Workshop, Snow Mountain, CO.

Central Intelligence Agency 2009, *A tradecraft primer: structured analytic techniques for improving intelligence analysis*, CIA, Washington DC.

Cheikes, BA, Brown, MJ, Lehner, PE, & Adelman L 2004, *Confirmation bias in complex analyses*, Technical report no. MTR 04B0000017, Mitre, Bedford, Massachusetts.

Clarke, MJ 2008, *Report of the inquiry into the case of Dr Mohammed Haneef: volume one*, Attorney-General's Department, Commonwealth of Australia, Canberra.

Cook, MB & Smallman, HS 2008, 'Human factors of the confirmation bias in intelligence analysis: decision support from graphical evidence landscapes', *Human Factors: The Journal of the Human Factors and Ergonomic Society*, vol. 50, no. 5, pp. 745–754.

Dean, G & Gottschalk, P 2007, Knowledge management in policing and law enforcement. Foundations, structures and applications, Oxford University Press, Oxford and NY.

Hammond, KR 2007, *Beyond rationality*, Oxford University Press, Oxford and NY.

Hawkins, SA & Hastie, R 1990, 'Hindsight: biased judgments of past events after the outcomes are known', *Psychological Bulletin*, vol. 107, no. 5, pp. 311–327.

Heuer Jr, RJ 1999, *Psychology of intelligence analysis*, Central Intelligence Agency, Government Printing Office, Washington D.C.

Intelligence and Security Committee 2009, *Could 7/7 have been prevented? Review of the intelligence on the London terrorist attacks on 7 July 2005,* Office of Public Sector Information, London.

Independent Police Complaints Commission 2007a, *IPCC independent investigations into complaints made following the Forest Gate Counter-Terrorism Operation on 2 June 2006*, Independent Police Complaints Commission, London.

Independent Police Complaints Commission 2007b, *Stockwell One. Investigation into the shooting of Jean Charles de Menezes at Stockwell underground station on 22 July 2005,* Independent Police Complaints Commission, London.

Klayman, J & Ha, Y-W 1987, 'Confirmation, disconfirmation, and information in hypothesis testing', *Psychological Review*, vol. 94, no. 2, pp. 211–228.

Leo, RA 2008, *Police interrogation and American justice*, Harvard University Press, Cambridge, MA.

Mears, DP & Bacon, S 2009, 'Improving criminal justice through better decision making: lessons from the medical system', *Journal of Criminal Justice*, vol. 37, no. 2, pp. 142–154.

Porter, L & Kebbell, MR 2009, 'Radicalisation in Australia: examining Australia's convicted terrorists', *ARC Centre of Excellence in Policing and Security (CEPS)*, issue no. 20, <http://ceps.edu.au/?q=Radicalisation-Australia-Examining-Australias-convicted-terrorists> <accessed 2 February 2010>.

Sjöstedt, G, & Långström, N 2001, 'Actuarial assessment of sex offender recidivism risk: a cross-validation of the RRASOR and the Static-99 in Sweden', *Law and Human Behavior*, vol. 25, no. 6, pp. 629–645.

Slovic, P, Fischoff, B & Lichenstein, S 1977, 'Behavioral decision theory', *Annual Review of Psychology*, vol. 28, pp. 1–39.

Tversky, A & Kahneman, D 1974 'Judgment under uncertainty: heuristics and biases', *Science*, vol. 185, no. 4517, pp. 1124–1131.

Wason, PC 1960, 'On the failure to eliminate hypotheses in a conceptual task', *Quarterly Journal of Experimental Psychology*, vol. 12, no. 3, pp. 129–140.

Wilson, TD & Brekke, N 1994, 'Mental contamination and mental correction: unwanted influences on judgments and evaluations', *Psychological Bulletin*, vol. 116, no. 1, pp. 117–142.

Zsambok, CE & Klein, GA (eds) 1997, *Naturalistic decision making*, Lawrence Earlbaum, Mahwah, NJ.

Insights from Adjunct Areas

Criminal Law
HON. TIM CARMODY SC

Introduction

The law is our most basic democratic institution. It is the standard operating environment for all regulatory and enforcement agencies. It dictates the who, what and why of civil and criminal liability and the how much, or quantum, of relief or punishment. In very broad terms the criminal law is a code or system of rules for social order and control based on prevailing moral values. Without it there would be anarchy and chaos. It creates and enforces mutually beneficial private and public rights and responsibilities. It is the sum of the mandatory restrictions accepted by a civilised state for controlling behaviour and determining relationships.

The source of all political power and judicial authority to make criminal or regulatory laws is the consent of the governed. Their compliance, however, is conditional on promised protection against harm being given and fundamental rights and liberties being respected. Bad laws fail to do one or the other of these. They inevitably lead to social unrest and eventually, civil disobedience. Revolutions usually have their beginnings in inequities in legal structures. Those with long law enforcement experience will know that whether or not people comply with the law depends on the kind of law they are expected to observe. If laws are unreasonable or ridiculous, then they will be treated with the contempt they deserve.

Clearly, social problems are not solved simply by passing more rules and regulations. Laws tend to be fixed and rigid. They either apply in a given case or they do not and are not easily modified to achieve a just, as distinct from strictly legal, result. A fairer alternative is needed to prevent hardship or even oppression, hence, the idea of justice. This is an abstract notion with a strong moral element. It is characterised by a sense of fairness, equality, evenness, openness, tolerance and balance. It is accessed by judges at their discretion when needed to not only do the right thing but to make sure the thing is done right.

The chief role of any criminal *justice* system is to prevent or penalise criminally offensive conduct. This is achieved by increasing the certainty of detection (actual or perceived) and imposing punishment severe enough to discourage others. Law enforcement agencies are responsible for the former while the courts deal with the latter. A characterising feature of the law, distinguishing it from a mere social convention, is enforcement. Breaking the law has to have consequences.

Both detection and imposing punishment have to be met consistently with traditional due process and procedural justice requirements. A person should walk free only if they are innocent and not because of some technicality or investigative deficiency. The blameless suspect, on the other hand, should never be bothered by unjustified official action or undeserved punishment. Furthermore, those who enforce the law must themselves respect it, including its hard won common law protections, even if they tend (or appear) to frustrate or defeat the fight against crime. This means that the balance between crime fighting and liberty is always in tension.

This balance is thrown into sharp relief when society seeks to prevent serious crime, such as by arresting suspected terrorists and I discuss this issue later in this chapter. I begin, however, by exploring a range of uncertainties that are widely applicable for imposing punishment across a range of serious crimes. First I deal with rule uncertainty and imprecision in the language of the law. I then move on to uncertainty in liability for punishment, uncertainty in court processes, the advantages and disadvantages of uncertainties associated with discretion and finally, luck. In the second part of the chapter I discuss legal issues associated with moving from punishment to prevention, elaborating on the possible impacts on freedom and liberties, as well as investigative power.

Rule uncertainty and imprecision in the language of the law

Criminal justice should be administered according to known rules properly interpreted. The law has an array of built-in mechanisms for removing interpretive doubts. The overriding function of a court interpreting statute is to ascertain and give effect to parliamentary intention and to do its best to attain the legislative objects. To achieve this, Acts are construed in line with fixed and universally accepted standards.

Once the purpose of legislation is clear, the judicial task—itself not always easy—is to give full force and effect to it, not to defeat or obstruct it. Courts also perform the important role of keeping the law in a serviceable state through an indispensible, ongoing process of reconsidering older principles to ensure that interpretation of the law is consistent with contemporary community values. Although fidelity to the law has a limiting influence on interpretation precedents, it is often ignored openly and correctly.

Despite built-in safeguards, so-called rule uncertainty or imprecision in the language of the law can be an instrument of injustice. Modern legislation is often complicated and hard for even the legally trained to understand and interpret. Words and phrases can have different meanings depending on the context and purpose. As J McHugh said in *Theophanous v. Herald and Weekly Times Ltd* (1994) 182 CLR 104 at 196:

> *The true meaning of a legal text almost always depends on a background of concepts, principles, practices, facts, rights and duties which the authors... took for granted or understood, without conscious advertence, by reason of their common language or culture.*

The English language is notoriously ambiguous and can often bear more than one meaning. Even using the same conventions for ascertaining meaning, experienced lawyers and judges disagree. Despite popular belief to the contrary, the law is not black or white but various shades of grey.

Uncertainty in liability for punishment

Being punished for socially bad or harmful actions depends solely on the notion of fault—a subjective mental element involving four recognised states of mind: intent, knowledge, recklessness and negligence. Knowledge of wrongness or, at the very least, heartless indifference as to the probable or possible outcome of action is required for a finding of criminal fault. Strict or absolute liability for offending behaviour irrespective of any state of mind is rare and generally found in public health, administration or safety contexts.

Yet these important states of mind cannot be proved directly or with absolute certainty. They can be admitted but otherwise can only be inferred from conduct. This involves unreliable behavioural interpretations and dubious social assumptions.

Uncertainty in court processes

The fundamental purpose of courts is to do justice according to law. This essentially includes applying the relevant law to proven facts. The most important function, of course, is ascertaining responsibility for and penalising crime-related wrongdoing. But criminal litigation is not a search for the truth. It is not about conclusiveness, but sufficiency.

In our adversarial tradition the alleging party is required to prove a contested charge by putting on so much supporting evidence so as to remove the protective veil of the presumption of innocence. The settled standard of proof is 'beyond reasonable doubt'. This is a formally undefined but well understood term. This is a lower degree of persuasion than certainty, but higher than probability and higher again than mere possibility. A precautionary principle is applied to guard against the applied greater social wrong of wrongful conviction.

Logic and reason apply but do not always rule or prevail. Decisions are often made based on unsubstantiated assumptions or received wisdom. For instance, as a general forensic rule, the unlikely is deemed to happen sometimes but not very often. Likewise, it is only when the likely is rejected that the improbable might be true (Young 1998). An allegation or case is not proved where the competing possibilities are of equal likelihood or the choice between them can only be resolved by conjecture. Thus, the more serious the allegation the surer the court needs to be before being satisfied of guilt. Grave suspicion or unsubstantiated but strong belief is insufficient.

The rules of evidence are designed to ensure fairness in the forensic process. Thus, irrelevant evidence is inadmissible. Exclusionary rules and discretions operate to reject overly prejudicial or insufficiently probative material for fear that it will give rise to impermissible lines of reasoning. For example, despite the logical relevance of a person's past misconduct to his culpability for subsequent similar conduct, the courts generally refuse admission because of the risk of misuse on the basis that past misconduct is not always the best predictor of future behaviour. Likewise, the sexual history of an alleged rape victim is not regarded as sufficiently relevant because it might distract from the issue of consent. Nevertheless, the rules of evidence can be applied differently, and sometimes unequally, due to the level of independence and discretionary scope judges have in procedural matters.

There are a range of other potential problems in court processes. Guilty people can look innocent and vice versa. Witnesses can be convincingly adamant about their own reliability, especially eye witnesses, and yet be completely mistaken as to identity. False witnesses can be almost impossible to spot or irresistibly charming. Science has clearly shown that body language or demeanour as indicators of the truth are overrated. For some witnesses lying is almost an art. Others tell the truth unconvincingly. Apparently neutral testimony can have an undeclared bias.

Not all relevant and probative information is automatically received. Faith in the veracity of those responsible for the enforcement of the law can be misplaced. For example, fabricated confessions or 'verballing' was a widespread police practice in the 1970s and 1980s.

Juries are also a source of unpredictability. Jury reasoning is totally protected from disclosure. Thus there is no way of forecasting how different juries will view the same set of facts or ascertaining the basis on which their decision was made.

In most property cases juries are asked to consider whether someone has behaved dishonestly, according to the standards of decent, honest members of the community. Strangely, however, research shows that there is no consensus in our society about what honesty is. A study by Drs Emily Finch and Stefan Fafinski of Brunel University found that women are more likely than men to see ethically dubious actions as dishonest but are less inclined than their male counterparts to convict a person charged with these actions. The research challenges the law's assumption that the majority of people hold the same views about what conduct is dishonest and found that there was a great deal of disagreement even in very basic situations. For example, 92% of women thought that it was dishonest to make an insurance claim for pre-existing damage to a car, compared with 85% of men. Only 47% of women, however, would be prepared to convict somebody of fraud on this basis compared with 55% of men. Age has an equally strong influence on perceptions of dishonesty. Older people take a tougher line. Finally, people are less likely to consider an action dishonest if they have done it themselves. Thus, under the present system, two defendants charged with the same crime may stand different chances of being convicted according to the sex and age profile of the jury and whether any juror has committed any similar acts themselves (Henderson 2009).

Peer pressure in the jury room can also influence people to change pre-existing strongly held views. In addition, in a climate of fear, unsatisfactory evidence can be given greater weight than it deserves for the sake of community protection.

Discretion

The competing and often conflicting concurrent demands of individual justice and the public interest in denunciation, protection and deterrence can create real dilemmas for judges. Although there are established ranges based on comparable precedents, no two cases are the same. People's personal circumstances can vary infinitely even when their offences are broadly similar. While many important areas of the law involve discretionary and, therefore uncertain, decision-making, criminal sentencing is one of the most common.

Discretion is the technique for contextualising legal decisions in a way which experience reveals is impossible by the use of rules alone (Evans 2001). It enables non-rule based decisions to be made within a rational framework. Its main virtue is its potential to produce morally sensitive and nuanced decisions in mediating between competing values and interests. There is a risk of serious injustice in preferring precedent to principle. Judges must not be prevented from doing justice in a particular case because of too strict adherence to precedent or legislative 'straight jacket' which leaves them with no fairer alternative.

The uncertainty associated with discretion has both positive and negative aspects. The positive effects are that a judge's sense of the moral answer to a question or to the justice of a cause has been one of the great shaping forces of the common law (*McFarlane v. Bayside Heath Board* (2002) 2 AC 59 at 85). Examples include the discussion by *Brennan J* in *Mabo v. The Queen (No.2)* (1991) 175 CLR 1 at 42 where the value of non-discriminatory treatment of indigenous interests influenced the majority conclusion that the extinguishment of rights based on social policy had no place in the contemporary law of Australia, even though it had not been previously recognised in the cases or statute. Another example is provided by *The Queen v. L* (1991) 174 CLR 379 where the High Court held that older authorities did not establish that marriage involved the irrevocable consent of the wife to sexual intercourse at the will of the husband. The majority considered that even if that proposition was supported by previous authority it could not longer be accepted because it is '…so out of keeping with the view that society now takes of the relationship between the parties to a marriage'. These cases demonstrate sound discretion guided by laws. Discretion must be governed by rule not humour, it must not be arbitrary, vague and fanciful, but legal and regular. It is not merely a matter of individual opinion. The objective fairness of an order is still assessable by reference to the judicial method.

Nevertheless, discretion can be inconsistent, confused and divergent. One of its most negative features is an increased scope for decision-makers to fall into error. It can also permit a judge to substitute his or her own personal standards rather than give effect to legal policy or legal value. In reality all discretionary decisions are laden with latent or undeclared attitudes or beliefs about social facts, values and trends. Judges are always making contestable choices between competing considerations and conflicting interests. There are core relationship values deeply imbedded so as to be almost merged with the organising concepts and principles used by the law to resolve disputes. Some are so obvious that they can be safely assumed to be taken for granted by everyone. In respect of others there is plenty of room for rational differences between honest and informed minds. Of course it does not follow that decisions or approaches which do not have a high level of community support must be wrong.

There is a strong presumption in favour of the correctness of discretionary decisions and conclusions, which adds a degree of certainty. Appeals against discretionary judgment can only properly succeed if founded on the application of wrong principle, mistaken facts or if significantly relevant factors were not taken into account. Otherwise, even a questionable discretion-based decision is immune from alteration even if a majority disagree with it.

Luck

Like all other human institutions criminal litigation is also at the mercy of luck. Neither greater knowledge nor superior skill guarantees success in every case. Nor does better preparation. Merits do not always prevail. Good cases are routinely beaten by weaker ones due to the unexpected or unanticipated, better legal representation or presentation, false but credible witnesses or documents, court or jury error, and bad tactical advice or strategic choices.

Not only are outcomes in the criminal arena uncertain; they are not even reasonably or rationally predictable. This is because the law is vague, ambiguous, internally inconsistent and lacking in clarity. It is imprecise, inexact, indefinite and liable to cynical manipulation and distortion giving rise to judicial divergence and dissent and deep confusion within the profession. Only in the legal realm, for instance, could you find a statement of allegation worded like this:

> *On an unknown date* [or should that be a date unknown?] *(the accused) murdered (the victim) at Brisbane or elsewhere in the State of Queensland.*

Then there are problems connected with unproved, unprovable, improbable or unknown facts and circumstances. Despite the inconvenience of these uncertainties there has been little interest or research into the notion of reducing levels of doubt in the law. This may be because the controlling doctrine of precedent, which requires identity of outcomes in cases that are relevantly the same, sees consistency, not certainty, as the key performance indicator. Or it may equally reflect resigned acceptance of the law's susceptibly to cynical manipulation by or on behalf of vested interest. Alternatively it might simply be due to the ongoing process of rejection and replacement of long standing values or ideals with new ones to keep pace with changing social conditions.

Future fears—moving from punishment to prevention

Harvard law professor and well known human rights activist, Alan Dershowitz, suggests shifting from punishing proven past wrongs to trying to prevent likely future harms, because the classic theory of deterrence is inapplicable in religious- or politically-based fanaticism. He suggests that pre-emption is not necessarily inconsistent with democratic ideals and argues prevention is the most efficient, effective and, in some cases the only, practical method of detecting and dealing with dangerousness. Nevertheless, the potential forensic value of pre-emption often tends to conceal the very real threat it represents to basic criminal process rights and democratic protections, including the freedom of speech and association, the right to liberty, reputation, privacy and personal security.

The problem with this thinking is that the prediction of possible future harm depends on drawing and acting on rational inferences drawn from past or existing facts. Evidence or information suggestive of the risk of something happening in the future because it might have happened in the past may be very useful in a law enforcement setting, but usually has no place in the court room. The issue for the law is whether or not a specific alleged event has in fact occurred. Very often for law enforcers it is whether something that has happened might happen again or whether something that might or might not have happened might happen again or for the very first time (Hirst 2005). However, the probability and gravity of assessed future crime does not justify depriving suspects of their liberty or denying them the same freedoms which their anticipated actions refuse their victims.

Nevertheless, there are examples of a risk assessment approach by the courts in a different context. In *Minister for Immigration and Ethnic Affairs v Pochi* (1980) 31 ALR 666 the issue was whether a long-term non-citizen resident of Australia with a minor drug conviction should be deported to his country of origin under migration laws in the national interest because of suspected involvement in the illicit drug trade. The decision was not governed by the criminal rules of evidence but was subject to procedural fairness constraints. This is also a good example of where uncertainty can give rise to judicial dissent, which is itself a cause of uncertainty in the law but is not without its own utility. Two members of the court held that, as a matter of law, conduct could not support a deportation order unless it was established as a probability. Suspected but unproved conduct should be excluded from the decision-making process. However, the minority judge held that suspected but unproven misconduct was sufficient when making determinations about the national interest and community risk. His Honour found that there was nothing contrary to the principles of natural justice or logic in placing real suspicion based on proven facts and to assessing its significance as part of the totality of the relevant matters in protecting the national interest and predicting future risks.

In other words, evaluating chance cannot be reduced to a scientific formula. It is not a determination about what will happen based on what has or might have happened in the past. Rather it is an informed opinion or discretionary judgment based on possibilities rather than probabilities. Probable previous offending can sustain a 'possible risk in the future' finding or alternatively possible past behaviour may support a 'probable future risk' finding.

Future risk is not capable of definite or scientific proof. It is founded on assumptions, conjecture, intuition, belief, suspicion and even guesswork. It is a forecast of 'what might be' based on 'what might have been' and other omens. The same body of evidence may produce two equally rational and reasonable but opposing conclusions, neither of which is exactly right or wholly wrong. It may rest on a lingering doubt or, to put it another way, an alleged but unproven, or possible not probable or conclusive, fact. Even doubt itself may be an indicator of future risk. The inability to know for sure may support a conclusion that there is a real risk not worth taking.

Freedom and liberties

Australia is a liberal democracy founded on common law principles and precedents (*R v The Secretary of State for Home Department; Ex Parte Pierson* [1998] AC 539 at 587) inherited on settlement from England. Government power and political authority is derived from the consent of the governed. Compliance with enacted laws is exchanged for and conditional on guaranteed protection against harm and the freedom of living without fear. A little liberty is sacrificed for larger advantages.

Everyone is subject to the law regardless of their wealth or power. The so-called rule of law is democracy's answer to the divine right of Kings. However, everyone also has a degree of 'inviolability' that even the welfare of society as a whole cannot override. Invasion of this space, even in the name of the law, is a wrong that cannot be made right, even by a greater good enjoyed by many.

The freedoms in this realm are deeply rooted in history and tradition and they are enjoyed by citizens conferred or recognised by the law and respected by the state under the terms of the social contract. Civil liberties differ from human rights which are the prerogative of citizens and non-citizens alike regardless of race or nationality. Their practical content was worked out over the centuries on a case by case basis by judges as a shield from official abuse and a safeguard against oppression of the weak by the strong. The practical operation of the law is subject to their observance.

Each is aimed at avoiding miscarriages of justice stemming from the enforcement of the criminal law and making officials exercising public discretionary power fully accountable for their actions. They exist because while laws are necessary they are insufficient on their own for a fair and just society. In this way society itself retains paramount authority, not those who make or enforce the law. Included in their ranks are all the implied criminal justice protections such as those against arbitrary search, arrest and detention, the right to a fair and speedy trial, the right of silence and privilege against self-incrimination without forensic disadvantage, trial by jury, proof beyond reasonable doubt and access to appellate review.

According to John Rawls (2005, p. 3) these fundamental civil liberties are uncompromising. None can be surrendered or diminished except and only to the extent needed to avoid an even greater injustice. The relevant concept of fairness is continually redefining itself to take account of changing circumstances so as to bring it into line with contemporary standards and values. However, being sourced solely in precedent and not constitutionally guaranteed, they are not strictly enforceable as legal rights. Thus, the judges remain their sole legal guardians. The presumption against unjustified modification of established implied common law freedoms was recently given practical expression by the Full Court of the Federal Court in *Minister for Immigration & Citizenship v. Haneef* (2007) 163 FCR 414.

Investigative power

In 2005, federal anti-terror legislation authorised administrative (i.e. non-judicial) preventative detention and incommunicado confinement of unconvicted terrorist suspects for the purposes of interrogation or preventing imminent attack. This 'better safe than sorry' attitude ignores a case by case analysis of the social costs and benefit of the loss of rights.

Despite fundamental common law-based objections, executive detention of terror suspects is now a common anti-terror measure. In what has become known as the terror age, there is a temptation to trade protection for freedom and to compromise traditional values. Extraordinary rendition and the euphemistic 'enhanced interrogative techniques' to procure intelligence or evidence are controversial examples. Though neither is justified in the civilised world, both have been widely practiced or condoned by western democracies in the last decade. Our common commitment to the rule of law and universal human rights were all suspended during this time. We forgot the answer to the question: what is wrong with torturing terrorists who would readily do the same to us if they could?

While an arguable case for permissible levels of pressure in questioning extremely dangerous suspects can be made, the war on terror, like the war on drugs, cannot be won by violating dignity, democracy and legality. By definition 'major crime' covers offending that is serious although not organised, and of significance to the community, requiring special investigative expertise or power. Such crimes include serial gangland-style killings, terrorist attacks, bomb threats, extortion and other threats to national security. However, we currently have no morally or legally effective way of deterring religious extremists or ideologues willing to die for their cause on the promise of rewards in the afterlife that cannot be matched in this one.

If extremism is not the answer to extremism, then how should an effective criminal justice system in a modern civilised world react within appropriate limits to those posing serious danger? When ordinary law enforcement powers and methods are rightly or wrongly seen as inadequate protection against crime, there are inevitable calls for tougher than usual responses. Desperate times are said to justify drastic measures. People have a right to feel safe and secure in their homes and homeland. The question is what action can, or should, a civilised country like Australia take to achieve this legitimate aim without drifting too far from its moral and legal moorings? Preventative detention as a social protection and control mechanism is an option. However, indefinite non-conviction-based detention should be used sparingly and only in clear cases— that is, where there is an unacceptable risk of future dangerousness.

The crime commissions set up at state and federal level in the 1990s to investigate and prevent the spread of organised and major crime in this country have a swag of unusually wide and far-reaching powers for investigation to aid them in discharging their important statutory duties. The most intrusive and controversial are their coercive capacities in conducting secret compulsory hearings involving inquisitorial rather than adversarial procedures, such as interrogation on oath without the traditional protection of the privilege against self-incrimination or right to silence.

Inquisitorial procedures (other than torture) can no doubt be justified when they produce more social good than harm. However, the use of coercive power has definite limits in the democratic criminal domain. The truth should not be pursued 'by any means' or at all costs, without moderation (*Whitehorn v. R* (1983) 71 A. Crim. R. 107 at 125). Truth, like all other good things, may be loved unwisely, pursued too keenly and cost too much (*Pearse v. Pearse* (1846) 63 ER 950 at 957).

Anti-terrorism measures and investigative hearings powers weaken the protection traditionally afforded by the common law to liberty of the individual and reflect a change in social values by favouring the administration of justice over human freedom and dignity. The hearing's powers should not be used routinely or be available in every justifiable case. They should be resorted to only when absolutely necessary for fear of destroying the very values said to be protected.

Nevertheless, the safeguards against over-exuberant use of the investigative hearings powers, including judicial review, are largely inadequate and fall well short of the strict judicial controls recommended. For example, the use of police brutality to elicit information about crime, as long as it was not used in court as evidence of guilt in criminal proceedings, is not technically a violation of the right to silence. The law steps in only to exclude the fruit of the poison tree from evidence, not to stop cruelty in interrogations. There is no constitutional guarantee against the use of torture to obtain involuntary confessions per se, only about their admissibility.

The mandatory principles of the common law would exclude an involuntary confession obtained by torture as not only unfair and contrary to acceptable standards of human decency but also unjust and unreliable (cf. *A & Ors v. Secretary of State* [2004] EWCA Civ 1123). There is also discretionary judicial power to reject illegal or improperly obtained evidence as a matter of public policy.

Conclusion

Uncertainties in the legal process and in policing serious crime intersect in important ways. Uncertainties commonly found when the law responds to serious crime—like rule uncertainty and discretion—can impact on the ultimate success of policing efforts.

In preventing and penalising such crimes of increasing community concern as terrorism, we must seek to prevent legal uncertainties from undermining the inherent values on which our legal system is based and ensure that judicial discretion continues to be available to deliver just outcomes in situations in which the law might otherwise operate to unjustifiably harsh effect.

Our approach to these emerging threats must necessarily continue to respect civil liberties and individual freedoms and uphold our society's fundamental tenets of democratic government and the rule of law. It is imperative that the response of policing and legal systems is subject to close scrutiny and that relevant policy is informed by political and public debate.

References

Dershowitz, AM 2006, *Preemption: a knife that cuts both ways*, WW Norton, New York.

Evans, S 2001, 'Defending discretionary remedialism', *Sydney Law Review*, vol. 23, no. 4, pp. 463–482.

Henderson, M 2009, 'Jurors find it hard to tell right from wrong, says study', *The Times*, 7 September, <http://business.timesonline.co.uk/tol/business/law/article6823915.ece> (accessed 19 January 2010).

Hirst, J 2005, '"Kangaroo Court": Family law in Australia', *The Quarterly Essay*, no. 17, p. 38.

Rawls, J 1999, *The theory of justice*, revised edn, Harvard University Press, Cambridge, MA.

Young, PW 1998, 'Practical evidence', *Australian Law Journal*, vol. 72, p. 21.

Politics
HON. CARMEN LAWRENCE

Introduction

Policing *is* highly political. What is defined as crime in legislation and how crimes are depicted are essentially political decisions. Similarly, the priority given to the detection and prosecution of various crimes and the resources devoted to those tasks are dependent on the perceptions that politicians and their advisers have of the risks to the public—and to their own political futures—posed by those crimes. These assessments are not necessarily dispassionate appraisals of the actual risks posed and can be seriously distorted by moral panics and fear campaigns.

I canvass the key issues in the psychology of uncertainty and risk assessment as a prelude to exploring the ways in which fear can be manufactured out of uncertainty and how this relates to the politicisation of crime.

Politics and uncertainty

Since we cannot see around the bend of time, except in our imaginations, uncertainty is inherent in everything we do; it pervades the mundane and the extraordinary, the personal and the political. Intrinsic to our psychology are strategies to deal with this uncertainty, since our survival depends on being able to reasonably anticipate what will happen next—to predict the actions of others in a changing environment and to make reasonably accurate judgments about the likely effects of our own actions. We cannot know at any moment precisely what the next will look like, although much of the time our predictions about what to expect are reasonably accurate.

The rest of the time, especially when we step outside the routines of daily life, our ability to anticipate events is less than perfect, particularly when we try to understand and foresee events well into the future. As Downs (1957, cited in Burden 2003, p. 7) has said, 'uncertainty is so basic to human life that it influences the structure of every social institution', and that includes political institutions. Some of those institutions are built to reduce uncertainty (e.g. bureaus of meteorology); others to reduce the impact of future destructive, unavoidable events (e.g. insurance).

The decisions of politics, whether they are about which policies are likely to produce desired outcomes or which political messages will appeal to voters, really amount to a series of experiments, conducted without a very substantial evidence base. They are experiments in which the 'stimuli' are generally more ambiguous than they are in our daily lives and over which we have even less control. Let us compare the personal decisions we make in buying a car, with those governments make in buying defence equipment, for example.

Generally speaking, the more information we have, the more confident we are that our expectations about the future are accurate; uncertainty is lessened. We take for granted the volume of evidence we have at our fingertips when making a decision, for example, like buying a new car. In that case we generally use a combination of our own driving experience, comparative advertising, motoring reviews, and word of mouth testimony from friends and colleagues. We may also convince ourselves that, in making our decision, we are logically assessing possible choices against carefully selected criteria, including price, comfort, fuel consumption, safety, resale value, appearance and speed. On the other hand, choosing defence equipment for a nation is of an entirely different order. As has been shown several times in recent Australian history, only a few military experts have the requisite knowledge for such a task and even they are constrained by the reality that the performance of new weaponry and equipment is uncertain and cost-benefit comparisons are difficult because of a lack of precise information. Mistakes are almost inevitable. And politicians like to avoid making mistakes—or at least, being seen to make mistakes.

It is uncertainty that makes political decisions something of a lottery and one of the reasons that politics is so challenging. As one observer put it, 'the necessity of decision-making makes uncertainty important…the ubiquity of uncertainty in decision making makes choosing difficult' (Burden 2003, p. 6). It is my experience that politicians and those associated with the political process become activists precisely because they are strongly motivated to reduce uncertainty through problem-solving.

With uncertainty comes risk; the risk of making the wrong projections, of missing important and even critical developments; the risk of misreading the unfolding landscape and implementing policies which have unlooked for or even harmful effects. One of the problems is that we humans make significant mistakes in trying to predict the likelihood that certain risky events will occur and, therefore, in designing strategies to mitigate risk commensurate with the actual risk posed. For example, while we can make probabilistic statements about the likely state of the world economy in 2020, nobody really knows what will be happening then or what policy makers will be doing in response. Just as almost no one in the game of economic prognosis saw the 2008–09 global financial crisis coming. And no one really comments on this failure.

Risk perception

As risk analyst Bruce Schneier (2008) has pointed out, our problem is that our brains evolved to handle 'the sorts of risk management decisions endemic to living in small family groups in the East African highlands in 100,000 BC', and not to living in modern societies. 'We make systematic risk management mistakes – miscalculating the probability of rare events, reacting more to stories than data, responding to the feeling of security rather than reality, and making decisions based on irrelevant context.'

There is now a substantial literature on the psychology of risk perception which needs to be taken into account in any analysis of uncertainty; it applies as much to politicians and policy makers as to anyone else. It exposes the systematic errors of reasoning which make it difficult for us to behave entirely rationally in the face of uncertainty. Perceptions of risk are influenced by emotion as much as by more analytic processes and depend, at least, in part on learned associations. For example, fear—arguably the most powerful of our emotions—is a genetically programmed, natural response to being threatened. But we also learn what to fear and can be conditioned by association to respond fearfully to events that are not, in themselves, dangerous, or not as dangerous as our reactions might suggest.

The analytic processes of risk assessment, while governed by more logical processes, are also susceptible to errors of reasoning which result from systematic biases and the employment of various rules of thumb (heuristics; see also the chapter by Mark Kebbell, Damon Muller and Kirsty Martin 2010). Our actuarial skills are pretty fast—but imprecise. In seeking to explain why people exaggerate or underestimate risks, researchers have examined how we employ these 'rules of thumb' to enable us to make decisions with reasonable economy and to make sense of our environment; they have measured how they influence the way we judge and respond to what is going on around us.

For example, if we can easily remember or have vivid images of certain events (availability), we will judge them as more of a risk than others for which we lack such images—a particular problem when judging the likelihood of being a crime victim, since our media are saturated with images of high impact, low frequency crimes. Because the media give prominence to the most horrific incidents of murder and rape, the public come to believe that these rare events are much more common than they are. This tendency is amplified by the use of devices like 'crime clocks' which calculate the number of rapes or murders per minute, taking no account of population changes.

One study showed that when people were asked about an illness which was 'becoming increasingly prevalent' they were more likely to believe that they would get the disease when the symptoms described were concrete and easy to imagine (Sherman et al. 1985). Events that could affect us, which we can readily imagine and which occur in the near future, are judged more risky.

When strong emotions are involved, people are inclined to ignore the fact that an event is highly unlikely. Again empirical research illustrates this phenomenon. In one study (Sunstein 2002), people were asked how much they would pay to eliminate cancer risks ranging from one in a million to one in 100,000. Some of the participants were given descriptions of the cancer as gruesome and intensely painful. The statistical risk mattered less than the vividness of the description in influencing the payment they were willing to make.

Research in a variety of settings also confirms the human tendency to discount the future: we generally prefer to take actions which confer lesser benefits now than those which give us greater benefits in the future. This attribute is obviously pertinent when trying to persuade people to take preventive action which may not have immediate rewards. Given the added influence of short electoral cycles, it is not surprising that we often see such discounting at play in policy decisions. Discounting is greatest when the future is distant and uncertain and when intergenerational distribution is involved, as it is with crime prevention, for example.

Of particular relevance here, is the fact that numerous studies in a variety of settings show that the way an issue is framed can markedly influence how people judge risk and what they are prepared to do to avoid that risk. For instance, investigations of people's reactions to the risks from various medical procedures, show that people react very differently to the information that 'ninety in one hundred are alive' than to the statement that 'ten in one hundred are dead'. In the former case they are more willing to undergo the procedure; in the latter case, they will not—the word 'dead' appears to have a special power! And physicians are equally prone to the error (Slovic 2000).

The power of fear

Uncertainty is fraught with emotional meaning and easily morphs into fearfulness. Our times have often been described as 'fearful' (Siegel 2005). Select any day's newspaper and TV headlines and it is clear that fear is pumped into our homes and workplaces every day. The media are saturated with apocalyptic warnings about crime, drugs, exotic diseases, global financial crises, threats to our way of life. The media exaggerate the risks we actually face and clamour for an instant response, especially from government, to threats that may never materialise. Health and crime risks in particular are often distorted. And politicians often join in.

In reality, the developed world has never been safer. Life expectancy in Australia is 40% longer in 2000 than it was in 1900. Childhood mortality has declined dramatically. We are better able to prevent and cure diseases than at any time in our history. Civil strife is rare and the murder rate is low by international standards and unchanged for over a century. We actually confront fewer threats to our safety than our grandparents did. There *are* serious threats to our planet—think climate change and pollution—but, interestingly, these appear to have far less traction than the threat of terrorism which actually poses a vanishingly small risk to the average person in the developed world.

Yet people often behave as if their lives were becoming more and more dangerous necessitating greater protection by the state; they personalise rather than calculate objective risks, exaggerating their vulnerability—frightened of their children being abducted if they step outside the front door; spending a small fortune on locks and alarms; allowing basic freedoms to be eroded because of the fear of terrorism and accepting accelerating intrusions into their privacy.

And some politicians are unable to resist using such fear as a political tactic. Historically, politicians of all persuasions have used fear as a technique for 'stampeding' citizens into supporting them and their policies. As HL Mencken (1922) once put it:

> *The whole aim of practical politics is to keep the populace alarmed (and hence clamorous to be led to safety) by menacing it with an endless series of hobgoblins, all of them imaginary.*

While, I would not go that far, more than a few of our leaders appear to have endorsed Hobbes' view that having control over human fears is a precondition for holding power; that we must place our trust in strong leaders to deliver us from insecurity, or otherwise face violence and social chaos devoid of human cooperation (Hobbes 2007). There are many politicians who are quick to alarm people about dangers they are unlikely ever to confront, seizing any opportunity to portray themselves as protectors.

Penal populism

The last few decades have seen a sustained fear campaign on law and order, with the result that people now have wildly exaggerated perceptions of the risks of assault, murder, child abuse and robbery. Inevitably, this campaign has distorted law and justice policies and misdirected public expenditure (Garland 2001).

Politicians and media populists are expert in using fear to exercise control and ratchet up their approval ratings. And big sections of the community have responded. What may have initially been justified as a response to public opinion, comes to shape it. The evocation of such fear appears to serve the two ends: as a means for political leaders to pursue specific political goals and as a threat to those who appear to challenge their power and status. In either case, the use of such fear may represent an intentional strategy to exploit public anxiety about crime and cultivate public resentment toward offenders or it may be a response to what is assumed to be public opinion—'doing what the community wants'.

Politicians often face a dilemma—you either promise what people want, even when their fears are not well based, and get yourself elected, or promise them what they really need, and start looking for a new job. Peter Schieder, President of the Parliamentary Assembly of the Council of Europe argued in 2003: 'it is the nature of the reaction (to fear in the community) that distinguishes a true representative of the people from a populist manipulator' (Schieder 2003).

These campaigns can seriously warp public policy priorities. Criminal justice budgets are growing at the expense of other public expenditure that could make a difference to crime rates. It is obvious that scaring people about the risk of them becoming the victims of crime will make them clamour for more and better resources for law enforcement agencies rather than for policies which might reduce crime in the long run.

Crime is one of those topics, as Altheide (2003) observes, where the repeated association with fear eventually means that simply to mention crime is to elicit fear. The fear is not just of the criminal acts—rape, murder, assault, burglary—but of social disintegration. Crime fear messages often carry the inference that 'enemies within' are intent on undermining our way of life.

The constant use of fear in communication about crime is part of a wider practice which pervades much popular culture and political debate. Fear and threat are pervasive elements in our entertainment and in the messages that shape our daily lives. Uncertainty and risk have become emotionally loaded terms. Research in the US has shown that the use of fear in the news media—in headlines and text—nearly doubled over the 20 years to 1994 (Altheide 2003).

Similar data from Australia have not, as far as I can discern, been collected. However, there are times when news bulletins appear to consist of nothing but crime stories. Under this sort of barrage, we develop the expectation that crime is a normal part of our lives. As Ferarro (1995) suggests, the major impact of the discourse of fear is to cultivate a sense of disorder and a belief that 'things are out of control'. Terror Management Theory (Pyszczynski 2004) tells us that when people believe they are being threatened, their disposition toward others becomes more hostile and they are more likely to see themselves as victims.

Since at least the mid 1980s, law and order politics (including 'the war on terror') have played a leading role in elections in Australia. Over time, the two major parties have converged on the position that we are under siege from burgeoning crime, that much more needs to done to combat crime and that the best remedies for dealing with crime are to employ more police, arm them with greater powers and punish offenders more harshly. This formula is not unique to Australia and has been embraced in varying degrees by much of the developed world. It has also been singularly ineffective.

What is going on here?

We cannot be entirely certain, but what we do know is that these 'tough on crime' policies are not a response to an escalating crime problem and cannot be justified by appealing to public attitudes toward punishment, which are not as enthusiastic as some of the 'shock jocks' (i.e. radio announcers who espouse extreme inflammatory views) would have us believe (Roberts et al. 2003). It is much more about ideology and political opportunism.

As Nicholas Cowdery (2002) put it:

> *Law and order is an easy thing for politicians to push. It makes them sound tough (and sounding tough is attractive to those voters who live in fear of crime and in ignorance of the causes and proper control of crime); it makes them sound powerful – as if they actually have the power to do something about crime; it is easy – it requires no detailed research, analysis, planning or even thought; it is instantaneous; and it is comparatively cheap.*
>
> *None of that makes it right; or even responsible politics. There are very few lasting benefits of such an approach - and a lot of costs not necessarily confined to dollars.*

As a result, it is rare today to hear statements about crime which attempt to unpick the power and resource differentials which are at play in the development of ideas about crime and the construction of criminal careers. It is deeply unfashionable, for example, to even speculate that the way we respond to crime may have as much to do with our conceptions of society as with the individual characteristics of the person who ends up in gaol. Yet, there is a very neat fit between the assumption that social position is entirely the result of a person's own effort and endeavour and the view that crime is the result of individual pathology.

By stripping crime of its social and economic context, such as race, poverty, mental illness and powerlessness, crime becomes a matter of perverse, individual 'choice'; it also becomes less amenable to understanding. And what you cannot understand is likely to make you afraid. Ignorant people are more susceptible to fear campaigns which promise to protect them from malevolent forces.

No recent government in Australia has been exempt from the charge of exploiting the community's fears about crime and all levels of government have attempted to exploit such fear for political advantage. For example, in the lead up to the 1998 election, the then Prime Minister raised the law and order issue (usually the province of the states), calling for harsher punishments and accusing judges of being 'soft' on crime. In New South Wales, former Premier Carr adopted a punitive rhetoric saying, amongst other things that drug traffickers would 'die in jail'. It has also become commonplace for politicians to line up at press conferences with senior police at their sides, presumably to give them—the politicians that is—greater credibility.

Over the last decade or more, a veritable fever of penal 'reform' gripped the state governments, usually in the heat of election 'auctions' designed to demonstrate that the purveyors of the policies were definitely not 'soft' on crime. Ministers under attack from the Opposition or vocal critics appeared to believe they had no option but to 'talk tough'; that unless they made compromises to 'penal populism' (Roberts et al. 2003), they would lose power and, with it, the chance to make beneficial changes to the system.

Bizarrely, even those in government have 'run against the state', alleging that judges, magistrates and parole boards are too lenient and that the existing laws are inadequate to deal with 'burgeoning' crime. This may have contributed to a worrying lack of public confidence in the courts and the legal system (Indermaur & Roberts 2005). Inevitably, in pushing for a more vengeful and punitive approach to lawbreaking, 'law and order' politicians also pit themselves against criminologists and social scientists who advocate a more nuanced and analytical approach to law and justice.

The key elements of the construction of a 'crime wave' appear to be: a sustained scare campaign by the media targeting marginalised 'others'; an hysterical public (and Opposition) response; a tragic trigger event and panic by the political leaders resulting in ineffective and even counterproductive legislation.

We saw many of these characteristics on show when the Northern Territory 'intervention' was announced (Lawrence 2008). The focus quickly shifted from child abuse, most of which occurs within families, to the responsible Minister's claims that 'paedophile rings' were operating in the Northern Territory. Such a fear slotted neatly into one of our society's currently exaggerated fears: the risk to our children of being abused (and abducted) by paedophiles. A subsequent investigation by the Australian Crime Commission found no evidence of organised paedophilia in Northern Territory indigenous communities (McKenzie 2009). The Minister's overreaction led to public alarm and the conduct of an 18-month multimillion-dollar investigation which diverted energy and resources from the Commission's specialised task of dealing with organised crime.

Because several cases before the courts were compromised by public panic, some members of the legal profession felt compelled to warn that if politicians and the media did not stop interfering in court cases involving paedophiles, more cases would be dropped and criminals would walk free. In fact, a Brisbane judge dismissed charges against a notorious paedophile partly on account of intense publicity which he said prevented a fair trial. The hysteria surrounding that decision saw a Queensland magistrate suppress the name of a man on child pornography charges a few days later for fear of a similar media frenzy (*The World Today* 2008). Such moral panics do not serve the community—or law enforcement—well.

As well as its directly distorting effects on criminal justice policy, disproportionate fear of crime causes great distress and harm to many in the community. Excessive fear may lead people to so constrain their lives that it may be said that it effectively imprisons them (House Standing Committee on Legal and Constitutional Affairs 2004); they withdraw from the community, curtailing their exposure to what they regard as risky environments. Older women are particularly likely to stay at home, avoid public transport and spend large sums on security measures. The tragedy is as people's daily lives become more 'armoured', the more the sense of threat and disorder is reinforced.

Another result of nearly two decades of unrelenting 'law and order' campaigns is that we are far too ready to gaol people rather than to seek other forms of sentencing. Too many politicians have been seduced into implementing costly and ineffective policies; they have enacted policies which are based primarily on their anticipated popularity rather than their effectiveness. We are, as a result, in the grip of a 'penal arms race', with each party offering tougher and tougher measures and little discernible public or political opposition to inflated criminal justice spending or to increasingly punitive sanctions.

There is substantial evidence, here and elsewhere, that prison, rather than reducing the chance of re-offending, actually makes it more likely. Conversely, community based sentences result in lower re-conviction rates. A review by the Canadian Solicitor General's office of 111 studies which looked at the relationship between various punishments and repeat offending concluded that 'harsher criminal justice sanctions had no deterrent effects on recidivism' and that 'compared to community sanctions, imprisonment was associated with an *increase* in recidivism'. Furthermore, the longer the sentence, the more likely the prisoner was to re-offend. He concluded that 'criminal justice policies that are based on the belief that "getting tough" on crime will reduce recidivism are without empirical support' (Public Safety Canada 2002).

Conclusion

At a time when it appears that conventional political ideologies fail to inspire, politicians appear to have succumbed to the temptation to employ the politics of fear as a way of buttressing their power and authority. The apparent expectation is that the desire for security will substitute for other more expansive political aspirations which might guide public policy.

This chapter draws on and updates a more extensive treatment of this topic in presentations made as the Fourth Freilich Foundation Eminent Lecturer in 2005, see http://www.anu.edu.au/hrc/freilich/events/archive/lawerence/lawrence.php

References

Altheide, DL 2003, 'Notes towards a politics of fear', *Journal for Crime, Conflict and the Media*, vol. 1, no. 1, pp. 37–54.

Burden, BC 2003, 'Introduction: everything but death and taxes: uncertainty in American politics', in BC Burden (ed.), *Uncertainty in American politics*, Cambridge University Press, UK, pp. 3–24.

Cowdery, N 2002, 'Tabloids and talkback have mugged sensible crime debate', *The Age*, 3 October, <http://australianpolitics.com/words/daily/archives/00000075.shtml> (accessed 26 January 2010).

Ferraro, K 1995, *Fear of crime: interpreting victimization risk,* State University Press, Albany, NY.

Garland, D 2001, *The culture of control: crime and social order in contemporary society,* Oxford University Press, Oxford.

Hobbes, T 2007 (1651), *Leviathan*, web edn, ebooks@Adelaide, Australia, <http://etext.library.adelaide.edu.au/h/hobbes/thomas/h68l/complete.html> (accessed 22 January 2010).

House Standing Committee on Legal and Constitutional Affairs 2004, *Report of the inquiry into crime in the community: victims, offenders, and fear of crime*, August, Parliament of Australia, Canberra,<http://www.aph.gov.au/house/committee/laca/crimeinthecommunity/report.htm> (accessed 23 January 2010).

Indermaur, D & Roberts, L 2005, 'Finding alternatives to imprisonment: drug courts in Australia', *Reform*, vol. 86, pp. 28–32.

Kebbell, MR, Muller, DA & Martin, K 2010, 'Understanding and managing bias', in G Bammer (ed.), *Dealing with uncertainties in policing serious crime*, ANU E Press, Canberra.

Lawrence, C 2008, 'The "emergency intervention" in Northern Territory Indigenous communities', *The New Critic,* issue 7, <http://www.ias.uwa.edu.au/new-critic/seven> (accessed 23 January 2010).

McKenzie, N 2009, 'Pedophile ring claims unfounded', *The Age*, 5 July, <http://www.theage.com.au/national/pedophile-ring-claims-unfounded-20090704-d8h9.html?skin=text-only> (accessed 12 March 2010).

Mencken, HL 1922, *In defense of women*, Alfred A Knopf Inc., New York, available online, <http://www.ibiblio.org/eldritch/hlm/defense.htm> (accessed 22 January 2010).

Public Safety Canada 2002, 'The effect of punishment on recidivism', *Research Summary*, vol. 7, no. 3, <http://www.publicsafety.gc.ca/res/cor/sum/cprs200205_1-eng.aspx> (accessed 23 January 2010).

Pyszczynski, T 2004, 'What are we so afraid of? A terror management theory perspective on the politics of fear', *Social Research*, vol. 71, no. 4, 827–848.

Roberts, JV, Stalans, LJ, Indermaur, D & Hough, M 2003, *Penal populism and public opinion: lessons from five countries,* Oxford University Press, Oxford.

Schieder, P 2003, 'Social cohesion or public security: how should Europe respond to collective feelings of insecurity?', speech to Council of Europe

Forum, Strasbourg, 23–24 October, <http://www.coe.int/T/E/Com/Files/Events/2003-10-social-cohesion/disc_Schieder.asp#TopOfPage> (accessed 23 January 2010).

Schneier, B 2008, 'Does risk management make sense?', October, <http://www.schneier.com/essay-240.html> (accessed 22 January 2010).

Sherman, S, Cialdini, R, Schwartzman, D & Reynolds, K 1985, 'Imagining can heighten or lower the perceived likelihood of contracting a disease', *Personality and Social Psychology Bulletin*, vol.11, pp. 118–127.

Siegel, M 2005, *False alarm: the truth about the epidemic of fear*, John Wiley & Sons, New York.

Slovic, P 2000, *The perception of risk*, Earthscan, London.

Sunstein, CR 2002, 'Probability neglect: emotions, worst cases and law' *Yale Law Journal*, vol. 112, pp. 1–107.

The World Today 2008, 'Paedophile case sparks lawyers' warning', radio program, ABC Radio, 7 July, <http://www.abc.net.au/worldtoday/content/2008/s2296476.htm> (accessed 26 January 2010).

Business
NEIL FARGHER

The disciplines of business seek to provide tools to deal with risk and uncertainty. Business leaders frequently need to manage within relatively finite resources and relatively unpredictable levels of demand or supply. This chapter provides an overview of uncertainty in business, with techniques for dealing with uncertainty and also some recent failures to do so. It concludes with a specific example of understanding organised crime as a business. Many business rules are relevant to how policing manages itself, as well as how policing understands and responds to crime.

Most business decisions are made within a context of uncertainty. Coping with uncertainty is necessary to maintaining a continuing business operation. For example, many software project decisions are made within a range of uncertainties, such as those regarding project requirements. The uncertainties inherent in software development can result in project failure, budget overruns and delayed delivery (e.g. Na et al. 2004). A response is to attempt to better specify requirements early in the software development process and during the development life cycle. Nevertheless, if something as seemingly predictable as software projects cannot run to time and budget, then how can an investigation into an unknown criminal?

In the business context, uncertainty refers to situations in which it is not possible to assign probabilities. The critical distinction is that the ability to assign probabilities allows a range of formal estimates related to risk and the resulting consequences. Tools and analyses can then be applied to manage quantifiable risks and to manage uncertainties with assumed characteristics. While the management of risk is well covered in standard business texts, this chapter considers the more difficult issue of the management of less quantifiable uncertainties. Many business questions of interest involve decisions with risk and uncertainty. Two classic economic theories of decision-making are Von Neumann and Morgenstern's (1947) expected utility theory of choice under uncertainty, and Samuelson's (1937) discounted utility theory.

Smithson et al. (2008) suggest the following classification of issues regarding responses to uncertainty:

- reduced (usually by gaining more knowledge)
- accepted or tolerated
- controlled, harnessed or exploited
- denied
- banished
- surrendered to.

Interestingly the Committee of Sponsoring Organizations of the Treadway Commission (2004) includes in their framework avoiding, accepting, reducing, or sharing risk as management responses to align risks with the entity's risk tolerances and risk appetite. This chapter uses examples from business to consider some of these responses to uncertainty.

Reduced

One approach to uncertainty is to invest in collecting and analysing the necessary information to reduce uncertainty. An area of recent research that has seen explosive growth is the development and application of data mining techniques that can provide information to resolve some uncertainty from an environment where there is too much data for easy handling (e.g. Agrawal et al. 1993; Agrawal & Aggarwal 2001). The ubiquitous Google software is the most obvious technique for identifying relevant information from the world of electronic data. The use of the internet to facilitate the legions of users searching through data to identify important information is an area with potential. For example, filings by Securities and Exchange Commission regulated companies in the United States are available electronically to financial analysts, academic researchers, journalists, retiree investors and third-party software companies on the internet (see www.sec.gov). Having more eyeballs surveying an uncertain environment can potentially identify problems that might otherwise go undetected. There is however no equivalent for Australian company and superannuation fund filings.

Data matching across data bases has also improved the ability of companies to link all the information for a given customer or supplier. The improved ability to match data can now be used to search for the possibility of insider trading, by connecting, for example, company news announcements with previous share options trades by a director's spouse. More efficient and effective access to data, with appropriate safeguards and procedures, potentially improves the ability to identify linkages and reduce uncertainties. For example, advertising can be directed at specific target groups, or tax audits facilitated by finding undisclosed or incorrectly disclosed sources of income (Bolton & Hand 2002).

It is always tempting when faced with a difficult management decision to attempt to reduce or eliminate the uncertainty. It is assumed, or perhaps hoped, that uncertainty can be converted into tractable problems of quantifiable risk management. More information can however uncover new uncertainties.

Similarly, when to stop gathering information is a difficult problem. There are academic tools that examine the optimal stopping point for gathering information in a range of decision contexts. The economic approach is that people continue to search for information until the marginal value of additional information exceeds the marginal cost of that information. Research has however found that such a rule is difficult to apply and therefore recent attention has been directed toward understanding the heuristics and rules that people use. For example, Browne et al. (2007) discuss the cognitive stopping rules used by people when terminating information search in online tasks. When a task is highly structured people will tend to use a single criterion or a mental list of items that must be satisfied prior to completing the search. When a task is poorly structured people tend to search until the new data is tending to confirm prior information, additional data is not altering their mental representation, or they judge that the quantity of information is sufficient.

When to stop information processing is also a difficult problem. Under time pressure, information-processing limitations and resource constraints, decision-makers frequently have to choose which information to pay attention to and which information to ignore. A simple example is the design of an information system to provide recommendations to shoppers browsing an online book store (Ho et al. 2008). Interestingly these authors find that while information systems can make more helpful recommendations after building a profile of a shopper's search criteria, shoppers take more notice of recommendations provided early in their information search.

It is however quickly apparent that searching for information to reduce uncertainty to quantifiable risk is avoiding the underlying problem of dealing with irreducible uncertainties. It is perhaps too easy too overinvest in the reduction of uncertainty. There are irreducible uncertainties that need to be managed or tolerated because they can not be eliminated. There are also reducible uncertainties that are not worth reducing. A greater emphasis on the management of uncertainty, in turn, helps us to understand the nature of the business and the ability to survive the unexpected outcome.

Accepted or tolerated

A basic assumption in business is that higher risk is expected to be associated with higher rewards. For example, an entrepreneur starting a new business will most likely fail. The rewards for success can however be very high, so risky investments will and must be made. Overly risk-averse management can lead to paralysis, the loss of business opportunities and even business failure. Risk and uncertainty must be accepted.

Representations of uncertainty potentially aid communication and improve perceptions of possibilities, threats and opportunities in a way that attempts at probabilistic estimation do not. Scenario analysis is a simple and valuable technique (Phelps et al. 2001). A recent example is the 'stress testing' of US banks (Federal Reserve Board 2009). There has been a return to the basics taught in MBA classes of examining the best and worst case scenarios as well as the expected case scenario. These analyses ask: 'What are the expected outcomes given a set of assumptions?' Such representations of uncertainty potentially aid communication and improve perceptions of possibilities, threats and opportunities.

Controlled, harnessed or exploited

Throughout history consumers and businesses have sought to limit the possible damage from uncertain outcomes. What does the management of uncertainty mean? What techniques are being revisited given the failure of some probabilistic measures of risk?

A problem familiar in both business and law enforcement is the coordination and deployment of resources. There is a need for robust planning, anticipating and confronting 'rude surprises' (Lempert et al. 2002, LaPorte 2007) and for reliable and resilient systems (Frederickson & LaPorte 2002). Frederickson and LaPorte argue that for commercial airline travel to be highly secure there must be high levels of technical competence; a sustained, high level of performance; regular training; structured redundancy; collegial, decentralised authority patterns; processes that reward error detection and correction; adequate and reliable funding; high mission valence (i.e. an attractive mission); timely, relevant and reliable information; and protection from external interference in operations.

A widely used coping mechanism is to pay a counterparty to assume some of the uncertainty. This can mitigate the potential losses from uncertain outcomes through insurance, derivatives, short selling and other techniques that limit one's loss given a possible outcome. Such techniques are however more likely to be provided where the counterparty can assess the risk being insured. Thus the uncertainty is shifted to another party willing to bear the risk. It is worth briefly considering the nature of these businesses that assume other peoples' uncertainties. Consider a typical insurance company. They stay in business because people want to avoid uncertain outcomes. They provide an essential service but these businesses can only succeed when they can successfully put structure around risk management. To the extent that uncertainties can be quantified and assessed, they can be priced so that an insurer can profit over the long run. Just like a bookmaker, the insurer must set the odds against the customer winning. To the extent that there is unquantifiable uncertainty, the insurer will either avoid such business, or charge a high premium for the uncertainty.

In recent decades derivative securities have become increasingly important. A derivative security depends on the value of more basic, underlying security. For example, a forward contract is an agreement to buy or sell a security or commodity for a certain price at a certain time in the future. A company that knows it has to pay an invoice in pounds sterling in ninety days time can enter into a contract today to buy pounds in ninety days. That is, the company removes the uncertainty arising from future changes in foreign exchange rates by taking a fixed price today for the debt it will pay in pounds in the future. For further examples refer to Hull (1989).

A stock option is a derivative security where the value is contingent on the price of an underlying share. Options on shares were first traded on organised exchanges in 1973 and their use has grown dramatically. A call option gives the holder the right to buy the underlying shares by a certain date at a certain price. Under specific assumptions, the Black-Scholes differential equation (Black & Scholes 1973) can be used to estimate the value of an option as a function of the current share price, time to expiry, share price volatility, and the risk-free rate of interest. Uncertainty can be valuable. While humans like to tame uncertainty, the value of options is increasing in share price volatility—the uncertainty in share price changes. All else being equal, the higher the volatility of the possible outcomes, the higher the value of an option over those possible outcomes. The simple intuition is that if you are in a losing position then it is the volatility of possible outcomes that can produce a profitable outcome.

Trading derivatives is a high risk activity. If a trader is in a losing position he or she can truncate the possible outcomes and take a loss with certainty now, or hold a position because a gain is still possible. Of course, a bigger loss is also possible and hence the use of derivatives can vary from offsetting companies' exposures to foreign exchange risk, prices of commodities, or other operating risks; through to speculation and the inevitable rogue traders who are found to double-up on their losing positions like any other gambler at the table (Jorion 1995; Leeson & Whitley 1996).

Multiple derivatives can be used for valuable purposes such as to create a 'collar' around the exposure to volatility. That is, contracts are entered into to set a maximum and minimum future price of the underlying security to which the buyer is exposed. An aspect of derivatives that has been revealed by recent financial collapses is the problems that arise from the complexity of strategies using these instruments. Multiple derivatives, and derivatives on derivatives, however quickly increase the complexity involved in understanding the risks being taken. Recent failures have highlighted how this complexity can hide the underlying uncertainty in the positions taken (e.g. Dash & Creswell 2008).

Denied

There are also examples of business managers denying uncertainty. Courtney et al. (1999) argue that executives take a binary view: either they underestimate the uncertainty in order to come up with required budgets and projections; or they overestimate the level of uncertainty, ignore all analysis, and go with their instincts. Unfortunately, in going with their instincts there is also evidence that managers are overconfident in their judgments. A fundamental of business analysis is that higher expected returns are associated with higher risk. Denying risk can lead to managers focusing on the high returns without considering the risks implicit in their businesses.

Banished

Business would be a much easier activity if uncertainty could be banished, set aside and not dealt with. A relevant concept in economics is that of externalities. An externality arises when the effect of production or consumption of goods or services imposes costs or benefits on others which are not reflected in the prices charged for the goods or services. An example is where uncertainties about environmental impacts of a manufacturing process are disregarded in costing the final product on the basis that the manufacturer is not liable for such impacts. The responses to this type of uncertainty include legislative responses to impose the cost of the externality on the manufacturer. Examples include the consideration of an emissions trading scheme that is intended to impose a cost for carbon emissions (Garnaut 2008).

Managerial responses can also avoid ignoring the costs of externalities. It is naïve and incorrect to assume that businesses will consider externalities for purely social benefit reasons. The directors' duty is to the shareholders, not to society at large. There are, however, many uncertainties regarding costs that are externalities today that may give rise to future liabilities for the business.

Such externalities should be considered in managing the company on behalf of shareholders over a longer term. Recent examples include the asbestos liabilities incurred by CSR Limited and James Hardy (Elks 2009). With respect to law enforcement there may be increasing need for sophisticated investigations linking problems of today to past corporate failures.

Further discussion

No discussion of uncertainty and business would be reasonable at this time without consideration of some of the mistakes that lead to the current global financial crisis and the resulting economic uncertainty. It is somewhat fashionable to refer to large, inexplicable 'black swan events' having occurred in 2007 and 2008. (The 'black swan' alludes to the once widespread belief that all swans were white—proved false when European explorers found black swans in Australia. A 'black swan event' is something extreme and unexpected (see Taleb 2007).) That is, large, unexpected events resulted in a global financial crisis (e.g. Grenville 2009). This provides an initial issue to consider whether such a large shift as the global financial crisis of 2007 was the result of unexpected events in a very uncertain business environment, wrecking the hubris of the investment bank 'masters of the universe' who denied the possibility of such events, or should these events have been foreseen and averted with prudent risk management?

As the evidence of events preceding the credit crisis of 2007 emerge, many of the explanations seem to suggest well known, but too soon forgotten, risks. Commercial and investment banks heavily exposed to a maturity mismatch by borrowing for the short term to buy assets maturing over a longer term, banks lending to borrowers with poor credit, rating agencies assuming that house prices only increase, banks hiding debt off balance sheet to avoid having to take prudent reserves for risk, analysts not considering the high correlation of asset price declines during recessions, and regulators maintaining a low interest rate environment for too long (e.g. Brunnermeier 2009). In hindsight, very few of the factors contributing to the initial period of recession were new. The primary lesson appears to have been the failure to adequately consider the magnitude of these imbalances. Perhaps the new aspect is the growing linkage of economies in an increasingly global community and therefore the high correlation between failures across the globe.

Once a recession starts, it is a well known phenomenon that business frauds, businesses with too much debt, and businesses with bad business models are all revealed more easily. During periods of high growth new business investment can hide past mistakes. During periods of recession bad business models, and outright frauds that rely on generating cash from new investors to pay off old investors, are revealed as the supply of new investment evaporates.

Economic uncertainty will continue to exacerbate the pressure on business and their owners and managers to do what is needed to survive. Recessions reveal past financial malfeasance, and also provide an incentive for management to perpetrate fraud in order to survive during a period of harsh business circumstances. Recent research on fraud (e.g. Dechow et al. 2009) highlights the frequency of top management involvement in major corporate fraud. The evidence suggests that there is an escalation of fraudulent behaviour to continue the perception of a successful business.

Conclusion

Economists rarely hang out with drug dealers. On the occasion that the books of a drug gang fell into the hands of an economist it was found that the gang worked a lot like most businesses. The particulars of the drug gang are covered in three papers by Venkatesh and Levitt (2000a, 2000b, 2001). Venkatesh and Levitt (2000b) track the evolution from independents to corporate super-gang. As with any business, the books were used as a tool for managing day-to-day operations and as a means for tracking operations for reporting to higher levels in the gang hierarchy. The gang systematically sought, acquired and distributed revenues, and managed an effective product distribution system. The organisational chart of the gang was very similar to that of a legitimate corporation. The results were however bleak. Over a four year period a junior gang member had a 1 in 4 chance of being killed.

If crack dealing is dangerous, why would anybody take the job for what worked out to a starting wage of $3.30 per hour? The results of this research suggested that crack dealing is similar to other extremely competitive professions. Just like professional sports or accounting partnerships, the junior employees participate in a tournament with uncertain outcome where those who reach the top are paid extremely well, but at low levels the financial compensation does not compensate for the risk and uncertainty. If I were to speculate how to help such a business to fail, my list would include an increased ability to access and cross-match financial data in order to identify and then penalise unexplained wealth acquisition of the higher level management.

Most business decisions are made within a context of uncertainty. Reward however is associated with risk taking. Overly risk-averse management can lead to the loss of business opportunities and even business failure. While some risks can be managed or insured against, other uncertainties must be accepted or even exploited for businesses to thrive. In an increasingly complex world, products such as insurance and derivatives can be used to manage and shift risk to those willing to bear it. These techniques do not however reduce the importance of understanding the uncertainties involved and the continued need to manage uncertainty.

Acknowledgements

With thanks to Damon Muller and Michael Smithson. All errors remain the responsibility of the author.

References

Agrawal, D & Aggarwal, CC 2001, 'On the design and quantification of privacy preserving data mining algorithms', *Proceedings of the twentieth Association for Computing Machinery Special Interest Groups on Management of Data, Algorithms and Computation Theory and Artificial Intelligence (ACM SIGMOD-SIGACT-SIGART) symposium on Principles of Database Systems*, May, pp. 247–255.

Agrawal, R, Imielinski, T & Swami, A 1993, 'Mining association rules between sets of items in large databases', *Proceedings of the Association for Computing Machinery Special Interest Group on Management of Data (ACM SIGMOD) conference on Management of Data*, May, pp. 207–216.

Black, F & Scholes, M 1973, 'The pricing of options and corporate liabilities', *Journal of Political Economy*, vol. 81, May–June, pp. 637–659.

Bolton, RJ & Hand, DJ 2002, 'Statistical fraud detection: a review', *Statistical Science*, vol.17, no. 3, pp. 235–249.

Browne, GJ, Pitts, MG & Wetherbe, JC 2007, 'Cognitive stopping rules for terminating information search in online tasks', *MIS Quarterly*, vol. 31, no. 1, pp.89–104.

Brunnermeir, MK 2009, 'Deciphering the liquidity and credit crunch 2007–2008', *Journal of Economic Perspectives*, vol. 23, no. 1, pp. 77–100.

Committee of Sponsoring Organizations of the Treadway Commission (COSO) 2004, *Enterprise risk management – integrated framework*, AICPA Publications, New York, NY.

Courtney, H, Kirkland, J, Viguerie, P, De Geus, AP & Christensen, CM 1999, *Harvard business review on managing uncertainty*, Harvard Business School Press, Boston, MA.

Dash, E & Creswell, J 2008, 'Citigroup saw no red flags even as it made bolder bets', *The New York Times*, 23 November, p. A1.

Dechow, PM, Ge, W, Larson, CR & Sloan, RG 2009, 'Predicting material accounting manipulations', working paper, University of California, Berkeley, <http://ssrn.com/abstract=997483> (accessed 19 November 2009).

Elks, S 2009, 'Hardie sues CSR over asbestos case', *The Australian*, 13 October, <http://www.theaustralian.com.au/news/nation/hardie-sues-csr-over-asbestos-case/story-e6frg6oo-1225786083164> (accessed 19 November 2009).

Federal Reserve Board 2009, *The Supervisory Capital Assessment Program: design and implementation*, Board of Governors of the Federal Reserve System, 24April, Washington, DC.

Frederickson, HG & LaPorte, T R 2002, 'Airport security, high reliability, and the problem of rationality', *Public Administration Review*, vol. 62, September, pp. 34–44.

Garnaut, R 2008, 'Garnaut climate change review: Emissions Trading Scheme discussion paper', March, <http://www.garnautreview.org.au> (accessed 19 November 2009).

Grenville, S 2009, 'Theory has failed: our hope is the real world', *The Australian Financial Review*, 11 May 2009, p. 20.

Ho, SY, Bodoff, D & Tam, KY 2008, 'Timing of adaptive web personalization and its effects on online consumer behavior', *Information Systems Research*, forthcoming.

Hull, J 1989, *Options, futures and other derivative securities*, Prentice Hall, Englewood Cliffs, NJ.

Jorion, P 1995, *Big bets gone bad: derivatives and bankruptcy in Orange County*, Academic Press Inc., San Diego, CA.

LaPorte, TR 2007, 'Anticipating rude surprises: reflections on "crisis management" without end', in DE Gibbons (ed.), *Communicable crises: prevention, management and resolution in the global arena*, Information Age Publishing, pp. 27–46.

Leeson, N & Whitley, E 1996, *Rogue trader*, Little Brown and Company, London.

Lempert, R, Popper, S & Bankes, S 2002, 'Confronting surprise', *Social Science Computer Review*, vol. 20, no. 4, pp. 420–440.

Na, K-S, Li, Z, Simpson, JT & Kim, K-Y 2004, 'Uncertainty profile and software project performance: a cross-national comparison', *Journal of Systems and Software*, vol. 70, pp. 155–163.

Phelps, R, Chan, C & Kapsalis, SC 2001, 'Does scenario planning affect performance? Two exploratory studies', *Journal of Business Research*, vol. 51, pp. 223–232.

Samuelson, P 1937, 'A note on measurement of utility, *Review of Economic Studies*, vol. 4, no. 2, pp. 155–161.

Smithson, M, Bammer, G & the Goolabri Group 2008, 'Coping and managing under uncertainty', in G Bammer & M Smithson (eds), *Uncertainty and risk: multidisciplinary perspectives*, Earthscan, London, pp. 321–333.

Taleb, NN 2007, *The black swan: the impact of the highly improbable*, Random House, New York, NY.

Venkatesh, SA & Levitt, SD 2000a, 'An economic analysis of a drug-selling gang's finances', *Quarterly Journal of Economics*, vol. 115, no. 3, pp. 755–789.

Venkatesh, SA & Levitt, SD 2000b, 'Are we a family or a business? History and disjuncture in the urban American street gang', *Theory and Society*, vol. 29, pp. 427–462.

Venkatesh, SA & Levitt, SD 2001, 'Growing up in the projects: the economic lives of a cohort of men who came of age in Chicago public housing', *American Economic Review*, vol. 91, no. 2, pp. 79–84.

Von Neumann, J & Morgenstern, O 1947, *Theory of games and economic behavior*, Princeton University Press, Princeton, NJ.

Commentaries from Practice

The Investigating Officer and the Investigation Manager
PETER MARTIN

Introduction

Serious crime investigations can be protracted, are usually complex and are often controversial. The circumstances of one crime differentiate it from another. The victim and location might be different, the *modus operandi,* or way in which the offence occurred, may also be different. Regardless of such differences the processes utilised in the major crime investigation can and usually do, follow a tried and true process.

Although as Sue Wilkinson identifies in her chapter (2010), there seems to be a limitless diversity of new and emerging crime types which confront and challenge contemporary police officers, the reality is that many of these 'new' types are innovative manifestations of old crimes using new technologies. For the majority of police officers this array of innovative crimes will be the domain of specialist investigators and high level task forces. Seldom, if ever, will the general duties officer on the street handle complex high level criminal investigations.

The uncertainties in serious crime are juxtaposed against a standard investigative process which is employed to move uncertainty or unknowns to the known investigative domain. It is the uncertainty that exists around crime issues that makes orientation of effort problematic from a strategic and operational perspective. Policing agencies have control over where resources are allocated, the optimum skill levels of their workforce, the strategic and operational approaches to respond to crime and the willingness to engage in partnerships. The challenge of employing a standard investigative methodology is to enable police agencies to bring the right resources, at the right time to the right investigative problem.

While the scale, nature and motivation of crime does change, there are many common aspects in terms of processes of investigations. The seriousness of the crime and the sophistication of that crime can make the degree of effort to ascertain the truth more critical and so too the resources which are allocated to the effort.

Further, the search for 'truth' occurs in an environment where much of the information crucial to a successful resolution is unknown. Ascertaining what occurred, the circumstances of how it occurred and who is liable at law takes place in environments where the political, media, community and internal 'authorising environments' are stakeholders in the outcomes. These stakeholders can bring tension and apply pressure to the investigation for both information and an expeditious outcome.

This chapter is written from the perspective of both the investigative officer and the officer managing the investigation. The policing of serious crime, as opposed to those that are less serious, can change the management of investigations. Not all investigations are the same. The scale and complexity of investigations or alternatively their level of community or political sensitivity, can lead to more significant management structures required to deal with this complexity or sensitivity. The senior investigator, rather than merely driving an investigation at the operational level and acting semi-autonomously, assumes more of a management role. This senior investigator not only sets the investigative priorities but assumes responsibility for human, physical and fiscal resource management. This can also mean that the now investigator/manager also assumes responsibility for managing the media and other peripheral but necessary functions such as political briefings.

This chapter covers two areas. First are the uncertainties pertinent to the investigative process itself, which I use to comment on the work of Smithson, as well as the chapters of Fargher, and Kebbell and colleagues. Second, I use the concept of the authorising environment to provide a focus for commenting on the chapter by Lawrence. A summary of these comments and suggestions for areas which would benefit from further research are provided in Table 1. But first I set the scene with the link between the investigation and the authorising environment.

The link between the investigation and the authorising environment—the who, how, when, where and why in context

Police officers are taught early in their training to apply their skills and ability to restore order in otherwise chaotic situations. The police role primarily is to enhance public safety, both perceived and real. In this way police officers respond to situations where they first, restore peace, second, ascertain what occurred and third, ascertain if an offence was committed. In cases where a breach of law has occurred, the police officer uses his/her discretion to determine whether it is in the 'public interest' to proceed with a prosecution or some other intervention.

Police are similarly taught that the aim of criminal investigation is to establish the 'who, how, when, where and why' of a matter subject to an investigation. These five framing questions have more to do with the arrival than the investigative journey. As important as it is to be able to get to the known dimension of each question, the process by which investigators arrive at this point is critical to a successful investigation. Criminal law and procedures and practices both internal to the police service and more broadly to the criminal justice system, provide the framework which guides the criminal investigation. Operating outside such frameworks can, at best, render evidence inadmissible or at worst, leave the investigator liable for an offence. In any event, this has the capacity to derail the prosecution of the wrongdoer and place the investigation in jeopardy. Therefore in the quest for certainty in dealing with serious crimes, the course that is adopted is one that is governed by rules, regulations, legislation and long established conventions. These are referred to by Mark Moore (1995) as the authorising environment.

As this description shows, it is not possible, or desirable, to disentangle the investigative process and the authorising environment. However I shall concentrate first on the investigative process and then on the authorising environment.

Moving the investigation from the unknown domain to the known

If we were to think about the known and unknown factors in a serious crime incident using a two by two matrix, as was done by Bammer et al. (2008, adapted from Kerwin, 1993), we would see that there were four permutations with one absolute known and three variations of unknowns (refer to Table 2).

Table 2: The known/unknown investigative matrix

		META-LEVEL	
		Known	Unknown
PRIMARY LEVEL	Known	Known knowns	Unknown knowns (tacit knowledge)
	Unknown	Known unknowns (conscious ignorance)	Unknown unknowns (meta-ignorance)

In the four quadrants or domains, the combinations can be expressed as:

Known-knowns—those matters for which the investigator is aware of the things that they know. From an investigative perspective these may be issues which are provable from hard evidence (physical evidence) or alternatively which can be inferred by provable facts (such as motivations for an offence gleaned through direct evidence of an offender).

Known-unknowns—The investigation usually focuses on what we know we don't know, otherwise described as investigative ignorance. Much of the investigation occurs in this domain.

Unknown-knowns—This situation can be described as tacit knowledge and applies to situations in which the investigator using intuition picks up on subtle cues in the investigation which may infer guilt or innocence.

Unknown-unknowns—This domain is sometimes described as meta-ignorance and is arguably the most difficult domain for the investigation.

The challenge is to move the investigation from the unknown domains, in whatever quadrant, to the known-knowns. The investigation needs to be mindful of testing the known-knowns to ensure that the investigation has not merely been self-serving in terms of its outcomes—involving many of the biases described in the chapter by Mark Kebbell, Damon Muller and Kirsty Martin (2010). Furthermore, presentation of the unknown will always be part of a 'solid' well-developed brief of evidence as it can demonstrate or assist with understanding the likelihood of achieving knowledge/opinion beyond reasonable doubt. Smithson (2008), in examining metaphors for 'uncertainty', identifies a common view that knowledge is power and ignorance is helplessness and impotence. While that might be so, from a criminal prosecutorial perspective it also shows objectivity and impartiality. Naturally, criminal investigations can be prone to the same extent of uncertainties as in other domains, such as the business world. In his chapter Neil Fargher (2010) identifies that if something as seemingly predictable as software development 'cannot run to time and budget, then how can an investigation into an unknown criminal?'

If 'necessity is the mother of invention', then it could be argued that, in investigating serious crime terms, that uncertainty is the mother of innovation and inspiration for truth/fact finding. Uncertainty, apart from being a frustration to an investigator, can be a source of opportunity. Smithson (2008) argues that uncertainty can motivate people positively and negatively and that people find uses for it (uncertainty) and do not always want to rid themselves of it. So too is uncertainty a potential opportunity. It can create willingness in the investigative team to think outside of the obvious. To explore what is possible as opposed to what is perceived as likely.

Unlike the Hollywood depiction of the criminal investigation, serious crimes are not usually solved by a charismatic intelligent investigator operating in isolation. In fact, most serious investigations are a team effort involving many people with a broad skill set in a range of disciplines. Increasingly, in an effort to defeat uncertainty, multidisciplinary teams with broad membership are employed to leverage off each other's skills, knowledge, expertise and, importantly, legislative regimes. The multidisciplinary approach is helpful in terms of analysing information and data but what usually occurs in major crime investigations is that the investigative team is hopelessly overwhelmed with information. Fargher (2010) also discusses this phenomenon in business and suggests that there are software solutions. Within a serious crime construct however, information needs to be individually analysed by an intelligence analyst. While technology is useful in this domain there is no currently effective surrogate for the human approach. Another important point related to too much information is that, given the nature of the investigation, it is often not possible to stifle the flow. Fargher describes the challenge for business managers of managing and effectively tasking finite resources in an environment of competing priorities and where there are 'relatively unpredictable levels of demand or supply'. The same is true for the serious crime investigation.

Intuition, heuristics and bias

When the senior investigator assumes the senior management role he/she then becomes the driver for identifying both the relevant uncertainty that exists with respect to the investigation and the methodology to defeat that which is uncertain. Experience, knowledge, skill and intuition combine to assist the investigative direction. In the case of experience, knowledge and skill, these are learned behaviours refined by internal and external training opportunities and practical on-the-job experience. Intuition on the other hand is a much more difficult skill to identify and define. The expert investigator through intuition may instinctively pursue an investigative course that may seem speculative to the less experienced.

Intuition is a highly prized resource in many fields of endeavour and it is equally highly prized in the management of serious crime. Length and breadth of criminal investigation experience are strong predictors of intuition, although not the only predictors. Individual perceptiveness is not solely determined by experience. To some degree, those individuals with high levels of intuition defy a complete scientific explanation, but their contribution to the investigation can be profound.

On the other hand, the real enemy of the investigator is the preconceived notion of 'truth'. When investigators take an erroneous belief that a situation occurred a particular way, and assume what the causal factors (motivation) were and who is likely to be responsible, then there can be an artificial conclusion before an investigation has run its course. In other words, generalisations are drawn based on aggregation of variables rather than compilation of the facts.

An investigation can be defeated and hopelessly compromised before it really begins, when investigators inexpertly and prematurely 'predict' the unknown factors. This is particularly the case where the evidence appears to fall within the known-known quadrant of certainty and can be accepted too willingly and not tested. The challenge for the principal investigator is to encourage objectivity at every stage of the investigation.

One way of maintaining objectivity is to document the process of the investigation. The major crime log not only details the outcomes of the inquiry but also the process employed and the evidence that was used or relied upon to inform the direction of the investigation. This is valuable both for its potential use in court proceedings and from the perspective of organisational and institutional learning. From a knowledge management perspective it is not just the arrival point that is important for the investigation but the journey of discovery.

In their chapter Kebbell and colleagues (2010) argue that there is a large amount of research which shows that that decision-making and informational processing abilities are not optimal because of contextual pressures which overwhelm cognitive ability and create bias. Intuition on the part of the investigator is important to the investigation, but can lead to bias. The challenge therefore is how to use intuition in such a way as to benefit the investigation and limit the potential for bias.

Bias is not only a relevant consideration for investigators themselves, but is also critical for assessing witnesses and others who have input into investigations. It is the natural human condition to want to make sense of uncertainty. Rumour and conjecture can be manifestations of an individual's attempts to provide certainty to uncertain situations. Either at a conscious or subconscious level the tendency is to defeat uncertainty by speculating or offering alternative scenarios which can bridge the divide to the unknown. This natural human condition can prove challenging for investigators. The overly 'helpful' witness who provides police with what they think will assist the investigation or the biased witness who is incapable or unwilling to take an objective view of the facts at hand, can significantly hamper an investigation. An extreme example is the case of Clare Werbeloff (otherwise colloquially referred to as the 'Chk-Chk Boom chick'), a 19 year old woman who sprang to international fame with her fictitious accounts of the shooting of a man in Sydney's Kings Cross in May 2009 (*The Sunday Telegraph* 2009).

Public value and the authorising environment

As indicated previously, the role of the investigation is to ascertain the truth of a situation. In doing so the investigation must also achieve public value. Public value from an investigative perspective involves the allocation of resources to give effect to the law and to achieve efficient outcomes. According to Moore (1995) public value is dependent upon operational capability, as well as what he calls an 'authorising environment'. The authorising environment is essentially the legislative and regulatory support for the investigation. But it can also have a downside through pressure to achieve results and demands for information about the investigation to be made public. This can serve to divert effort from the investigation to meet political and media needs. Such diversion of effort can also impact on the perception of impartiality or create the belief that a particular outcome is wanted. This is a highly undesirable situation that can run counter to the quest for truth. In terms of serious crime, the media are in a unique position. The media have the potential to exaggerate risks and demand from governments instant responses to theoretical threats. As Carmen Lawrence (2010) argues in her chapter '[t]he media exaggerate the risks we actually face and clamour for an instant response, especially from government, to threats that may never materialise'.

It is unsurprising that there is a discrepancy between the levels of actual crime and exaggerated perceptions of crime that both Lawrence (2010) and Robyn Attewell (2010) describe in their chapters. The media play a significant role in creating the context in which individuals asses risk to themselves, their families and the community in which they live. Lawrence argues that people behave as if their lives were becoming more and more dangerous and that they personalise rather than calculate objective risk, often exaggerating their vulnerability—this can then lead politicians and the media to exploit public anxiety about crime and cultivate public resentment towards those who offend.

The role of politicians in the authorising environment has another dimension. It is important to have an appreciation of the intentions of the lawmakers who both drafted and enacted particular legislation that the investigation relies upon to extract its authority. The spirit and intent of legislation is critical to the investigator in the management of serious crime. The fundamental question when applying a particular offence provision is, what wrong was to be corrected by enacting this particular piece of legislation?

Moore's work (1995) on public value, not only highlights the importance of the authorising environment, but also provides focus on the term 'public'. In particular, the public interest test is an important consideration. Despite the fact that police may be working feverishly to uncover the truth of a matter and may have uncovered a set of circumstances where prosecution may occur, it may not be in the public interest to prosecute. This occurs to a lesser extent with serious crime than low-level matters. There can be a host of mitigating factors which may make prosecution unviable, including the minor or technical nature of the offence and the age or mental competence of the offender. In some serious crimes (e.g. euthanasia) defining public interest is difficult.

But the 'public interest' test in terms of prosecution is not the only impact from the public. The perceived wishes of the public in terms of serious crime are often strong drivers. In some cases they can be strongly influential and need to be managed, thereby further diverting the investigation effort towards public perception management. On the other hand, the mood of public sentiment might be against prosecution where the evidence would otherwise support such prosecution. An example is assisted suicide investigations.

There are many driving factors in investigations. From the perspective of the authorising environment, what is important is that there is certainty as to who the stakeholders are and that there is clarity in terms of their motivations. Importantly for the investigation, there needs to be a clear and unambiguous message from those who make up the 'authorising environment' in the Police Service to those managing and undertaking the investigation. One such significant message is the need to maintain objectivity by embracing and using uncertainty to investigative advantage.

Conclusion: strategies to manage uncertainty

All investigators seek to find certainty, yet investigations usually have varying degrees of uncertainty attached to them. Strategies that should be considered in attempting to provide clarity to that which is uncertain could include, but are not limited to, the following:

1. at the commencement of the investigation an adherence to the philosophy of objectivity and to embrace uncertainty
2. a clear statement of intent with respect to the investigation (What is wanted to be achieved, when and by whom?)
3. a management and investigative structure that supports the investigation
4. a diversity of skills and talents which can objectively assess available information and weight it in terms of accuracy, objectivity and evidentiary worth
5. clarity concerning what the internal authorising environment expects from the investigation
6. an appreciation of the community, media and political interest in the investigation and an ability to use this interest to the benefit of the investigation
7. a carefully considered and well articulated investigative plan
8. leveraging off others, both internal and external, in an effort to finalise the investigation
9. objectively assessing the available evidence and making decisions to prosecute on an evidence basis, having regard for the criminal standard of proof and the public interest
10. the need to capture the learnings from the investigation to inform future practice in this area—combining knowledge management with continual improvement.

Almost all serious crime has elements of uncertainty. Even in the most seemingly clear-cut of matters, there are elements that are unknown where an investigative process needs to be employed to both elicit the circumstances of the matter and do this in such a way as not to render the evidence inadmissible in a court. Usually however, much to do with the serious crime is unknown to the investigator, at least initially.

The challenge is to respond to the crime in the first instance with sufficient resources and expertise so as to maximise the evidentiary value of any exhibits from the scene of the offence. The role of the principal investigator is to assemble sufficient resources (human, physical and intelligence) to enable a sustained effort for conducting an investigation having regard for the circumstances of the case.

Above all else, the investigator must be armed with objectivity. Arguably, objectivity and intuition are the investigator's greatest assets. Investigations can and do go awry. A significant risk point in most investigations is early in the investigatory life-cycle. A biased investigation which makes assumptions about the circumstances of the matter is unlikely to be made good with the passage of time. Time and effort are not, of themselves, enough to bring an investigation back from the brink of contamination. A professional and balanced investigation which has regard for the rule of law must be the starting point for any investigation and particularly those dealing with serious crime.

Rather than uncertainty being seen as a burden and something that confounds investigations, it should be construed as an opportunity: an opportunity to examine parallel scenarios which might explain motivations and behaviour; an opportunity to work with other agencies and those with expertise in other areas in a multidisciplinary context; and to advance the organisational knowledge that exists on such matters.

The views expressed in this chapter are those of the author and do not represent those of any agency including the Queensland Police Service or Queensland University of Technology.

Table 1. Summary of comments on the other chapters and critical areas that warrant further research

Author	Ideas or methods for dealing with uncertainty	Critical areas that warrant further research
Attewell	Police further adopting statistical principles and incorporating scientific methodology into research and practice	Strategies to encourage reporting in an effort to defeat the 'dark figure' of crime
	Links between underreporting of crime and 'uncertainty' generally, particularly in the knowledge gap that exists	Effective strategies to address the lack of balance and restore objectivity in arguments about crime given potential bias in media reporting
	Media reporting and the link to community fear despite the evidence (e.g. crime statistics)	
Fargher	Difficulty of managing in environments where there is too much data (much of which is contradictory)	
Jarrett & Westcott	Considering risk identification (e.g. likelihood and consequences) as determinants of allocating police resources	Consideration of a trial of advancing arguments based on cost-benefit equations and gauging the public reaction to such arguments (e.g. management of serious crime and search and rescue operations)
	Considering cost-benefit calculations in determining police effort (managing public, media and political reality of such 'clinical' scientific decision-making)	
Lawrence	Identifying and understanding the factors which lead to the politicisation of crime	The extent that the community is prepared to trade-off freedoms to deal with serious crime uncertainties
	Perceptions of risk are influenced by emotion as much as they are by more analytic processes and are dependent upon learned associations	
	The critical role of media in shaping and elevating uncertainty into fear and therefore driving political 'non-evidence-based' decision-making	
	Acceptance of fear leading to strategies to defeat such fear such as intrusive invasions into privacy	
	The criminal justice system walking the 'tough political tough talk' about getting tough on crime	
Milroy	Developing sound definitions for nationally significant crimes and analysis mechanisms to make informed assessments of areas to direct resources	Appropriate levels of training for personnel performing key roles in serious crime investigations
		Identification and implementation of strategies to reduce cognitive bias in serious crime investigations
Smithson	Reducing the likelihood of an individual's guilt to mathematical terms	Disease models and pro-activity for police—using mathematics generally and probability specifically to calculate activity of greatest benefit from a preventative perspective
	Reducing standards of proof (e.g. beyond reasonable doubt) to mathematical proportions (e.g. blood and DNA examples)	
	Applying the learnings from medical science in terms of applying preventative effort into statistically more likely areas of concern (can apply to proactive policing effort)	
Wilkinson	The rise in use of technology by organised crime and the corresponding use of technology by police to defeat uncertainty	Enhancing and managing the exchange of information and intelligence between law enforcement agencies, domestically and internationally
	International agreements and conventions with respect to the sharing of information to deal with uncertainty across jurisdictional boundaries	Anticipating the next wave of 'cyber-crimes' given the presumption that this is a mix of 'old crimes' using new technologies

References

Attewell, R 2010, 'Can statistics help', in G Bammer (ed.), *Dealing with uncertainties in policing serious crime*, ANU E Press, Canberra.

Bammer, G, Smithson, M & the Goolabri Group 2008, 'The nature of uncertainty', in G Bammer & M Smithson (eds), *Uncertainty and risk: multidisciplinary perspectives*, Earthscan, London, pp. 289–303.

Fargher, N 2010, 'Business', in G Bammer (ed.), *Dealing with uncertainties in policing serious crime*, ANU E Press, Canberra.

Jarrett, R & Westcott, M 2010, 'Quantitative risk', in G Bammer (ed.), *Dealing with uncertainties in policing serious crime*, ANU E Press, Canberra.

Kebbell, MR, Muller, DA & Martin, K 2010, 'Understanding and managing bias', in G Bammer (ed.), *Dealing with uncertainties in policing serious crime*, ANU E Press, Canberra.

Kerwin, A 1993, 'None too solid: medical ignorance', *Knowledge: creation, diffusion, utilisation*, vol. 15, no. 2, pp. 166–185.

Lawrence, C 2010, 'Politics', in G Bammer (ed.), *Dealing with uncertainties in policing serious crime*, ANU E Press, Canberra.

Milroy, AM 2010, 'Law enforcement agencies which respond to nationally significant crime', in G Bammer (ed.), *Dealing with uncertainties in policing serious crime*, ANU E Press, Canberra.

Moore, M 1995, *Creating public value: strategic management in government*, Harvard University Press, Cambridge, MA.

Smithson, M 2008, 'The many faces and masks of uncertainty', in G Bammer & M Smithson (eds), *Uncertainty and risk: multidisciplinary perspectives*, Earthscan, London, pp. 13–25.

Smithson, M 2010, 'Understanding uncertainty', in G Bammer (ed.), *Dealing with uncertainties in policing serious crime*, ANU E Press, Canberra.

The Sunday Telegraph 2009, 'Chk-Chk Boom chick Clare Werbeloff made up Sydney shooting account', <http://www.news.com.au/technology/story> (accessed 30 September 2009).

Higher Education in Policing
TRACEY GREEN AND GREG LINSDELL

Introduction

We are interested in the relationships between higher education, uncertainty and the investigation of serious crime while acknowledging that there is 'higher education' and then there is 'higher' education. The investigation of serious crime has changed considerably, but having to deal with uncertainty is the one element that can be predicted with certainty. It is no coincidence that higher education has taken on more and more importance in the policing profession and this chapter will reveal some of the reasons for this without intending to take away from or diminish the importance of 'service developed and delivered' training. Indeed this chapter will argue that the contemporary investigation of serious crime needs a collaborative approach to both training and education with practitioners and researchers providing new approaches and innovative solutions to what are very difficult and complex problems, namely the investigation of serious crime in uncertain times.

This chapter begins with a brief discussion of the development of police-specific higher education and explores the contribution higher education makes to policing. It briefly outlines how scientific breakthroughs and the quest for certainty have revolutionised policing, but also demonstrates how some of these certainties are illusory. The chapter then explores how higher education assists in the understanding and management of uncertainty in policing and demonstrates intersections with the ideas proposed in the other chapters in this book. We conclude by exploring uncertainty as an ally to policing and describing how the higher order skills provided by higher education become obvious in practice. A summary of suggestions for areas which would benefit from further research is provided in Table 1.

The emergence of police-specific higher education

The progression towards higher education in policing in Australia can be traced back to 1981 with the Lusher Report in New South Wales (NSW) (Lusher 1981) which identified policing as a profession which would benefit from higher educational standards. The report advocated improving educational standards and processes within police training and encouraging police to undertake university education. A 1997 Royal Commission into the NSW Police Service (Wood 1997) voiced concerns about police training and professional standards, police culture, and transparency and accountability. It suggested that the involvement of an external agency—a university—in police education would be effective in addressing these problems, particularly through:

- raising educational standards and expectations
- making police education transparent to the wider community and more open to the values of that community
- encouraging a culture of reflective practice, professional autonomy and accountability.

Initially the take-up was limited to the ambitious, but over time a more general acceptance of higher education in policing has developed. In response to the growing awareness across the policing profession of the value of higher education, there has been a growth in policing-specific education programs (Wood & Bradley 2009). Unfortunately, not all of the programs have sought to enhance the development of policing as a profession or to develop a body of knowledge specific to the discipline of 'policing' (Chambers 2004) and this has reduced the willingness of many practitioners to engage with universities.

Sections of the higher education sector identified the demand from the police to source new knowledge and develop their skills, however rather than recognising the need for a new and emerging discipline they chose to offer a mixture of traditional and established programs in areas such as criminology, law, business or sociology. Whilst obviously there is underpinning knowledge to be drawn from many disciplines, these readily available courses were not tailored to policing and were merely given a 'blue rinse'. Not surprisingly they did not meet the needs of a discerning new breed of practitioner.

Today we can best describe contemporary higher education for policing as being delivered in a three tiered yet totally combined 'club sandwich' approach. On a very basic level there are three fundamental aspects to professional education. First is the underpinning knowledge which supports the foundations of the discipline of policing. Drawn from a multitude of traditional discipline areas, this knowledge feeds the second, and new, level—applied evaluation, reflection and research—which as it develops is creating the new discipline of policing. Of most concern to practitioners is the third level, that of application. A useful analogy is education for medical students, who study foundational knowledge, topped up with current research and then applied practice. This is a very effective way to develop and evaluate best practice and drive forward change and innovation. In much the same way policing is beginning to forge its own destiny and recognise that, without the evidence to support the critical decision-making and analysis of the current and future needs, they will make little progress towards a truly recognised professional status. This approach has two major benefits. First, it demonstrates how higher education has evolved to meet the needs of the profession without losing its commitment to the higher order skills. Second, it demonstrates the willingness, on behalf of policing, to engage in serious debate and analysis of its own practice to establish new approaches and determine future options for more effective policing.

For their part, universities have developed many policing-related courses and some criminologists have focused their research in ways that can help police achieve their goals rather than in ways which criticise police methods and are of little assistance. Fortunately policing research is moving away from being conducted 'of police, not with police', as if they are laboratory rats to be studied and commented on. Research needs to be of an applied nature to help investigators work with uncertainty. Further, practitioners need to make sure that they come together to share best practice and capture it for the future. These issues were neatly summarised by Bratton recently when he said, 'I understand research for research sake and believe that it has its place; but in order to be useful to the practitioner, researchers need to understand practitioners' needs and should consider the potential impact of their study on the audience. Otherwise we just might end up having academics writing to impress each other with no long-term lasting effect on what is actually happening in the field' (Bratton 2007).

For an improved partnership between practitioners and researchers to occur, the practitioners also need to change focus. They need to realise that their insights and experience have real value and can contribute to the overall body of knowledge. They need to move beyond thinking that 'knowledge is power' and be prepared to share their knowledge, as well as to recognise that they alone do not hold all the answers. For police to stop being the 'observed' and become the 'observers' they need to embrace all aspects of higher education and recognise that there is value there for them and their practice. Professional practitioners, if engaged in the research, have the opportunity to interpret findings, ask meaningful questions and apply their knowledge to ensure meaningful outcomes. These can still be critical and objective, but will amount to more than many current four-year studies which simply develop statements of the 'bleeding obvious' to those engaged in policing (Bratton 2007).

The role of higher education

Higher education has three fundamentals at its core. These separate it from other forms of training. Three underlying tenets, as defined in the Oxford English Dictionary (2000) are:

- *critical thinking*—analytical evaluations, being diagnostic and discriminating, fastidious, perceptive and precise. Making judgments using intelligent thought, assessment, opinion and rational reasoning
- *analysis*—to investigate or interpret
- *research*—systematic investigation to establish facts or collect information on a subject, to analyse and examine.

Most would agree that these skills and abilities are the core of what is required in contemporary investigation. Interestingly, this is not a recent realisation. For example, Isaac Newton was engaged to investigate a particularly complex fraud against the Royal Mint and the Bank of England because of his analytical and strategic thinking abilities (Levenson 2009), demonstrating that methods of reasoning can outweigh investigative zeal alone. It should come as no surprise that there is a very clear link between the core skills required for investigation and rigorous research. They can be considered to be one and the same, as both are a 'search for the truth' (Ord et al. 2008). Whether studying psychology or archaeology, these 'higher order' skills are what is most valued in higher education and are what gives higher education its edge. Knowledge and technology will constantly change but these skills will give their recipient the ability to inquire, evaluate, research and develop accordingly. The 'evidence-based' trend, which began with evidence-based medicine and swept across to policing in the late 1980s is an example of the influence of higher education, and the skill sets it brings, on various professions.

There are two additional roles that higher education will ideally fill. One is to help police stay abreast of the changing demands on and challenges for the profession, as described in Sue Wilkinson's chapter. She discusses the many new crime types which are now emerging as issues for law enforcement and the fact that globalisation has changed the nature of modern organised crime which now, 'tends to be international, multilayered, multicultural, highly developed, ambitious, profitable and technologically sophisticated' (Wilkinson 2010).

Whilst collated crime statistics and annual reports from the various policing agencies present a somewhat 'clinical' and often distorted picture of what is occurring, research within communities and key service providers can provide a much clearer picture of the 'actual' levels of criminality. In his chapter, Alastair Milroy (2010) argues that the way crime data is collated and reported provides little or no guidance as to future trends. The people most likely to be able to identify emerging trends are the practitioners dealing with the new crimes. Internally policing needs to be able to identify and respond to changes which are sometimes rapid, surprising and somewhat unpredictable. This must be matched by external research in predicting this kind of trend.

Higher education programs in both the strategic intelligence and leadership areas provide police practitioners with the requisite skills to identify future trends and use traditional research skills to predict the issues they are likely to be facing. For example, the development of 'Strategic Intelligence Assessments', required by police commanders, is now part of the higher education intelligence practitioner course and postgraduate assessment. Such practical application is continued through to the leadership and management higher education programs, where police leaders learn to recognise the importance of responding to trends by ensuring that they have adequately trained staff and the resources to combat emerging crime types. Obviously this is not always the case in practice and uncertainty is forever playing its part as the predicted trends are dynamic and constantly changing.

The focus on changing trends emphasises the requirement for investigators to be skilled in determining appropriate and measured responses to an evolving range of problems which are all competing for the same limited resources. Wilkinson (2010) outlines the need for police to have sound and robust analysis and risk assessment methodologies to determine appropriate police responses which can withstand scrutiny. Such assessments are being employed at many levels simply to determine the necessary response by law enforcement agencies to emerging serious crime.

The second role for higher education is to help police effectively manage the internal and external pressure on investigations—the authorising environment that Peter Martin (2010) describes in his chapter. In their chapters Carmen Lawrence (2010) and Sue Wilkinson (2010) examine the political impact on uncertainty in investigations, describing shifts in focus and effort (both escalating and reducing) to meet political whim. A good example of this kind of dynamic situation can be found in the recent spate of publicity and public outrage in relation to the number of Indian students being attacked in Australia. The possibility of this being a future issue was identified two years earlier by some higher education students when conducting strategic assessments. The prediction was ignored, possibly because of some of the issues raised in the chapter by Mark Kebbell, Damon Muller and Kirsty Martin (2010) in relation to cognitive bias. The statistical analysis was largely ignored because of uncertainty about the nature and reporting involved in the collection of the data, in line with issues suggested in the chapter by Richard Jarrett and Mark Westcott (2010). Lawrence makes the point that only when it became a huge political issue did the police leadership respond.

Uncertainty and higher education in policing

In the preceding discussion, we have highlighted the following roles for higher education in policing. First, the 'club sandwich', which combines underpinning knowledge relevant to policing, ongoing research and evaluation, and application. Second are the three tenets relevant to all layers of the club sandwich, which are critical thinking, analysis and research. Third is staying abreast of changing demands and effectively dealing with the authorising environment. Understanding and managing uncertainty are critical to each of these roles. The emphasis to date has largely been to turn uncertainty into certainty and this has led to significant revolutions in policing. Examples of key developments are described next. We then comment specifically on the other chapters in this book from the standpoint of higher education.

Scientific 'certainty'

Scientific breakthroughs have completely changed the way that police investigate serious crime and have had a great impact on the debate around uncertainty for policing and the way certain evidence is regarded. Remarkable breakthroughs starting with the first blood tests and fingerprints have seen crime scenes change from a quick wander around the scene to see if anything has been left behind to the extensive and intensive searching in sterile conditions which is currently the norm. However, as barristers and courts are ever vigilant in examining and challenging the certainty of such scientific advances, invariably doubts and uncertainty are reintroduced.

DNA analysis, once described by the FBI as infallible (Rossmo 2009), has been proven to have an error rate (Gigerenzer 2007). DNA should be seen as a starting point of an investigation in the same way as fingerprint and trace evidence, rather than the end. Obviously if there are further developments which do question the certainty of science, then it is imperative that these are revealed to prevent miscarriage of justice based on scientific evidence alone. Work with juries has discovered that scientific evidence holds enormous weight in their decision-making (Goodman-Delahunty & Newell 2004). The area of scientific certainty therefore needs to be fully explored. Investigative officers and judiciary can become 'blinded' by science and ignore other lines of inquiry if they feel the case has been established by condemning evidence such as DNA (Kebbell et al. 2010). Scientific evidence from research and pathology, for example, is easy for investigators to engage with and accept as it is much more black and white, or at least it appears to be.

It is therefore of particular concern that, as scientific certainty increases within an investigation, the willingness of investigators to conduct searching interviews or consider other possibilities reduces. Research suggests that the more evidence there is, particularly scientific evidence like DNA and fingerprints, the more likely it is that investigators will approach the interview in a narrow-minded fashion and not give the suspect the opportunity to deny the crime or explain their involvement, if any, in it (Dixon & Travis 2007). This can result in weaknesses in the prosecution case and, potentially, in unsound convictions. In the infamous case of *R v Chamberlain*, the alleged 'trace' evidence, which was later discredited, was pivotal to the conviction of Lindy Chamberlain (Lowndes 1995). More recently, there is the case of Dr Haneef described by Kebbell et al. (2010), where intelligence was taken at face value without a complete objective analysis—resulting in 'deafness' to the pleas of innocence from Dr Haneef (Clarke 2008). Numerous other alleged miscarriages of justice, such as *R v Mallard* (O'Donnell 2005) stem from similar issues around investigator mindset or tunnel vision brought on by the investigators' search for 'certainty' rather than 'the truth' of the matter under investigation.

This phenomenon is easy to understand and provides a very tempting path to follow. As Michael Smithson highlights '[h]umans both want and do not want unknowns' (2010) and most investigators want to be convinced of the guilt of the offender they are prosecuting. Science and technology provide far more certainty than do other sources of information and intelligence, however, it is the other sources that complete the picture and bridge the gaps in logic. For example a DNA sample, or fingerprint, purportedly provides a certain fact, but this is insufficient without the answers to the surrounding questions, such as how did that DNA sample come to be there or why was the fingerprint at the crime scene. These questions can usually only be answered by using various other sources of information, derived from related inquiries, witnesses, suspects or others with some involvement in the incident. None of these, however, provide the absolute certainty sought by investigators. The shades of grey remain and this is why the ability to analyse and evaluate the information available is all-important. The pitfalls of investigator mind set are well documented and researched. Kebbell et al. (2010), Rossmo (2009) and others discuss this phenomenon at length.

Improving the way uncertainty is dealt with in policing higher education

The other chapters in this book provide a starting point for thinking about the way uncertainty is dealt with in policing higher education and how this could be enhanced for practitioners. As stated by Cavanagh (1993):

The challenge to professional education is to improve the integration of academic scholarship with an educational process suitable to preparing professionals for contemporary service-oriented dynamic and demanding practice environments.

It is important to recognise that that 'policing' is now an emerging discipline and body of knowledge in its own right (Chambers 2004). Australia is, in many ways, the leader in terms of real engagement with policing in higher education providing a wide range of undergraduate and postgraduate programs specifically designed for police. In a number of other comparable countries like the UK and Canada, there is nowhere near the same level of opportunity for police and law enforcement officers to link their police training in an articulated sense to the higher education sector. New Zealand has specific links to university programs but Australia is one of the few countries seriously recognising the training and expertise of police officers and allowing that to be formally linked to higher education.

Junior police officers (recruits), at least in NSW, join the police service by way of a collaborative higher education program between NSW Police and Charles Sturt University. The Associate Degree in Policing brings together police and university staff to co-develop and deliver a practical training and education program for new recruits. In other words the students are not simply taught 'what to do' in their role but also why and when it is appropriate for a particular course of action. This basic level preparation of new police involves awareness of serious crime issues and the dangers of investigative mindset and heuristics (Kebbell et al. 2010) as well as the importance of their autonomous role in dealing with uncertainty, and the inevitable 'grey areas of the law' in relation to practice as discussed in the chapter by Tim Carmody (2010).

Beyond the probationary years officers often develop particular areas of interest and specialisation. In relation to the investigation of serious crime, officers wanting to become detectives in Australia undertake a National Diploma in Investigation delivered 'in force' by their own state or jurisdiction. Many officers also take up the opportunity to study bachelors level programs tailored for police to advance their knowledge of investigation, as well as to increase their chances of promotion. The specific programs offered for police usually provide advanced standing for the training to become a detective and include specifically bachelors degrees in policing, forensic science and justice studies. Some officers also elect to study a variety of associated degrees such as criminology or law. The qualifications specifically tailored to policing discuss at a higher educational level many of the issues raised in the various chapters of this book. Whilst set in a policing investigative context, the issues of emerging crime raised by Wilkinson (2010), cognitive bias discussed by Kebbell et al. (2010), as well as aspects of the law and the complexity of the judicial environment are examined from a national and international perspective. The use of case studies to illuminate the learning is common practice and the students themselves are encouraged to be reflective practitioners on their own professional development. Even at this still relatively junior stage of development, the impact of politics on policing and the role of leadership is not ignored (Lawrence 2010) with students being only too aware of the pressures upon them to deal with emerging crime or incidents with particular political interest attached.

Beyond the level of the bachelors degree, postgraduate programs currently specifically developed and offered to law enforcement students particularly address many of the issues raised in the chapters of this book. Intelligence practitioners at the strategic level attend a National Strategic Intelligence Course, which is a collaborative venture of the Australian Federal Police, the Australian Crime Commission and Charles Sturt University. This course is seen as the national benchmark for strategic analysis throughout Australia. The program also provides a pathway to higher education for intelligence practitioners.

Students in these programs study applied statistical analysis, which is based on the kind of work presented by Smithson (2010). This analysis is used to determine new and emerging crime types and trends (Wilkinson 2010). However students also study a broader range of research methods to ensure that they not only know how to conduct research but are also capable of being 'critical users' of research. Analysts in policing rely on secondary information from numerous sources ranging from National Crime Statistics to the information provided by a human source or listening device. All of this information has to be analysed to determine credibility, reliability and usefulness. This is why very rigid mathematical formulae, such as the one presented by Smithson, are very difficult to apply as a sole point of reference in policing. There is always the 'uncertain' human aspect involved. For example, in the case of Smithson and Muller's research into missing persons (which Smithson describes), the statistics quite clearly show that there is very little chance of a missing person being found dead. However, although the chance is small, it is not zero and in policing it is impossible to ignore the risk! However statistical analysis does form not only an indicator as to the solvability, but also quite often contributes to the investigative outcome. The analysis of phone record data and frequency correlations often provide convincing and compelling evidence in a court room where science will often impress the judge or jury (Goodman-Delahunty & Newell 2004).

An officer's ability to provide mapping, cluster analysis, descriptive stats and graphs, described by Robyn Attewell (2010); and the quantification of risk, discussed by Jarrett and Westcott (2010); is not restricted to the intelligence analysis field. Senior investigators are taught to make open and transparent decisions based on information and relevant data rather than their 'gut feeling'.

As Kebbell et al. (2010) discuss investigative mindset or tunnel vision, often fuelled by some aspect of scientific or other 'evidentiary' information is a very dangerous path for any investigation. The lessons learned from numerous previous miscarriages of justice are utilised in postgraduate investigation management programs to enlighten investigators of serious and serial crimes of the dangers of failing to keep an open mind and to consider all possible avenues of investigation. The theories of criminology and psychology are used to help investigators develop strategy around the entire investigative processes and to accurately record decision-making in relation to risk and uncertainty. Students are taught that the use of accurate validated research, and the use of such tools as mapping and cluster analysis, are essential if they are to argue successfully for additional resources or for continuing, or winding down, an inquiry.

Specialists in the areas of terrorism safety and security have the opportunity to study in a number of postgraduate programs which are currently offered in both Australia and overseas. Many law enforcement agencies are supporting staff to study in these programs which involve students developing a much broader range of understanding of fundamental issues involving religion, politics, history and current conflicts occurring around the world. These programs better equip officers to prevent and respond to terrorist threats and provide a much broader understanding of the current level of uncertainty and threat in relation to terrorism.

Police leaders are currently engaging in higher education programs which prepare them for the positions they either currently hold or aspire to. Here the focus on leadership and responsibility embraces many facets of risk and performance measurement. Business principles as described by Neil Fargher (2010), which can equally be applied to organised crime gangs or police, are incorporated into policing leadership programs. Modern policing and crime investigation is often considered a business with similar budgetary constraints prone to influence from global markets, technology, infrastructure and, most expensive of all, human resources. The use of all resources must be justified, accountable and open to public scrutiny. The only point of difference is the measures against success which serious crime investigation needs to consider.

Police leaders also learn about the legal implications of serious crime investigation (Carmody 2010), which grow more complex all of the time. What appears to deliver some form of certainty by way of scientific method can become inadmissible in a very short space of time. The issues surrounding admissibility and probity are a constantly changing feast. Police leaders also need to be very aware of the political environment in which they operate. As Lawrence (2010) outlines in her chapter police are influenced at every level by politics and suffer a high level of interference despite the so-called 'separation of powers'. Whilst this situation is arguably somewhat more of a problem in some states than others, well-educated investigators need to be politically astute and prepared to support their decision-making with well-researched evidence and reasoning. Officers need to be confident in their own judgments and not become the risk adverse puppets of whatever political regime is in place. Students study this level of interference and are challenged to suggest ways of dealing with both the media and the politicians in a productive and professional way.

Finally there is a wide range of research currently being undertaken by police officers at the masters, professional doctorate and PhD levels. This self-initiated research is an excellent platform for police to become—as was stated above—'the researchers, not the researched'. Police engagement in scientifically credible empirical research into their own professional practice is essential if the discipline of policing is to grow. Examples of current research being undertaken by police at Charles Sturt University range from a Detective Inspector in the Netherlands studying the 'role of hostage negotiators in international kidnap situations', to a Chief of Police in Ottawa conducting an evaluation of 'tenure policies in Canadian policing'. This diverse pool of police not only become experts in their own areas of study, but also engage in all the earlier mentioned aspects of higher education: critical thinking, analysis and research. It is these skills which underpin modern police education and provide the police who involve themselves in the various programs on offer with the skills to deal with the uncertainty of police investigation.

'Uncertainty' as an ally

Policing in Australia, as in other areas of the Western world, has undergone a 'shake-out' phase with Royal Commissions, statutory bodies and ad-hoc inquiries in most states and territories seeking to purge corrupt officers. Accountability and transparency have become catch-words and bodies with draconian powers have been established to police the police. The scrutiny of the 1990s arguably led to a tendency toward risk aversion among officers while at the same time the 'certainty' of scientific evidence created an illusion that criminal cases are easily solved through the use of scientifically verifiable evidence (Moston & Fisher 2006). This so-called 'CSI effect' (Goodman-Delahunty & Newell 2004; Mirsky 2005) has resulted in an avoidance of other more risky and uncertain methods of investigation such as the use of human sources and even formal and informal interviewing of witnesses, victims and suspects, as outlined earlier.

We argue that the higher level skills associated with higher education can improve the investigation of serious crime by reducing or preventing cognitive bias or tunnel vision. Investigators who are practiced in the disciplines of critical thinking, analysis and research are more likely to consider all of the information and evidence, be less likely to ignore information which is contradictory to their original hypothesis and be more prepared to keep an open mind to all lines of inquiry.

In addition, the key attributes of a higher education encourage investigators to embrace rather than avoid issues of uncertainty. As previously discussed, the idea of 'certainty' in serious crime investigation is a very comfortable one and an obvious aim for investigators, but comes with risk. The idea of being certain of a person's guilt is very attractive and rewarding. However, it can also lead to 'cognitive bias', 'confirmation bias' and a lack of understanding of one's own heuristics (see Kebbell et al. 2010). Properly understood and approached, uncertainty actually brings great benefits to the investigation of serious crime. Understanding that 'there is nothing as certain as uncertainty' can lead to a more thorough and open investigation process which maintains all lines of inquiry.

Higher order skills in action

Finally, we talk about those higher order skills as the attributes of the modern investigator and how the fruits of higher education will be seeded in the capacity of investigators to think critically, analyse and research.

Recently an example of these higher order skills occurred in the UK during a review of a 1993 missing person inquiry. The review meeting involved a wonderful example of collaborative and innovative thinking. The senior investigating officer had gathered a group of experts to assist in the development of a strategy to reinvestigate the missing person. The group included a forensic scientist, geographic profiler, investigative interviewing advisor, search specialist, investigation review advisor and family liaison officer. The net outcome of the meeting was a strategy which brought a completely new approach to how this case could be elevated to a murder investigation. The group basically conducted research of all of the facts and information prior to the meeting and then conducted a critical analysis of all of the intelligence and evidence. They then all shared their findings and developed a very innovative, practical and thought provoking strategy which brought an entirely new perspective for the senior investigating officer. This was not a traditional academic exercise by any means, but was action research, providing very practical and invaluable results in the fight against serious crime. What was very interesting was that all members of the group had undertaken higher education in their area of expertise and agreed that the combination of training and higher education had developed their ability to conduct this very practical form of review and analysis of serious crime cases.

Conclusion

The investigation of serious crime, like policing generally, is continually faced with the challenge of uncertainty on many fronts. Technology provides advances to both the criminal and the investigator. Uncertainty will remain for investigators as, for example, the international community becomes more mobile and borders become more porous, home-grown terrorism emerges in marginalised communities and the private sector continues to develop its own responses to crime and insecurity. In this environment higher education will continue to develop and the higher order skills that form its base will become more valued as the battle for control of law and order continues.

Academics and practitioners in law enforcement both have a lot to offer in maintaining a dialogue around the area of 'uncertainty' in the investigation of serious crime. However, for this dialogue to have real meaning and benefit it requires a great deal of collaboration and a deeper appreciation of each other's expertise and value.

Table 1: Summary of critical areas that warrant further research

Author	Critical areas that warrant further research
Kebbell et al	How does cognitive bias impact on decision-making in serious crime cases? In depth case reviews of serious crime cases and interviews with the investigating officers could be very helpful. This could include some questions around both 'gut feeling' as opposed to 'scientific' certainty to determine the main drivers for investigators. This could also feed into the proposals for formal formative review processes in serious crime.
Lawrence	This area of policing is fundamental to the future direction of Australian policing and a great project would be to look at the extent of political interference—both real and perceived/assumed—across the jurisdictions. This could link into the aims of the Australia New Zealand Policing Advisory Agency to provide the Commissioners with a 'single voice' and could demonstrate what is 'real' interference and what is anecdotal and how this impacts on decision-making of senior police in relation to serious crime.
Smithson	Some of this work could be used to look closely at the data and information currently being collated by police to see if there is room for improvement in the quality of collection and the nature of the information collected to give national standards for data gathering.
Wilkinson	Importantly, it would be beneficial to undertake some work regarding the dangerous state of borders and separate jurisdictional data bases, lack of information being shared and how this can be improved across the country and internationally.

References

Attewell, R 2010, 'Can statistics help', in G Bammer (ed.), *Dealing with uncertainties in policing serious crime*, ANU E Press, Canberra.

Bratton, W 2007, 'Bratton speaks out: what is wrong with criminal justice research – and how to make it right', edited by N Ritter, *National Institute of Justice Journal*, no. 257, <http://www.ojp.usdoj.gov/nij/journals/257/chief-bratton.html> (accessed 27 January 2010).

Carmody, T 2010, 'Criminal law', in G Bammer (ed.), *Dealing with uncertainties in policing serious crime*, ANU E Press, Canberra.

Cavanagh, SH 1993, 'Connecting education and practice', in L Curry, J Wergin & Associates (eds), *Educating professionals responding to new expectations for competence and accountability*, Jossey Publishers, San Francisco, pp. 180–212.

Chambers, R 2004, 'Collaborative police education - a report', unpublished paper presented to the World Association for Collaborative Education conference, Rotterdam.

Clarke, J 2008, 'Clarke inquiry into the case of Dr Mohamed Haneef. Report of the inquiry', <http://www.attorneygeneral.gov.au/www/ministers/RWPAttach.nsf/VAP/(966BB47E522E848021A38A20280E2386)~clarke+inquiry.pdf/$file/clarke+inquiry.pdf> (accessed 27 January 2010).

Dixon, D & Travis, G 2007, *Interrogating images. Audio-visually recorded police questioning of suspects*, Sydney Institute of Criminology, Australia.

Fargher, N 2010, 'Business', in G Bammer (ed.), *Dealing with uncertainties in policing serious crime*, ANU E Press, Canberra.

Gigerenzer, G 2007, *Gut feelings: the intelligence of the unconscious*, Viking, New York.

Goodman-Delahunty, J & Newell, B 2004, 'One in how many trillion?' *Australasian Science,* August, pp. 14–17.

Jarrett, R & Westcott, M 2010, 'Quantitative risk', in G Bammer (ed.), *Dealing with uncertainties in policing serious crime*, ANU E Press, Canberra.

Kebbell, MR, Muller, DA & Martin, K 2010, 'Understanding and managing bias', in G Bammer (ed.), *Dealing with uncertainties in policing serious crime*, ANU E Press, Canberra.

Lawrence, C 2010, 'Politics', in G Bammer (ed.), *Dealing with uncertainties in policing serious crime*, ANU E Press, Canberra.

Levenson, T 2009, *Newton and the counterfeiter: the unknown detective career of the world's greatest scientist*, Houghton, Mifflin & Harcourt, London.

Lowndes, J 1995, *Analysis & findings of the third coroner's inquest, into the death of Azaria Chamberlain*, 13 December, NT, <www.law.umkc.edu/faculty/projects/ftrials/chamberlain/lowndesreport.html> (accessed 27 January 2010).

Lusher, EA 1981, *Commission to inquire into New South Wales Police administration*, Parliamentary paper no. 179, Government Printer, Sydney.

Milroy, AM 2010, 'Law enforcement agencies which respond to nationally significant crime', in G Bammer (ed.), *Dealing with uncertainties in policing serious crime*, ANU E Press, Canberra.

Mirsky, S 2005, 'Crime scene instigation', *Scientific American,* May, <http://www.scientificamerican.com/article.cfm?id=crime-scene-instigation> (accessed 27 January 2010).

Moston, S & Fisher, M 2006, 'Defining the limits of police interrogation techniques with criminal suspects', in M Ioannou & D Youngs (eds), *Explorations in investigative psychology and contemporary offender profiling*, IA-AP Publishing, London.

O'Donnell, M 2005, 'High Court overturns Mallard murder conviction', ABC television, 15 November, <http://www.abc.net.au/7.30/content/2005/s1507471.htm> (accessed 27 January 2010).

Ord, B, Shaw, G & Green, T 2008, *Investigative interviewing explained*, 2nd edn, LexusNexus, Sydney.

Oxford English Dictionary 2000, 2nd Edition, Volume III, Clarendon Press, Oxford.

Rossmo, DK 2009, *Criminal investigative failures*, CRC Press, London.

Smithson, M 2010, 'Understanding uncertainty', in G Bammer (ed.), *Dealing with uncertainties in policing serious crime*, ANU E Press, Canberra.

Wilkinson, S 2010, 'The modern policing environment', in G Bammer (ed.), *Dealing with uncertainties in policing serious crime*, ANU E Press, Canberra.

Wood, JRT 1997, *Royal Commission into the New South Wales Police Service*, final report, Government of New South Wales, Sydney.

Wood, J & Bradley, D 2009, 'Embedding partnership policing: what we've learned from the Nexus policing project', *Police Practice and Research*, vol. 10, no. 2, pp. 133–144.

Consultancy to Build Capacity in Dealing with Uncertainty in Law Enforcement

STEVE LONGFORD

This chapter is based on research and anecdotal feedback aggregated over the past eight years in order to develop some of the training that New Intelligence provides to law enforcement, compliance and national security agencies, as well as the higher end of the corporate sector. It highlights the main kinds of issues that have driven the development of this training—both about the problems police face and about methods they can use to enhance their ability to deal with uncertainty.

Everyday, in all aspects of their lives, people are constantly making decisions. These decisions are an integral part of life, and the outcomes will be a reflection of each person's decision-making ability and technique. Sometimes individuals are called upon to justify important decisions, while at other times the decision is as simple as what they are having for dinner and requires no justification at all. The consequences of a decision tend to dictate how important it is and this may or may not affect how it is derived. As with most human interactions, individuals have varying ability to make decisions and the outcomes reflect how good the decision was. An individual's ability to explain how they arrived at a particular decision can be a significant indicator of their capabilities. This difficult and complex area constitutes the key area of exploration of uncertainty in terms of developing training and capacity building for agencies and organisations.

Making critical decisions represents the greatest source of uncertainty experienced by law enforcement officers in the investigation of serious and organised crime for a number of reasons including:

- the public rely on the decision-making capability of law enforcement
- the outcomes of many law enforcement decisions are life or death
- there is a perception that law enforcement officers are excellent decision-makers, whereas in reality law enforcement officers do not receive adequate training in decision-making
- the consequences of decisions made by law enforcement are not always open to examination, nor are they obvious

- scrutiny of law enforcement decision-making is at its greatest when things go wrong.

Compounding these issues are the hidden factors in decision-making, including the effects of bias which distort how decision-makers perceive and deal with inputs to decision-making. Such hidden factors include:

- the propensity to use personal and organisational avoidance mechanisms in the face of uncertainty
- the effects of uncertainty on the confidence of decision-makers
- the way that decisions are assessed both individually and organisationally and how that contributes to uncertainty.

It does not require any substantial research to assert that decision-making is a significant component of the function of law enforcement. It is our experience that decisions also represent the greatest source of uncertainty experienced by law enforcement officers in the investigation of serious and organised crime. The essence and aim of our courses and the research that underpins them is to increase understanding of how biases impact upon decision-making and to provide a framework, guidelines and tools that assist with more effective decision-making. This chapter therefore examines some of the key points that link decision-making with uncertainty. It concludes with a discussion about how a consultancy service such as ours deals with insights identified in the other chapters in this book in order to improve our ability to build capacity among police to make good decisions in the face of uncertainty.

Decisions

We define a decision as: 'a choice made among alternative courses of action'. Both uncertainty and a decision are psychological constructs and cannot be seen but only inferred from behaviour. In practice, an integral part of the role of the critical decision-maker is decision-making under conditions of both certainty and uncertainty. There are a number of tools and techniques for reducing uncertainty. Before they can be understood and applied, however, it is important to understand what a decision actually is and how uncertainty arises throughout the decision-making process.

Decision process

In order to increase the validity of a decision, an officer should ensure that they utilise a reliable and valid process and that it sits within a logical framework. Decision-making can be viewed as the process involved in making a choice between alternatives that have varying consequences attached to them.

Choice can be defined as the opportunity to make a selection from a number of alternatives. If there is no choice, there is no decision to be made.

Alternatives can be defined as possible courses of action or situations from which a choice is made. If there are no alternatives, there is no choice to be made and hence no decision to be arrived at.

A *consequence* can be defined as something that logically or naturally follows from an action or condition, or more simply, the outcome of an action or situation. If there are no consequences to an alternative, it is most likely an invalid alternative and therefore should not be under consideration.

There are often *limitations* to what can happen and these can impact on the decision process by restricting or eliminating alternatives. There are also *factors* that must be taken into account when assessing *risk* associated with both the likelihood of something occurring and its impact.

Finally consequences are assessed against *criteria* which are defined as characteristics or requirements that a consequence must possess to a greater or lesser extent. Usually the validity of a consequence is dictated by how many criteria it possesses and often these criteria are associated with a certain outcome. Another way of viewing criteria is as the characteristics of a good decision. Potentially the most important aspect of decision-making revolves around not only establishing criteria but prioritising these criteria. This is the area of decision-making process that tends to require the greatest effort.

As highlighted in Figure 1, any decision is not simply a matter of choosing between alternatives. Each alternative has consequences and some alternatives may result in shared consequences or even consequences that are exactly the same. A decision is made by comparing each of the consequences against the relevant criteria and choosing the alternative that possesses the greatest number of valid consequences bearing in mind factors, limitations and risk. Uncertainty can arise at any of the points in the process but tends to be most prevalent when trying to forecast consequences, assess risk, and most importantly, establish and prioritise criteria.

Figure 1: Decision process model

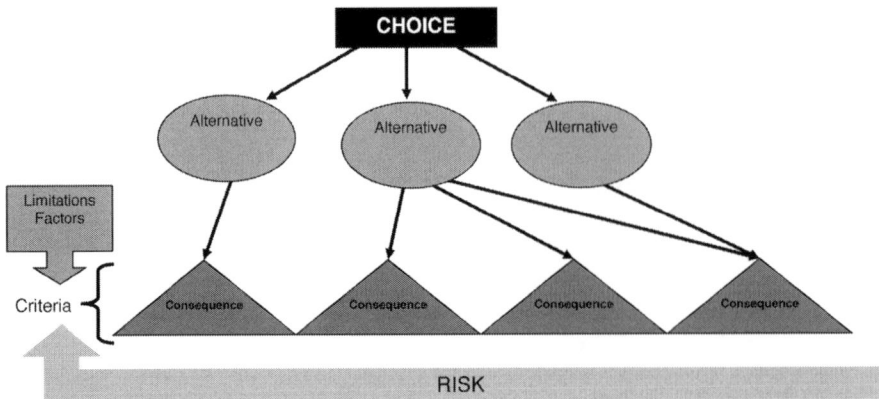

Bearing each of the attributes of the Decision Process Model in mind, there are a number of decision situations that can be more fully explained and understood. The most significant of these is the situation in which decision-makers believe or state that they 'had no choice'. If there are truly no alternatives to a course of action then there is no choice. If, on the other hand, there is simply an apparent lack of alternatives, it may be an indication that there is an insufficient amount of information or a lack of thoughtful application to identifying more alternatives. Similarly, it may be that the officer does not like the consequences of an alternative and so removes it from the options. Finally, the criteria that the officer is setting for the alternatives may be too narrow, uninformed or derived from a set of untested assumptions.

Difficulty in decisions

Decisions themselves are often characterised by how difficult they are to make. We tend to see some decisions as being easier to make than others, yet there is an important distinction to be made. There is a difference between the ease with which a decision can be made and the ease with which it can be implemented. Although the two are connected, this chapter will not attempt to address implementation issues. This section will talk about the factors that influence the ease with which a decision can be made, known as decision factors or decision attributes. The following section will deal with how the decision environment contributes to decision difficulty by creating uncertainty.

The relative difficulty of making a decision is influenced by the following factors:

- previous decisions made
- nature of problems and solutions
- existence of alternatives
- impact of consequences
- reversibility
- rules.

These factors have been identified through research and analysis of various decision-making situations and are a symptom of the decision itself. Generally, easier decisions tend to be described as programmable, whilst more difficult decisions are described as unprogrammable.

Programmable decisions

Programmable decisions are routine and repetitive. The response can be decided ahead of time, and the action taken is the same each time the decision has to be made. Definite systematic procedures can be established for making the choice. The difficulty is to judge whether or not the decision is sufficiently routine to be classified as programmable. Despite the fact that a programmable decision might be routine, it must nevertheless not be taken too lightly. Circumstances change continually and, accordingly, each decision must be addressed individually. However, if it can be determined that a decision falls within certain standard parameters, a routine procedure can be used.

A programmable decision can be made by applying a set of rules. These rules can be determined as a result of experience with other similar problems or situations.

Unprogrammable decisions

Unprogrammable decisions are less structured than programmable decisions. A completely unprogrammable decision is unique in that it has no rules; it has a completely individual set of circumstances, consequences and alternatives. There are no rules or guidelines for handling this kind of decision and therefore the unprogrammable decision requires better decision-making ability. Often, the consequences of this type of decision are far more serious than those pertaining to the programmable ones.

By determining whether a decision is programmable or unprogrammable, the decision-maker can allocate time accordingly. Unprogrammable decisions will generally require more time and examination and obviously tend to create more uncertainty. Importantly there is a tendency for decision-makers to try to transform unprogrammable decisions into programmable ones, usually by engaging emotion, succumbing to bias, applying rules (criteria) or oversimplifying the process. Another option is to manage the environment in which the decision is to be made.

Decision environment

The environment within which a decision is made can strongly influence the speed, accuracy, validity and reliability of the decision. Not only can the environment trigger situational biases, but it can also corrupt the decision-making process by interfering with the proper application of the various steps of the process.

The decision environment is influenced by the incident(s) around which the decisions are made. For example crossing the road in the face of oncoming traffic is what is known as a fast burn decision. That is to say, the incident requires a quick decision, the consequences of which will be known in the very near future. On the other hand, buying a new apartment off the plan is a slow burn decision, where there is more time to make the decision and the consequences of it will not be known for some time. Problems arise when the two become confused especially when slow burn decisions are treated as fast burn decisions.

The decision environment is also made up of:

- decision layers
- complexity
- ambiguity
- sensitivity
- context
- preparedness.

The decision environment contributes to the difficulty of making any particular decision and directly contributes to the most common confounding factor of good decision-making—uncertainty.

Bias

The definition of bias is *a preference or an inclination (mental leaning), especially one that inhibits impartial judgment*. Bias has been most practically examined by Heuer (1999) as applied in the role of intelligence analysts. Signficantly, bias can contribute to decision-making by both increasing and reducing uncertainty, however where bias reduces uncertainty it tends to be at the expense of validity.

There are a variety of types of bias. In our research and training courses, we concentrate on the following:

- cognitive bias
- situation bias (also known as situational bias)
- personal bias

Cognitive bias

Cognitive biases are consistent, predictable mental errors caused by implementing simplifying strategies to ease the burden of mentally processing information to make judgments and decisions. However, even if the person is aware of these mental errors or cognitive biases, this will not necessarily increase the accuracy of their perception or objectivity. Cognitive biases are those biases that are built up by an individual, that they may or may not be aware of, and that influence behaviour and attitudes both consciously and unconsciously.

For example, Moston et al. (1992) found that if a police interviewer knew an interviewee had previous convictions, they were less likely to give them the benefit of the doubt and more likely to try to obtain a confession as opposed to the truth, often using an accusatorial interview style.

Situation bias

Situation bias is where particular situations can impact upon a person and the decisions they make. In short, the effects of the people, circumstances, pressures and factors that make up every situation have the potential to change the way a person behaves. Often people have to work and collaborate with others, which has many benefits, limitations and biases that stem from the working environment. In and of itself this enviroment can create within an individual a tendency to behave in certain way and one of the most common yet powerful examples of this is 'group think'. Group think describes a psychologically proven principle that states that individuals will tend toward consensus despite evidence that contradicts such a postion. Whilst there are many examples of this, the position taken by the American military (before their entry into the Second World War) that Pearl Harbour was unlikely to be attacked is one of the most famous.

Personal bias

Personal bias is a product or an outcome of situational bias. In other words, personal biases are shaped by the world in which we live or the situations that are present in everyday life. Unfortunately, personal biases are formed from a very early age but become more dominant and entrenched through puberty into adulthood. As with cognitive biases, personal biases can be explained by referring to the theory of bounded rationality which states that there is too much information in the world and that in order to process some of it and remain sane, people must take short cuts (Simon 1972). One of the most common examples of this type of short cut is the evolution of 'isms', or stereotypes, for example racism, sexism and ageism. Stereotypes and prejudices tend to occur after exposure to an issue that deeply impacts on the individual and they tend to judge all similar future experiences by those same criteria. Although considered to be the exception rather than the rule, prejudices and stereotypes can be subconscious or even unconscious. More commonly, however, they are known to the individual but are suppressed due to 'political correctness' or for other social reasons.

Personal biases tend to be deeply ingrained and influence thinking at a fundamental level. Prejudices and stereotypes are not necessarily wrong or bad, but they are powerful. The best way to deal with personal biases is to be honest about issues that obviously impact on the individual, but more importantly to try to gain awareness of those that are not so obvious. However being aware of personal biases is not enough. Conscious steps are required to effectively manage such biases.

Decisions under conditions of certainty and uncertainty

Most decisions require the decision-maker to estimate or predict the future consequences of alternatives under consideration. This estimation or prediction can be based on information such as historical trends and data about current situations. Crystal ball gazing is always dangerous because predictions made about the future are necessarily based on past and current information. This means that all decisions, even programmable decisions, carry with them a certain degree of uncertainty. Therefore the conditions under which decision-making is performed can be classified in terms of certainty or uncertainty.

To be an effective decision-maker, however, it is important to understand just one fact about certainty and uncertainty. Both are a state of mind—a cognitive state. People do not live in an uncertain world; the world is certain enough. How individuals deal with the potential for change over time creates uncertainty.

Without delving too far into the psychology of confidence, it is not difficult to recognise that conditions of uncertainty tend to diminish the confidence of those experiencing the uncertainty. Extrapolating this observation, it is possible to draw an inverse correlation between uncertainty and confidence—as uncertainty increases confidence diminishes and vice versa. It is important to note that operating under conditions of low confidence increases stress and reduces effectiveness for most people. Techniques for increasing confidence alone do not tend to be effective or practical in critical situations. Dealing with uncertainty, on the other hand, can be achieved through clear understanding of the decision process in conjunction with use of various guidelines or principles.

Under conditions of certainty, the decision-maker feels they have enough data to be able to quite accurately predict the outcomes of the various choices. Generally, decisions made under conditions of certainty are programmable.

Most decisions, however, are made under conditions of uncertainty. In these situations, there are a large number of factors to consider and there is likely to be an additional group of unidentifiable factors. The circumstances are also probably in a state of change or flux. The decision-maker must use greater judgment, intuition and experience to assign the correct probabilities to different alternatives and their consequences. There are five main factors that increase uncertainty in decision-making. They are:

- the type of decision to be made
- the process used for making a decision
- the filters (biases)
- the framework (critical thinking)
- the inputs (information).

Decisions made under conditions of uncertainty may be either programmable or unprogrammable, but are more likely to be unprogrammable. Knowing what type of decision the decision-maker is faced with can assist in determining how the choice or problem should be approached and help reduce uncertainty.

Mitigating uncertainty

Problem-solving

Traditionally, problem-solving has been taught as a fundamental aspect of analysis and, whilst many aspects of problem-solving are important in terms of tools and techniques for use during analysis, it is important to delineate between problem-solving and decision-making as functions. Simply stated, problem-solving is about finding answers—the solution—whilst decision-making is about choosing the best alternative in light of the information at hand. On one hand good problem-solving is an important part of decision-making, but on the other there is no substitute for critical thinking in decision-making.

Good problem-solving requires problem definition followed by problem breakdown. This should result in a series of questions that, when correctly answered, provide a solution to the overall problem. If done properly, the problem-solving technique should result in a series of specific questions that the decision-maker seeks to find specific answers for. These answers, when re-aggregated, provide a solution as opposed to a product.

When information is incomplete or missing the decision-maker can use one of the five basic types of problem-solving:

1. analogy—evidence found in parallel cases
2. deduction—identify patterns from a reasonably complete set of data (move from the general to the particular)
3. extrapolation— forecasting process whereby data are extended beyond a series
4. induction—identify patterns from a limited set of data (move from the particular to the general)
5. interpolation—providing the missing link in a set of data.

Critical thinking

Critical thinking should not be confused with being argumentative or being critical of other people and their ideas. Although critical thinking skills can be used in exposing fallacies and bad reasoning, critical thinking can also play an important role in cooperative reasoning and constructive tasks. Critical thinking can help decision-makers acquire knowledge, improve theories, and strengthen arguments. As a general rule, critical thinking involves developing some emotional and intellectual distance between the decision-maker and ideas, whether their own or those of others, in order to better evaluate their truth, validity, and reasonableness.

Critical thinking is an effort to develop reliable, rational evaluations about what is reasonable to believe and reject. Critical thinking makes use of the tools of logic and science because it values scepticism over gullibility or dogmatism, reason over faith, science over pseudoscience, and rationality over wishful thinking.

Critical thinking is the ability to think clearly and rationally. It includes the ability to engage in reflective and independent thinking. Decision-makers with critical thinking skills are able to do the following:

- understand the logical connections between ideas
- identify, construct and evaluate arguments
- detect inconsistencies and common mistakes in reasoning
- solve problems systematically
- identify the relevance and importance of ideas
- reflect on the justification of one's own beliefs and values.

Critical thinking is not a matter of accumulating information. A decision-maker with a good memory and who knows a lot of facts is not necessarily good at critical thinking. A critical thinker is able to deduce consequences from what they know, and they know how to make use of information to solve problems, and to seek relevant sources of information.

Critical thinking is a skill. Like the acquisition of many other skills, there are three main factors involved in learning critical thinking:

- theory
- practice
- attitude.

Decision-makers differ in their natural talent for good reasoning. Psychologists have discovered persistent biases and fallacies in human reasoning. Acquiring explicit knowledge of these cognitive limitations and the principles of good reasoning can help us improve our critical thinking.

However, merely knowing the principles that distinguish good and bad reasoning is not enough. One might acquire an understanding of the theories of good tennis, and yet fail to apply and make use of such theories in actual game play. Similarly, to improve critical thinking skills, it is necessary to develop the ability to internalise the principles decision-makers have learnt in normal reasoning, and to develop the disposition and ability to apply such principles in daily life.

Good critical thinking skills require more than occasional practice and knowledge of theory. Persistent practice will bring about improvements only if a decision-maker has the right motivation and attitude. To improve a decision-maker's thinking they must recognise the importance of reflecting on the reasons for belief and action. They must also be willing to engage in debate, to make mistakes, to break old habits, and to deal with linguistic complexities and abstract concepts.

There are a number of key skills and tools which are necessary for thinking critically. I deal with each of them in turn.

Open-mindedness

A decision-maker who wishes to think critically must be open-minded. This requires being open to the possibility that not only are others right, but also that the decision-maker may be wrong. Often decision-makers argue their point, however, it is in reviewing or developing their analysis, without taking any time to consider that they may be mistaken in some element of their thinking or the process involved where the problem is caused.

It is possible to be too open-minded, as not every idea is equally valid or has an equal chance of being true. Although decision-makers should allow for the possibility that others are correct, all claims should be supported to a sufficiently high level or else they should be dismissed.

Differentiate emotion from reason

Even if decision-makers have clear, logical and empirical reasons for accepting an idea, there may also be emotional and psychological reasons (i.e. cognitive biases) for accepting it. As discussed earlier, it is important that decision-makers learn to separate the two, because the latter can easily interfere with the former.

A decision-maker's emotional reasons for believing something may be quite understandable, but if the logic behind the belief is wrong, then ultimately their belief is irrational. If decision-makers are going to approach their beliefs in a sceptical, fair manner, then they must be willing to set aside their emotions and evaluate the logic and reasoning independently—possibly even rejecting their beliefs if they fail to live up to logical criteria.

Argue from knowledge, not ignorance

Because decision-makers often have an emotional or other psychological investment in their beliefs, it is not unusual for them to step forward and try to defend those beliefs, regardless of whether the logic or evidence for them is weak. Indeed, sometimes decision-makers will defend an idea even though they really do not know a great deal about it—they think they do, but they do not.

A decision-maker who tries to practice critical thinking, however, should avoid assuming that they already know everything they need to know. Decision-makers should recognise that someone who disagrees with them can teach them something relevant and refrain from arguing a position if they are ignorant of important, relevant facts. A general maxim 'There is always someone better' is relevant.

Probability is not certainty

There are ideas that are probably true and ideas that are certainly true, but while it is nice to have an idea that belongs in the latter category, decision-makers must understand that the latter group is far, far smaller than the former. However preferable it might be, decision-makers cannot be absolutely certain about the bulk of matters—especially those matters that are the focus of many intelligence debates.

When a decision-maker exercises scepticism and critical thinking, they should remember that just because they can show a conclusion is probably true, that does not mean they have shown or can show that it is certainly true. Certain truths require firm conviction, but probable truths require only tentative conviction—that is to say, decision-makers should believe them with the appropriate strength that the evidence and reason allow.

Possibilities and probabilities

Extrapolating that probability is not certainty, it is important that decision-makers deal in probabilities rather than possibilities. The propensity of some to explore what might be possible is a constant source of uncertainty, especially in light of the fact that nearly anything is possible. The requirement to state any potential situation or scenario in terms of probabilities limits the potential for extreme and highly unlikely scenarios to impact on decision-making. It does not preclude extreme or highly unlikely scenarios, but just forces the officer to recognise the potential rarity of the scenario and to express the reasoning and support for that particular decision in terms that can be readily compared.

Occam's Razor

Occam's Razor, stated simply, posits that all things being equal, the simplest explanation for a given situation is the best one. Looking for the 'hard' or clever answer can often be a waste of time and effort, especially considering that, for a large proportion of time, decision-makers are 'satisficing', that is finding the immediate good-enough solution that deals with their specific issue rather than the best solution.

Intelligence and evidence

The last 20 years has seen the advent of intelligence as a mainstream tool used by law enforcement. Its relatively recent arrival, however, has dictated that understanding of both the intelligence process and any resulting product are limited, especially by investigators and those who manage them. This can best be expressed as follows: evidence can be intelligence but intelligence can never be evidence. In simple terms, we define evidence as anything that can be proven, or more specifically proven in a court of law, and we define intelligence as anything that supports the discovery or evidence, or provides direction and focus to an investigation. The sometimes murky divide between the two often forms the basis for poor decision-making when attempts are made to apply the certainty of evidence to the fluid, dynamic uncertain nature of intelligence (Longford 2008).

The role of anchoring

Nothing happens in a vacuum, especially decision-making. Therefore it is important to understand how some of the information we use to make decisions affects us. There are many ways in which this occurs but one of the most common and powerful is that of *arbitrary coherence*. Arbitrary coherence refers to the way that an initial piece of information that is arbitrary, which becomes established in our minds, tends to shape how we view any subsequent information. In other words this piece of information becomes an *anchor* around which all other information is assessed.

Anchoring is an attempt by the brain to help reduce uncertainty but is in reality partly a cognitive bias and partly lazy thinking. Anchoring can be very subtle and often unperceived by the decision-maker.

Decision quality

Unfortunately decisions viewed in this way tend not to differentiate between false positives and false negatives. A false positive is when a result is shown or believed to be positive when in fact it is negative and vice versa for a false negative. These two terms tend to be used when speaking about the validity of a scientific test, experiment or process. If decision-making as a process is viewed as either valid or invalid, then the quality of a decision can be rated more fairly despite the outcome.

This view of decision quality becomes increasingly important as the potential or actual requirement to defend a decision escalates. There is a direct correlation between the validity of a decision's underlying process and its ability to be defended. The Decision Quality Matrix (Figure 2) shows that an actual positive and a false positive may not need to be defended, however an actual negative as well as a false negative will. It is very difficult to defend a bad decision, however, it is possible to defend a false negative decision that has been perceived as bad. Decision-makers should seek to increase the validity of their decisions accordingly because this tends to ensure two things; a higher probability of achieving a 'good' decision and greater defensibility when a decision is perceived as 'bad'.

For example after getting a tip and deciding to bet on a horse, a punter confuses the race number 2 and horse 3 and bets on horse number 2 to win in race 3. The horse wins and pays a handsome dividend, however, for the actual tip, in race 2, horse 3 came second last. This was a good outcome but the underlying process was flawed. On the other hand, the same punter gets another tip for another horse and two days before betting checks the form of the horse. He discovers that it runs well on wet, slow tracks and is at very long odds of 100 to 1 and rated as very unlikely to win on a standard dry, fast track. The two favourite horses are at odds of 2 to 1 and 3 to 1 one, respectively. On the day of the bet he contacts the course to discover that it has rained over night and that the track has been rated as slow, and the odds of the horse have come in at 20 to 1. He makes his bet as an each way bet (win and place) and the horse comes in third and pays a reasonable dividend. Although the outcome was not as good, the decision was based on sound process.

Therefore it is possible that a 'good' decision may not be a valid one in terms of process and a 'bad' decision may be very sound as far as the manner in which it was arrived at was concerned. Figure 2 shows how this can occur.

Figure 2: Decision Quality Matrix

	Valid Process	Invalid Process
Good Outcome	Positive (Good Decision)	False Positive (Bad Decision)
Bad Outcome	False Negative (Good Decision)	Negative (Bad Decision)

Decision practice

The practice of decision-making tends to be unconscious except when the criticality or difficulty of it becomes so overbearing that it is impossible to miss. When confronted with a decision, officers should first try to understand the importance of the decision.

In order to determine the importance of a decision, answering the following questions can assist the decision-maker:

- What effect will the decision have on the goals of the unit or organisation?
- Will the decision further the achievement of those goals?
- How many people will be affected?
- What resources are involved?
- What are the ramifications of the decision?
- Will the decision create other problems in other sections of the organisation or will it create other problems within the immediate unit or task force?
- What is the relative frequency of the decisions?
- What is the time pressure?

The amount of time and effort spent making a decision should directly correlate with the importance of that decision. Decision-makers work with limited resources, particularly in terms of available time. Time must be budgeted carefully. It is pointless and inefficient for decision-makers to spend a disproportionate amount of time on decisions of minor importance and yet make major decisions without properly examining the circumstances or all the alternative choices.

When an urgent decision is required, a decision-maker can only immediately choose among the alternatives that they have identified. Due to time constraints, the choice may be an 'either/or' situation. In these cases, it is quite possible that a less than optimal decision is made because not all the alternatives have been identified. Therefore, it is preferable that the decision be structured so that later, if necessary, further action can be taken to begin to reduce the uncertainty under which such decisions are made.

Biases, frameworks, inputs and decisions

As the level of criticality or difficulty of the decision increases, so does the possibility of the introduction of an extra dimension that cannot be ignored—sometimes decisions are just not made. In some situations the decision maker does not resolve the issue of choice and fails to complete the process. In many cases the impact of not making a decision outweighs that of making a bad or invalid decision. Therefore in every case there are six potential outcomes as shown in Table 1.

Table 1: Decision quality

Process	Outcome	Quality
Valid	Successful	Positive
Valid	Unsuccessful	Positive
Invalid	Successful	Negative
Invalid	Unsuccessful	Negative
No Decision	Successful	Negative
No Decision	Unsuccessful	Negative

Table 1 highlights four decision processes that have negative quality ratings. For these types of decision processes, 'invalid' and 'no decision' tend to be the result of errors, flaws or undue influence in terms of biases, frameworks and information.

Biases, as described earlier, are the unconscious processes that are continuously occurring within people's heads and are indicative of their mental patterns and cognitive processes. Frameworks that support decision-making revolve around critical thinking. Critical thinking refers to those kinds of mental activities that are clear, precise, and purposeful and aimed at achieving a real or potential outcome.

Input issues, primarily those related to information, can include factors such as:

- information overload
- information quality
- too many alternatives
- insufficient alternatives
- low visibility of consequences
- unattractive consequences.

Ultimately these factors contribute to uncertainty which, as a cognitive state, is subjective for the individual. This tends to be a personality or bias issue that can be difficult to deal with. There are, however, tools and techniques to help deal with these factors and they all tend to fall under the banner of intelligence, including behavioural intelligence and intelligence analysis.

Behavioural intelligence allows officers to understand the impact of their own biases and to mitigate and manage for them. Intelligence methodology creates greater visibility of new or better alternatives that may not have been considered, and subsequently illuminates potential consequences that were not previously apparent. Utilising the intelligence process, a good decision-maker will be able to readily define the scope of alternatives immediately available and, drawing on a wide range of resources, generate further imaginative, innovative and practical alternatives. The potential consequences of these alternates can have increased visibility and subsequently levels of uncertainty can be reduced.

Where to next?

How does our education and research intersect with the insights from the other chapters? Clearly some of the topics are more relevant than others.

Robyn Attewell's (2010) work on statistics has provided some very useful insights. Reasoning by analogy she draws very interesting comparisons between disease and crime. There is clearly room to draw further upon this comparison in order to try to understand how tools and techniques used to deal with disease, especially identification of root cause and subsequent spread, could have application when dealing with uncertainty in crime. More practically, her approach to statistics—and how they both contribute to uncertainty but may be used to help reduce it—is significant. This is especially so when we consider that the use of statistics within the intelligence arena has been crude and in many cases misleading. Clearly there is a role for the use of statistics in reducing uncertainty and the challenge is to devise ways to use them to easily and practically enhance decision-making.

While the chapter by Carmen Lawrence (2010) deals with issues that are largely outside the sphere of decision-making that we work in, she highlights some important synergies. One is her statement that, '[i]n reality, the developed world has never been safer' which is in line with our position that uncertainty is a cognitive state, and that, whilst external events contribute to uncertainty, the uncertainty itself originates in the mind. Where we would disagree, however, is on the value of problem-solving as a tool to reduce uncertainty. It is our experience that whilst problem-solving can be helpful, it is often problem identification that contributes more significantly to reducing uncertainty.

Lawrence's examination of how fear contributes to uncertainty and the way this is used in politics would seem to warrant more research. In our consultancy work on decision-making we explore the role of fear through avoidance and the impact of emotion. Lawrence demonstrates that police have to deal with the fear of others (politicians, other police, the public), as well as their own fear and this is something we will explore further in our training programs.

A number of other papers spend varying proportions of their time positing risk management as a mechanism for reducing uncertainty. Anecdotally there appears to growing evidence that effort put into risk identification may contribute more significantly to reducing uncertainty, especially in policing. This point is inadvertently alluded to by Neil Fargher (2010) in the conclusion of his paper, and more succinctly by Richard Jarrett and Mark Westcott (2010).

Jarrett and Westcott also make a very interesting attempt to provide a better understanding of uncertainty by quantifying some of the contributing factors such as risk and consequence, both of which are key to the decision-making process. They identify both alternatives and consequence as key factors in uncertainty, both of which our model (Figure 1) of decision-making posit as key components.

Of most interest is their formula for quantifying risk which ultimately multiplies consequence by likelihood. The formula itself appears valid, however, as with their attempts to reduce many situations to simple outcomes such as cost, their position fails to account for the complexity and difficulty associated with assessing likelihood. Evaluating and accounting for likelihood is one of the key areas that can be earmarked for future research.

Similarly, Sue Wilkinson's (2010) assertions in regards to interoperability present an obvious avenue for research. Anecdotally, most interstate or national operations elevate the levels of uncertainty for individual police, especially when two key issues arise: competing priorities and failure to share information. A greater understanding of exactly how these two issues impact on uncertainty would provide a significant springboard for more pragmatic approaches.

Finally, Michael Smithson's (2010) paper generates more questions than it answers, yet provides the most significant avenues for exploration. The practical value of these may not be immediately obvious, yet they have the greatest potential for modifying how we approach uncertainty in general and decision-making more specifically and certainly warrant further examination. The ideas that call for discussion are:

1. The relationship between uncertainty and ignorance, including Smithson's 1989 taxonomy. From the perspective of the work we undertake, there is no doubt that ignorance can contribute to uncertainty, but they differ in so far as ignorance tends to describe a discrete lack of knowledge or information whilst uncertainty describes a cognitive state.
2. The focus on alternatives, especially partitioning. From a decision-making perspective, this highlights the problem of decision-makers failing to pursue consequences. Whilst the examination of partitioning is entirely valid in terms of alternatives, it fails to provide any direction for those engaged in the assessment of consequences, specifically about risk and limitations. Yet it may be that very examination that results in a more clinical approach to

what could be considered one of the more subjective aspects of decision-making.

3. The exploration of guilt and innocence tends to fall outside the purview of police, however, it is important to recognise that even the inclusion of a 'third option' fails to account for a system which has always been based on the paradigm that it is better that ten guilty men go free than one innocent man be convicted. In effect the system is designed for this.

4. The exploration of the issues of probability, as they relate to the decision to investigate a homicide, correctly discredits any attempt to develop any formula for the instigation of an investigation. On the other hand it supports the concept of Standard Operating Procedures as a set of guidelines to be interpreted according to the individual situation each decision-maker encounters.

The rest of Smithson's paper either subtly, or inadvertently, supports the role and function of intelligence as an essential tool to support the management of uncertainty in the investigation of serious and organised crime. He identifies and articulates, in some deal of complexity, issues and factors that will never be examined by many decision makers, yet they speak to the heart of how intelligence may change the way decisions are made in law enforcement. Intelligence provides tools to assist with the reduction, evaluation and collation of raw information and thereby increases its utility in managing uncertainty. Smithson has started to provide some of the questions that, if answered effectively, could guide the development of the way intelligence is used to reduce uncertainty. Of greater significance is that an increasing understanding of Smithson's proposals illuminates the void between the worlds of academia and officers, and how the narrowing of this chasm may be the most important outcome of this book.

Finally, there are assertions by some of the papers that humans either do not know or do not want to know certain things. This may be true and, in effect, may constitute an attempt to deal with uncertainty by reducing the amount of information a particular individual has to deal with in to order to make a decision. It does fail to take into account that, whilst the amount of information may contribute to levels of uncertainty, it is the way each individual deals with the amount of information that is at the core of how uncertainty affects decision-makers. Uncertainty is a cognitive state and the relationship between it and the key to many human interactions—confidence—is an inversely proportional one. Ultimately it will be research into the mechanisms and techniques whereby individuals manage and mitigate their own levels of uncertainty and subsequently deal with their own levels of confidence, or indeed self esteem, that will provide the most important and pragmatic inroads into how uncertainty can be dealt with.

Conclusion

If, as a result of this chapter, it becomes apparent that decision-making constitutes one of the most significant contributions towards the inherent nature of uncertainty in law enforcement, then it should be obvious that any measures that seek to make decision-making either easier or more accountable have a reasonable degree of value in dealing with uncertainty. The real value of this chapter and, more importantly, the approach of this book lies in attempts to engage a multidisciplinary approach to improving decision-making and dealing with uncertainty. As Smithson and others rightly point out, the emphasis should not be so much focused on eliminating or even reducing uncertainty, but learning to deal with it in a way that is efficient, effective and justifiable.

Uncertainty is a constant factor in life. It makes life, particularly that of a law enforcement officer, difficult. A multidisciplinary approach has great potential for making life easier.

References

Attewell, R 2010, 'Can statistics help', in G Bammer (ed.), *Dealing with uncertainties in policing serious crime*, ANU E Press, Canberra.

Fargher, N 2010, 'Business', in G Bammer (ed.), *Dealing with uncertainties in policing serious crime*, ANU E Press, Canberra.

Heuer Jr, RJ 1999, *Psychology of intelligence analysis*, Central Intelligence Agency, Government Printing Office, Washington DC.

Jarrett, R & Westcott, M 2010, 'Quantitative risk', in G Bammer (ed.), *Dealing with uncertainties in policing serious crime*, ANU E Press, Canberra.

Lawrence, C 2010, 'Politics', in G Bammer (ed.), *Dealing with uncertainties in policing serious crime*, ANU E Press, Canberra.

Longford, S 2008, 'Uncertainty in decision-making: intelligence as a solution', in G Bammer & M Smithson (eds), *Uncertainty and risk: multidisciplinary perspectives*, Earthscan, London, pp. 219–230.

Moston, S, Stephenson, GM & Williamson, TM 1992, 'The effects of case characteristics on suspect behaviour during police questioning', *The British Journal of Criminology*, vol. 32, pp. 23–40.

Simon, HA 1972, 'Theories of bounded rationality', in CB McGuire & R Radner (eds), *Decision and organization*, North-Holland Publishing Company, Amsterdam, pp. 161–176.

Smithson, M 2010, 'Understanding uncertainty', in G Bammer (ed.), *Dealing with uncertainties in policing serious crime*, ANU E Press, Canberra.

Wilkinson, S 2010, 'The modern policing environment', in G Bammer (ed.), *Dealing with uncertainties in policing serious crime*, ANU E Press, Canberra.

Law Enforcement Agencies which Respond to Nationally Significant Crime

ALASTAIR M MILROY

The purpose of this chapter is to present the uncertainty of investigating and responding to nationally significant crime from a law enforcement agency perspective and to use that perspective to comment on the other chapters. Responding to national crime threats involves a multitude of agencies, but my knowledge and experience is predominately law enforcement related and this paper is from that viewpoint.

The paper is practical and describes four major uncertainties that I was confronted with at the Australian Crime Commission in responding to nationally serious crime. The paper acknowledges there is no scientific method to achieve a successful outcome against serious crime.

To demonstrate the uncertainties of responding to crime I have used 'illicit drugs' as a nationally significant crime type and an Asian criminal drug syndicate as an example of a special investigation throughout the paper to highlight the issues for the law-makers (governments), the law enforcement decision-makers (Commissioners of Police and Chief Executive Officers of law enforcement agencies) and the law enforcement agencies that investigate the crimes.

The four uncertainties listed below are by no means the only uncertainties dealt with by the Australian Crime Commission or law enforcement agencies in responding to serious crime.

Four major uncertainties

1. What nationally significant crimes should the Australian Crime Commission pursue in accordance with the Australian Crime Commission Act 2002?
2. Will government and the Australian Crime Commission Board support the crimes identified by the Commission for a law enforcement response?
3. Will the Australian Crime Commission have the capabilities to impact on the nationally significant crimes identified?
4. Will the operational results meet stakeholder expectations?

My approach and predisposition to responding to serious crime is governed by my background and experiences as a detective and police officer. My ideas and thoughts are not supported by rigorous research but reflect my experience in the context of thirty-seven years in state, federal and international law enforcement activities. Much of the insight in this paper stems from the period I spent as Chief Executive Officer at the Australian Crime Commission from 2003 to 2009.

The Australian Crime Commission is a statutory body working nationally with a range of federal, state and territory agencies in partnership to counter serious and organised crime. The commission was established to address federally relevant criminal activity, which is defined in Section 4 of the *Australian Crime Commission Act 2002* as:

- an offence against a law of the commonwealth or a territory; or
- an offence against a law of a state that has a federal aspect.

In practical terms, federally relevant criminal activity generally equates to 'serious and organised crime'.

The governance framework for the Australian Crime Commission is extensive and includes the Minister for Home Affairs, the Inter-Governmental Committee (commonwealth, state and territory police/justice ministers), the Parliamentary Joint Committee (members of the Senate and House of Representatives), the Australian Commission for Law Enforcement Integrity and the Australian Crime Commission Board.

The Australian Crime Commission Board, which is chaired by the Commissioner of the Federal Police, consists of eight state and territory police commissioners and five commonwealth agency heads being: The Director General of the Australian Security and Intelligence Organization, the Chair of the Australian Securities and Investment Commission, the Chief Executive Officer of Customs, the Secretary of the Attorney-General's Department and the Chief Executive Officer of the Australian Crime Commission who is the only non-voting member.

The aim of the Australian Crime Commission is to bring together all arms of law enforcement intelligence gathering to unite the fight against serious criminal activities. A primary objective of the Australian Crime Commission in partnership with other law enforcement agencies is to disrupt significant criminal groups and individuals by arrest, seizure of illegal drugs, firearms and proceeds of crime action. Simultaneously the Australian Crime Commission acts to break down criminal behaviour and the continuity of the criminal enterprise.

What nationally significant crimes?

The first uncertainty for the Australian Crime Commission is to identify nationally significant crimes that should be pursued in accordance with the *Australian Crime Commission Act 2002*. As Sue Wilkinson (2010) described in her chapter, in Australia organised crime is acknowledged as a key part of the national security statement and strategy. The Australian Crime Commission Act interprets the meaning of 'serious and organised crime', describing it as involving two or more offenders, involving substantial planning and organisation; using sophisticated methods and techniques; committed in conjunction with other offences of a like kind; and a serious offence within the meaning of the *Proceeds of Crime Act 2002* (Australian Crime Commission Act 2002).

The true extent and nature of nationally serious and organised crime in Australia is relatively uncertain. As Sue Wilkinson (2010) highlights, '[o]rganised crime does not necessarily follow a logical process, a plan'.

Law enforcement is uncertain about the number of nationally significant criminals or criminal groups that are operating within Australia. A recent Parliamentary Joint Committee Inquiry heard that there is limited agreement over how serious and organised crime should be defined (Schloenhardt 2009). For example, the Australian Institute of Criminology refers to organised crime as usually being a structured group of three or more people that exists over a period of time with the aim of committing serious crime offences with profit as a motive (Australian Institute of Criminology 2004).

The Australian Crime Commission's main functions under the Act involve collecting, correlating, analysing and disseminating criminal intelligence and information. This intelligence function is the basis of the threat and harm assessment processes. The Australian Crime Commission undertakes the threat assessment process to consider the impact of a range of nationally significant criminal issues and activities on Australian interests. The threat assessment process informs law enforcement decision-makers and aids their process of determining and prioritising national criminal law enforcement efforts and targets.

The Australian Crime Commission Board provides strategic direction and determines the national criminal intelligence priorities. The decisions by board members of priorities and measures to respond to serious and organised crime can differ due to varying jurisdictional concepts of serious and organised crime, different political pressures and conflicting agendas.

As Carmen Lawrence (2010) indicates in her chapter, what is defined as crime in legislation and how crimes are depicted are essentially political decisions. Similarly, the priority given to the detection and prosecution of various crimes and the resources devoted to these tasks are dependent on the perceptions that politicians and their advisors have of the risks to the public —and to their own political futures—posed by those crimes. Perhaps, as Kempton (1998, cited in the chapter by Richard Jarrett and Mark Westcott 2010) suggests, if government members and other decision-makers were better educated in interpreting risks they would be less dependent on their perceptions of the law and order risks to the community. We need research on how to teach decision-makers interpretive estimates and how to encourage them to apply the methodology to their decision-making.

In summary, how serious and organised crime is defined determines, to an extent, how serious and organised crime will be approached (Parliamentary Joint Committee on the Australian Crime Commission 2009).

Support by management board

The presentation to the Australian Crime Commission Board of suitable criminal groups for a law enforcement response comes with its own uncertainties.

Inconsistencies in reporting and intelligence data retrieval methodologies prevent accurate assessment of the nature and extent of serious crime. The absence of a nationally coordinated database prevents the collection and exchange of information, intelligence, advice and warnings between key stakeholders. Using police data to compile national statistics comes with incompatible data sets and as a consequence the statistics can lack parity.

This comment finds support in Robyn Attewell's (2010) chapter. She highlights that, despite the wide availability of administrative police databases and survey information, both nationally and internationally, these empirical sources are limited by problems of scope and coverage, and inconsistent definitions across jurisdictions. Attewell argues that often there is no data to work with, either 'events are sparse (terror attacks), difficult to classify consistently (disruption of organised crime activity), difficult to detect (people smuggling), there are no complainants (drug trafficking and organised crime) or the data are generally only accessible through liaison with other agencies (cyber-crime, drug importation)'.

Establishing that a crime group is worthy of a special investigation must meet legislative requirements and the threshold of 'whether ordinary police methods of investigation into the matters are likely to be effective' (*Australian Crime Commission Act 2002*, 7C (3)). The Australian Crime Commission is required to prove to the Australian Crime Commission Board that traditional police methods have been ineffective based on an incomplete intelligence collection process.

To provide insight into the differing views of law enforcement, a submission to an Australian Parliamentary Joint Committee inquiring into the future impact of serious and organised crime on Australian society disclosed a lack of uniformity by the nine law enforcement agencies. These agencies were asked to identify the current and future threats by organised crime groups. Only one type of crime—'illicit drugs'—was common to every agency as a threat. The submissions identify that there are differences in opinion about how organised crime is to be countered and that serious crime in one jurisdiction may not have the same degree of influence in another jurisdiction (Sullivan 2007).

Defining and assessing significant national criminals is based on information and intelligence systems that have inconsistencies. As a result there are no assurances that the governments involved and/or the Australian Crime Commission Board will support the actions suggested by the Australian Crime Commission for action.

On most occasions if the law enforcement decision-makers agree to collaborate against a nationally significant criminal group there is usually an obligation to commit resources and funds to achieve a positive outcome for the Australian community. Commissioners of Police constantly argue insufficient police numbers, high employee attrition rates and insufficient annual appropriations to conduct business. Police unions agree and argue poor police-to-population ratios.

The pressures on police budgets are highlighted by the increasing importance of outside sources of revenue to police agencies, despite real increases in the budgets of many police jurisdictions.

> *The tightening of police budgets clearly has implications for police responses, both in relation to dealing with law and order, and in respect of the way in which police organizations are managed. It affects police priorities and how low priority tasks are dealt with (Ayling et al. 2009, p. 17–18).*

Some, such as Lawrence (2010), argue that the widely exaggerated perceptions of risk of crimes, generated through fear campaigns, have inevitably distorted law and justice policies and misdirected public expenditure.

It is necessary in practice to find a balance between the expectations of governments, law enforcement decision-makers, commentators and the community on crime reduction and the reality of insufficient police resources, funding and legislation.

Capabilities to impact on nationally significant crime

Without the support of state, territory and federal police forces and other law enforcement agencies, the Australian Crime Commission's capabilities to respond to significant crime would be limited to its in-house resources. The appropriate capabilities mix required to impact on a national or transnational target is extensive. Developing a response capability without appreciating the full extent and nature of the criminal activities can have resource implications and influence the effectiveness of the intelligence operation or investigation.

Even with thorough information gathering by the Australian Crime Commission and presentation of a detailed picture of criminal group/s activities, there are still gaps in intelligence relating to the criminal identities and their methods. By using the example of the Asian drug syndicate it is possible to highlight the uncertain lines of inquiry that exist at the commencement of a national investigation and the difficulties of determining the resources required to impact on a criminal group.

Asian drug syndicate—uncertainties and gaps in intelligence

- extent of the global illicit drug distribution network
- harm caused by the illicit drug criminal network on the Australian community
- identity of the overseas principals
- methodologies used to source and transport illicit drugs into Australia
- preferred illicit drugs types
- volume of illicit drugs imported and distributed within Australia
- distribution networks throughout Australia
- identity of network members
- number of Australian based syndicates ordering and distributing illicit drugs
- geographical areas of operation within Australia
- methods for ordering illicit drugs and payment
- identity of local and/or overseas officials facilitating the illicit drug importations
- extent of money laundering and methodologies
- identity of the money facilitators
- types of technology used to facilitate crimes
- history of attempts to disrupt the syndicate by local and overseas police

- extent of intelligence and information held by law enforcement agencies
- the level of cooperation that could be expected from overseas and local law enforcement agencies.

In relation to the Asian drug syndicate, sufficient intelligence and agreed priorities by Australian Crime Commission Board members allowed a national task force capability to be formed to disrupt the activities of the criminal syndicate. Building a case for a whole of law enforcement response is impeded by uncertainties and inconsistencies including lack of common legislation, as well as differing interoperability standards, skill competencies, police powers and procedures, criminal codes, information sharing protocols, jurisdiction management and cultural issues, to name a few.

Coordination and cooperation of the national task force involves utilising the resources from state and federal government agencies. The formation of the task force is based on the knowledge and assessment of current criminal activities, the type of operation to be conducted, proposed tactics, coercive powers, time frames, geographical locations, available funds and skills required to achieve the objectives of the investigation.

Formation of a task force to deal with the Asian drug syndicate involved nine agencies collaborating, including the Australian Crime Commission, Victoria Police, New South Wales Police, New South Wales Crime Commission, Western Australia Police, Austrac, Australian Taxation Office, Australian Customs Service and the Australian Federal Police.

If law enforcement agencies do not work together there is the potential to work against each other. Turf wars between state and federal agencies are common with the sharing of information and intelligence both locally and overseas complicated due to lack of trust and long-standing police cultural barriers. A response by multiple agencies can exacerbate jealousies and conflicts over who has jurisdiction—who is in command—or it can produce 'buck passing' where no agency wants to take responsibility. Lack of cooperation can mean crimes remain unsolved and criminals remain free to commit further offences (Prenzler 2009).

Prenzler (2009, p. 43) also highlights that the International Association of Chiefs of Police Code requires that 'police officers will cooperate with all legally authorised agencies and their representatives in the pursuit of justice'. In practice the Chiefs of Police Code is not always the behaviour displayed by law enforcement officers.

There are always many issues to overcome to achieve success from cross-jurisdictional task forces. As Wilkinson (2010) points out, it is often said that criminals take advantage of borders and jurisdictional barriers but police are hampered by them.

Uncertainty is an inescapable ingredient of investigating crimes, as there are many ways to tackle a crime problem. The task force involved in the Asian crime syndicate investigation involved sworn and unsworn investigators, physical and electronic surveillance operatives, analysts, accountants, lawyers and support staff drawn from the contributing agencies.

The jealousies that can exist between agencies can also exist between the various professionals assigned to the task force. Investigative cultures can isolate individuals into silos, which can impede cooperation, information sharing and impact on the ultimate success of the task force investigation (Dean and Gottschalk 2007).

Once the investigation was commenced, the Asian task force was confronted with information and intelligence that had omissions, duplications, gaps, classification restrictions, qualified releases and poor information sharing practices. The uncertainty associated with not enough information versus too much information is an interesting concept for law enforcement decision-makers. In his chapter, Michael Smithson (2010) provides examples of where additional information increases uncertainty by creating conflict or being irrelevant. This is true. Each additional piece of information in an investigation has the capacity to be in conflict with information already gathered or it can be irrelevant. However, the benefit of gathering information and the associated intelligence process also assists in reducing that uncertainty (Longford 2008). Disinformation, deception, incorrect information, walls of silence, Chinese whispers, miscommunications and secrecy are all features of the intelligence gathering and investigative phases for joint agency task forces. The methods used by intelligence officers and investigators to identify a trend or explain the trend, highlight the risks, as well as identify the alternatives and gaps, are all processes used to reduce uncertainty in an investigation.

There was compulsory regular reporting of operational results, legal compliance, use of coercive powers, professional integrity, and resource usage to the Inter-Governmental Committee, the Parliamentary Joint Committee and the Australian Crime Commission Board. The release of sufficient information to inform decision-makers without compromising ongoing operations is a tricky balancing act. Providing written reports and operational updates involves managing sensitive data among many individuals with different agendas.

Management of the media is never certain; editors control headlines and dull headlines do not sell newspapers. The media have an obligation to inform the community and governments want to appear active in reducing crime and catching criminals. If not properly managed, the media can engender fear, distort the facts and betray confidences. The media can exaggerate the risks the community actually face and clamour for an instant response, especially from government, to threats that may never materialise. Health and crime risks in particular are often distorted and politicians often join in (Lawrence 2010).

During the task force operation, when substantial seizures or arrests were made, relevant information was released to the media usually through the minister's office. Cross-jurisdictional agency media releases involving ministers and law enforcement agency heads at times can fail due to grandstanding and not recognising the efforts of all agencies involved. A media release can be reported by the media in line with their agenda and as Lawrence (2010) suggests politicians can line up beside senior police to give them (the politicians) greater credibility.

Operational results and stakeholder expectations

In February 2009, after a two-year investigation, the full results of the task force were made public. The task force investigated 26 cases of money laundering and 72 criminals were charged involving 139 charges. Sixteen criminal syndicates were disrupted and over $1 billion worth of illicit drugs and drug making chemicals were removed from Australian streets. In business financial terms, the government's investment in this task force and special investigation translated to a rate of return of 6500%, but who can put a real value on removing that amount of drugs from the community? This question is supported by Wilkinson (2010) who states the harm caused by organised crime is often insidious and hard to quantify. I indicated in a media release in 2009 that the greatest return for the government dollar and for the community is to solve crime as effectively and efficiently as possible.

This investigation highlighted to governments and the Australian Crime Commission Board the methods used by money laundering criminals to channel funds to overseas locations. Like all successful investigations, the intelligence and knowledge gained on the global and national criminal network caused a shift in law enforcement methods used to attack similar criminal networks.

Based on the original uncertainties and gaps in this investigation, the extent of the results for governments and partnering law enforcement was seen as extremely successful. While the task force followed the investigative plan, met key performance indicators, stayed within budget, achieved substantial arrests and charges, the overall impact on serious crime will never be known.

Uncertainty in police investigation is time consuming. In an investigation, uncertainty extends the investigation period, but at the same time—because of the uncertainty—the investigator/s are required to look further and to be more thorough. The saying 'the more you know the more you don't know' is very true; however, uncertainty can enhance both the intelligence and investigative process.

Ultimately the task force must present sufficient evidence to convict the Asian criminal syndicate and convince a judge and jury that a maximum sentence is appropriate. As Carmody (2010) highlights in his chapter 'juries are a source of unpredictability' and 'there is no way of forecasting how different juries will view the same set of facts'. Is it possible to know the truth about a crime and if all the evidence has been gathered? Carmody suggests that criminal litigation is at the mercy of luck where neither greater knowledge not superior skill guarantee success in every case. Nor does better preparation.

Questions of ethical behaviour by officers and/or noble cause corruption can be raised in relation to any investigation. Is a full confession by a criminal the truth, or has it been toned down to reduce the impact of the penalty? Are the witnesses credible or have the investigators confused facts with fiction, created biases or acted on hunches, theories and/or mindsets.

As Mark Kebbell, Damon Muller and Kirsty Martin (2010) point out in their chapter, ensuring task force team members have appropriate training and awareness of cognitive biases could mitigate some of these concerns. However, answers to these questions are all part and parcel of the prosecution process and are uncertainties that may present in the next stage of the law enforcement cycle.

Managing uncertainties more effectively

In Table 1, I summarise the key intersections with the other chapters in the book, along with critical areas that warrant further research. I describe some of these in more detail here, as well as raising other issues related to uncertainty that require research and practice attention.

One of the key uncertainties that law enforcement faces in combating serious and organised crime is collecting statistics about and mapping trends in organised crime due to the difficulties in defining and measuring organised crime. Even with cooperation from all law enforcement agencies, an accurate picture of the scale of serious criminal activity is difficult to ascertain, as private sector victims can be reluctant to declare their losses or may even treat losses as a bad debt.

For the decision-makers, including myself, the uncertainties exist in the lack of a national uniform intelligence database on crime trends to support our decisions to pursue one crime type over another and to determine the most urgent policing priority for the community. Such a national system needs agreed information and intelligence sharing protocols that would assist in producing a more accurate national picture of organised crime within Australia. Research that identifies a standardised classification system for crime that is acceptable both nationally and internationally would benefit future decision-makers. Further, a national uniform intelligence database would see the full benefits of the available statistical tools that Attewell (2010) describes in her chapter.

Even with an improved crime classification system for information and intelligence, there would need to be enhanced decision-making skills for determining future policing priorities. Although a threat and risk assessment methodology was used at the Australian Crime Commission to identify strategic and operational priorities, there can still be disagreement on the importance of the different types of criminal harm within a geographical region or relative to another region. Richard Jarrett and Mark Westcott (2010) provide an example of how risk scores can be used for a range of hazards that are geographically dispersed and of different types. They suggest having defined consequences, likelihood and risk scores, which allow risks to be combined to produce an interpretable result. Improving the skills of decision-makers by providing them with new tools such as interpretative estimates of risk is another area conducive to future research.

Greater awareness of the decision-making process can also be achieved by exposing decision-makers to the type of arguments presented by Smithson (2010) in his chapter. These include the impacts on a decision of the number of alternatives or outcomes, that reducing uncertainty is not always worthwhile, that more information can increase uncertainty, and that the right analytical tool is required to make decisions. Raising decision-maker awareness of biases as suggested by Kebbell and his colleagues (2010) is another opportunity to improve the decision-making process for law enforcement.

Nevertheless, the fact that the national task force was formed and achieved substantial results proves serious crime can be impacted upon in a coordinated manner in spite of jurisdictional differences, flawed decision-making, gaps and uncertainties in the national information and intelligence framework. The differing legislative tools, including criminal laws, proceeds of crime and variety of police powers, increase the complexity for the decision-makers in supporting a law enforcement response to serious crime. Impacting on serious and organised crime is a complex composite of policy and intelligence issues that are beyond the capacity of any one jurisdiction or agency. Harmonisation of law enforcement efforts can reduce displacement of criminal activities to other jurisdictions.

In investigating this particular syndicate it is not possible to guarantee that the Australian Crime Commission task force detected all criminals involved within Australia and overseas. If a method to quantify harm of organised crime on the community had been available, the Australian Crime Commission could have measured its performance more precisely. Successful drug law enforcement disrupts market supply creating a void for the re-emergence of criminal groups. If that void is filled by a new criminal group the uncertainty cycle starts again and law enforcement agencies must attempt to identify the methods that the new criminals have adapted to defeat the laws.

Table 1: Summary of comments on the other chapters and critical areas that warrant further research

Author	Ideas or methods for dealing with uncertainty	Critical areas that warrant further research
Attewell	Geospatial analysis—crime mapping and movement of funds Cluster analysis—fraud Process control—management of internal productivity Descriptive statistics Enforcement prioritisation index	Ways to monitor activity associated with money laundering that could lead to detection How can statistical methods be utilised in the investigation of serious crime? Identification of a standardised classification system for crime acceptable by jurisdictions (nationally and internationally)
Fargher	Data mining techniques—intelligence Scenario analysis—best and worst case Cross-matching financial data to unexplained wealth Exploitation of uncertainty—improves investigation The uncertainty of future costs associated with externality arising from production of goods or services	A framework for investigation of future externalities generated by business How can the exploitation of uncertainties in serious crimes support the investigation?
Jarrett & Westcott	Quantitative risk rating methods Movement of risks—across jurisdictions The need for decision-makers to be better educated in interpreting estimates of risk Attractiveness of targets	How can interpreting estimates of risk be adopted by decision-makers for policing priorities?
Kebbell et al.	Cognitive abilities and potential biases—information and intelligence process Heuristic based methods—cognitive short cuts Mechanisms for debiasing	How to manage risks associated with cognitive biases in investigating serious crime?
Lawrence	When uncertainties are reducible, they may not be worth reducing Reducing one uncertainty may increase or generate other uncertainties More information can increase uncertainty—intelligence Applying resources to investigations Consequences of partitioning Survival analysis—event history analysis 'Near-miss' incident reporting Ignorance assessment	How to take the politics out of responding to serious crime?
Smithson		How can the 'ignorance assessment' be developed into the decision-making process for policing?
Wilkinson	Risk and harm assessments Partnerships Interoperability	A way to quantify harm of organised crime A partnership model that will incorporate law enforcement, governments, public sector and community to address future policing needs

References

Attewell, R 2010, 'Can statistics help', in G Bammer (ed.), *Dealing with uncertainties in policing serious crime*, ANU E Press, Canberra.

Australian Crime Commission Act 2002, Part 1 – Preliminary, 4, Interpretation (1), <http://www.austlii.edu.au/cgi-bin/sinodisp/au/legis/cth/consol_act/acca2002289/s4.html?query=serious%20and%20organised%20crime> (accessed 31 January 2010).

Australian Institute of Criminology 2004, 'The worldwide fight against transnational organized crime', *Australia-Technical and Background Paper-No. 9*, AIC, Canberra.

Ayling, J, Grabosky, P & Shearing, C 2009, 'Lengthening the arm of the law', *Enhancing police resources in the twenty-first century*, Cambridge University Press, Melbourne.

Carmody, T 2010, 'Criminal law', in G Bammer (ed.), *Dealing with uncertainties in policing serious crime*, ANU E Press, Canberra.

Dean, G & Gottschalk, P 2007, *Knowledge management in policing and law enforcement: foundations, structures, applications,* Oxford University Press, Oxford.

Jarrett, R & Westcott, M 2010, 'Quantitative risk', in G Bammer (ed.), *Dealing with uncertainties in policing serious crime*, ANU E Press, Canberra.

Kebbell, MR, Muller, DA & Martin, K 2010, 'Understanding and managing bias', in G Bammer (ed.), *Dealing with uncertainties in policing serious crime*, ANU E Press, Canberra.

Lawrence, C 2010, 'Politics', in G Bammer (ed.), *Dealing with uncertainties in policing serious crime*, ANU E Press, Canberra.

Longford, S 2010, 'Consultancy to build capacity in dealing with uncertainty in law enforcement', in G Bammer (ed.), *Dealing with uncertainties in policing serious crime*, ANU E Press, Canberra.

Parliamentary Joint Committee on the Australian Crime Commission 2009, *Inquiry into the legislative arrangements to outlaw serious and organized crime*, Parliament of Australia, Canberra, <http://www.aph.gov.au/senate/committee/acc_ctte/laoscg/index.htm> (accessed 31 January 2010).

Prenzler, T 2009, *Police corruption: preventing misconduct and maintaining integrity*, CRC Press, USA.

Schloenhardt, A 2009, *Inquiry into the legislative arrangements to outlaw serious and organized crime*, submission to the Parliamentary Joint Committee on the Australian Crime Commission 2009, Parliament of Australia, Canberra, http://www.aph.gov.au/senate/committee/acc_ctte/laoscg/submissions/sub01.pdf (accessed 31 January, 2010).

Smithson, M 2010, 'Understanding uncertainty', in G Bammer (ed.), *Dealing with uncertainties in policing serious crime*, ANU E Press, Canberra.

Sullivan, S 2007, 'The adversarial intelligence model', *Journal of the Australian Institute of Professional Intelligence Officers*, vol. 15, no. 3, p. 81.

Wilkinson, S 2010, 'The modern policing environment', in G Bammer (ed.), *Dealing with uncertainties in policing serious crime*, ANU E Press, Canberra.

List of Contributors

Editor

Gabriele Bammer, Professor, National Centre for Epidemiology and Population Health, ANU College of Medicine, Biology and Environment, The Australian National University

Gabriele Bammer is convenor of the Knowledge Integration research program of the Australian Research Council Centre of Excellence in Policing and Security and a Research Fellow in the Program in Criminal Justice Policy and Management at the John F Kennedy School of Government at Harvard University. She is developing the new discipline of Integration and Implementation Sciences to improve research strengths in synthesis of disciplinary and stakeholder knowledge, understanding and managing unknowns and providing integrated research support for policy and practice change (see http://i2s.anu.edu.au).

Contributors

Robyn Attewell, Coordinator, Performance Analysis, Internal Audit and Business Analysis, The Australian Federal Police

Robyn Attewell is an accredited statistician who has been with the Australian Federal Police (AFP) since December 2007. The AFP is an Industry Partner of the Australian Research Council Centre of Excellence in Policing and Security. She is responsible for the development and maintenance of the performance framework for the AFP. Regular reporting to management, compliance with government accountability requirements and coordination of internal and external satisfaction surveys are key components of this role. Previously Robyn worked as a biostatistician in occupational and environmental health and consulted for a range of academic, government and private industry clients. Prior to joining the AFP she was responsible for biometrics in the Asia Pacific region for a global contract research company focused on pharmaceutical drug development and marketing. She has co-authored over 60 publications in the medical and public health literature.

Simon Bronitt, Director, Australian Research Council Centre of Excellence in Policing and Security

Simon Bronitt was previously a Professor of Law in The Australian National University's (ANU) College of Law and Director of the ANU's Australian Centre for Military Law and Justice. Between 2006 and 2009 he served as the Director of the National Europe Centre, Research School of Humanities, at the ANU. Drawing on comparative and interdisciplinary perspectives, Simon has published widely on criminal justice issues, including counter terrorism law and human rights, covert policing, telecommunications interception and international criminal law. His publications include *Principles of criminal law* (2nd ed., Law Book Co, 2005) and *Law in context* (3rd ed., Federation Press, 2006). He was the lead Chief Investigator of ARC-funded Discovery Project on counterterrorism law (2005–2008), which culminated in the publication of Miriam Gani & Penelope Mathew (editors), *Fresh perspectives on the 'War on Terror'* (2008).

Hon. Tim Carmody SC, John Jerrard Chambers, Brisbane

Tim Carmody is a former judge of the Family Court (2003–2008). He was admitted to the Queensland bar in 1982 and took silk in 1999. Tim holds a Bachelor of Laws (1982) and Master of Laws (Hons) (1977) from the Queensland University of Technology. He was Queensland Crime Commissioner (1998–2002) and held key positions on numerous state and federal committees and advisory boards. He is an adjunct professor of law and has contributed to many professional journals on topics ranging from pre-emption options against terrorism to the law of forgery and family law specific subjects such as international relocation law and private arbitration. In 1999 he was Queensland University of Technology's Alumni of the Year Winner for outstanding professional achievement and community service. He was awarded the Centenary Medal in 2003 for distinguished service to the law.

Neil Fargher, Professor, School of Accounting and Business Information Systems, The Australian National University

Neil Fargher's research interests are in the areas of auditing and accounting. He has a particular interest in how risk is measured, how risk is communicated to the market, and how investors respond to such communication. Neil has studied a range of specific issues relating to the measurement of types of risk, leverage, hedge effectiveness, valuation, audit report qualifications and assurance services. Neil joined the ANU in 2008 from Macquarie University. He has previously held positions at the University of New South Wales, the University of Oregon and the University of Arizona. Prior to becoming an academic he worked with CSR Limited and Canadian telephone company AGT Limited.

Tracey Green, Associate Professor and Associate Dean (Policing), Australian Graduate School of Policing, Charles Sturt University

Tracey Green is a member of the Research Advisory Committee of the Australian Research Council Centre of Excellence in Policing and Security (CEPS). Charles Sturt University is one of the four key nodes of CEPS, linking in the teaching program of the Australian Graduate School of Policing. Tracey has 22 years police experience as a sworn officer in the UK. Serving to the rank of detective inspector, she has extensive experience in the areas of serious and serial criminal investigation, in particular homicide, drugs and police corruption. Tracey is a strong advocate of policing as a profession and, since joining Charles Sturt University, has developed a history of collaboration with police and law enforcement agencies ensuring that educational and research opportunities are relevant and aligned to policing. She has been instrumental in the development of postgraduate courses in the areas of investigation, intelligence, terrorism and police leadership, all of which involve research by the practitioner into their own area of professional expertise. In her position of Associate Dean (Policing and International) Tracey has overall responsibility for the School of Policing Studies which is located within the NSW Police College at Goulburn, and the Australian Graduate School of Policing which is co-located with the Australian Institute of Police Management at Manly. Her research relates to human source management and investigative interviewing and her co-authored text book *Investigative interviewing explained* is currently released as a 2nd edition.

Richard Jarrett, CSIRO Mathematics, Informatics and Statistics, Adelaide

Richard Jarrett is an accredited statistician and has been with CSIRO for the last 10 years. Prior to that, he was Professor of Statistics at the University of Adelaide. His particular research interests are in experimental design, risk analysis and reliability models. In recent years, he has worked on asset management for water distribution systems, but more recently on the provision of risk management research and services for government and industry. Recent major clients include Melbourne Water, Sydney Water, Orlando Wyndham, the Commonwealth Bank of Australia, the National Bank of Australia, the Australian Customs Service and the Australian Federal Police.

Mark Kebbell, Associate Professor, Australian Research Council Centre of Excellence in Policing and Security, Griffith University

Mark Kebbell is a Chief Investigator with the Australian Research Council Centre of Excellence in Policing and Security (CEPS). His expertise and research is in the area of investigative psychology, particularly the investigation and prosecution of serious crime. Within CEPS he is the lead investigator in the areas of risky people and intelligence methods. In addition, he and colleagues are working on an investigative interviewing project with the Victoria Police Service. His previous work has included co-writing the guidelines for police officers in England and Wales for the assessment of eyewitness evidence and a review of factors associated with violent extremism for the National Policing Improvement Agency commissioned by the Office for Security and Counter

Terrorism in the UK. He has worked on more than seventy criminal cases, principally involving murder or serious sexual assault, and has given expert evidence on numerous occasions. He was award a British Academy Postdoctoral Fellowship for Outstanding Younger Scholars. He is co-editor of the book *Practical psychology for forensic investigations and prosecutions*, published by Wiley.

Hon. Carmen Lawrence, Professorial Fellow, Institute of Advanced Studies, University of Western Australia

Carmen Lawrence trained as a research psychologist at the University of Western Australia and lectured in a number of Australian universities, before entering politics in 1986, serving at both state and federal levels for 21 years. She was at various times WA Minister for Education and Aboriginal Affairs and was the first woman Premier and Treasurer of a state government. She shifted to federal politics in 1994 when she was elected as the Member for Fremantle and was appointed Minister for Health and Human Services and Minister Assisting the Prime Minister on the Status of Women. She held various portfolios in Opposition, including Indigenous Affairs, Environment, Industry and Innovation and was elected national President of the Labor Party in 2004. She retired from politics in 2007. She is now a Professorial Fellow at the University of Western Australia where she is working to establish a centre to research the forces driving significant social change in key areas of contemporary challenge, as well as exploring our reactions to that change. The centre will also seek to expose for public discussion the processes most likely to achieve social change where that is a desired objective.

Greg Linsdell, Academic Associate and Senior Lecturer, Australian Graduate School of Policing, Charles Sturt University

Greg Linsdell teaches across a range of policing subjects including executive leadership and effective operational command. He is a former superintendent with Victoria Police with a strong operational background predominantly within the Special Operations Group. Greg has Masters Degrees in Law, Criminology and Education and is currently writing a reference text for police operational commanders. Charles Sturt University is one of the four key nodes of the Australian Research Council Centre of Excellence in Policing and Security, linking in the teaching program of the Australian Graduate School of Policing.

Steve Longford, Managing Director, New Intelligence

Steve Longford is a former police officer appointed as a Detective, Senior Intelligence Analyst and Behavioural Analyst. He retired after 16 years with Queensland Police as head of the Violent Crime Analysis Unit. He has tertiary qualifications in psychology and intelligence. For five years after his departure he was involved with the development of investigation management and intelligence management software and consulted on capability development for enforcement and intelligence agencies. Steve has also developed and delivered training to Executive members of law enforcement and compliance agencies from Australia and 18 other countries including the United States, Singapore, China and the United Kingdom. He has consulted directly to the Australian Federal Police (various), Indonesian National Police (Bali bombing) and Commonwealth Departments of Immigration and Citizenship and Foreign Affairs and Trade. He is now the Managing Director of New Intelligence, a Canberra-based company which specialises in developing and providing niche training programs. Along with his colleagues he has spent the last 8 years developing various training packages including interview, intelligence analysis, decision-making and most recently the human skills training program, the only program of its kind in the world.

Kirsty Martin, PhD student, Australian Research Council Centre of Excellence in Policing and Security, Griffith University

Kirsty Martin's doctoral research focuses on the identification, exploration and evaluation of decision-making processes utilised by criminal intelligence analysts. She has a Bachelors Degree (with Honours) in Criminology, majoring in crime prevention and human behaviour.

Peter Martin, Assistant Commissioner, Ethical Standards Command, Queensland Police Service

Peter Martin is a member of the Research Advisory Committee of the Australian Research Council Centre of Excellence in Policing and Security. The Queensland Police Service is an Industry Partner. Peter is a career police officer, having served with the Queensland Police Service for 30 years. He was promoted and appointed to his current position in early 2008. Previously he was the Operations Coordinator at Metropolitan North Region which has operational responsibilities for the Central Business District and a large area in the central and north Brisbane areas. His other recent roles in the Service have included: District Officer, Brisbane West District (2005–2007); Chief of Staff to the Commissioner of Police (2000–2005); and the Officer in Charge of the Drug and Alcohol Coordination Unit (1996–2000). Peter has an Executive Masters in Public Administration through the Australian and New Zealand School of Government and Griffith University. He also has a Bachelor of Arts in Justice Administration with a major in Police Studies and Adult and Vocational Education. He is currently undertaking a PhD in the Faculty of Health, School of Psychology and Counselling at Queensland University of Technology investigating the police role in reducing drug and alcohol related harm in and around licensed premises. Peter was awarded the Australian Police Medal on Australia Day 2008 for his contribution to policing and the community of Queensland.

Alastair Milroy, Executive-in-Residence, Australian Research Council Centre of Excellence in Policing and Security

Alastair Milroy has had a distinguished and varied career in law enforcement spanning over 37 years serving with the New South Wales Police, National Crime Authority, New South Wales Royal Commission into the Building Industry, the New South Wales Drug Enforcement Agency and the United Nations International Criminal Tribunal. In the private sector he was the National Security Manager for Brambles Security Services and operated a consultancy that provided investigations and security risk management for public companies. During 2003–2009 he returned to the public sector as the Chief Executive Officer of the Australian Crime Commission responsible for national criminal intelligence and operational responses to fight serious organised crime in Australia. Alastair provides advice to the Australian Research Council Centre of Excellence in Policing and Security as the part-time 'Executive in Residence'. He serves on the Australasian Policing Forum that is engaged in expanding knowledge on policing, security and public safety to inform governments, law enforcement and the community. Alastair holds an Associate Diploma in Justice Administration and a Graduate Diploma in Police Management. He is a member in the General Division of the Order of Australia for his services to national crime investigation and prevention.

Damon Muller, Postdoctoral Fellow, Australian Research Council Centre of Excellence in Policing and Security, National Centre for Epidemiology and Population Health, ANU College of Medicine, Biology and Environment, The Australian National University

Damon Muller is currently conducting research into understanding and managing uncertainty in policing and security. He received his PhD in criminology from the University of Melbourne. He previously worked for the Australian Institute of Criminology researching bushfire arson and as a sessional lecturer at the University of Melbourne. He has published research in areas including homicide and homicide solvability, arson, criminal profiling and juvenile justice.

Michael Smithson, Professor, Department of Psychology, The Australian National University.

Michael Smithson is an Associate Investigator of the Australian Research Council Centre of Excellence in Policing and Security. He received his PhD from the

University of Oregon. He is the author of *Confidence intervals* (2003), *Statistics with confidence* (2000), *Ignorance and uncertainty* (1989), and *Fuzzy set analysis for the behavioral and social sciences* (1987), co-author of *Fuzzy set theory: applications in the social sciences* (2006) and co-editor of *Uncertainty and risk: multidisciplinary perspectives* (2008) and *Resolving social dilemmas: dynamic, structural, and intergroup aspects* (1999). His other publications include more than 100 refereed journal articles and book chapters. His primary research interests are in judgment and decision-making under uncertainty, social dilemmas, applications of fuzzy set theory to the social sciences, and statistical methods for the social sciences.

Mark Westcott, Senior Principal Research Scientist, Optimisation in Air Transport Management Team, CSIRO Mathematics, Informatics and Statistics, Canberra

Mark Westcott has been with CSIRO for over 30 years after a period as an academic in the UK. He has been involved in many areas of mathematical and statistical modelling and analysis, including such diverse projects as estimating the average fuel temperatures at Australian service stations and optimal power management in a hybrid petrol/electric vehicle. His recent work has included projects on aspects of airspace risk for Qantas and Broome International Airport, and he has collaborated on a paper about risk analysis in the defence arena.

Sue Wilkinson, Executive Director, Australia New Zealand Policing Advisory Agency

Sue Wilkinson is a member of the Research Advisory Committee of the Australian Research Council Centre of Excellence in Policing and Security. The Australia New Zealand Policing Advisory Agency is an Industry Partner. Sue took up her current post in November 2007. She was previously a Commander in the Metropolitan Police in London, where she was responsible for a wide portfolio of serious and organised crime. Sue has a degree in History from University College, London, and has postgraduate qualifications in change management and criminology. In 29 years of policing, Sue has served in a variety of roles—uniform, detective, strategy and policy.

Printed in Great Britain
by Amazon.co.uk, Ltd.,
Marston Gate.